Foreign invasions had destroyed the old world. Radical new ideas, seemingly at open conflict with the traditional frame of reference and with each other, were flooding the universities. Scholars and students were in ferment; old questions were being answered with new solutions. A confused world was trying to rebuild on the foundations of the old, and the result was chaos.

This is a description not of the tumultuous twentieth century, but of the thirteenth century, the time when the Dominican scholar Thomas Aquinas was writing his masterpiece, SUMMA THEOLOGIAE—an intellectual synthesis of two divergent philosophical schools hitherto considered incompatible. With this intellectual marriage of faith and reason, Aquinas gave to his own era a foundation upon which to advance and gave to all men of every era a model of intellectual insight and method undisputed in its precision, clarity, and totality.

Today *our* universities are in ferment, *our* traditional ways of thinking are crumbling before the onslaught of new philosophical approaches, *our* attempts at rebuilding on the foundations of the old are doomed to failure. Now is the time to look back to the great classic which, by bridging the old and the new, occasioned an advancement in Western civilization unrivaled in its impact. As a historical work, the SUMMA is unsurpassed; as a method of thought, it is worthy of study; as an example of synthesis, it is a source of hope.

This Image edition of SUMMA THEOLOGIAE comes at a time when Aquinas' position as a master of philosophical insight is recognized anew. Using the translation of the definitive Blackfriars edition (widely acclaimed for its accuracy, faithfulness to the original, and pure scholarship), it is a work to be welcomed by all interested in the work of the man whom the New York *Times* called "the greatest philosopher and theologian of his age."

Thomas Aquinas

SUMMA THEOLOGIAE

VOLUME I

The Existence of God

PART ONE: QUESTIONS 1–13

GENERAL EDITOR

THOMAS GILBY, O.P.

Blackfriars, Cambridge

IMAGE BOOKS

A DIVISION OF DOUBLEDAY & COMPANY, INC.

GARDEN CITY, NEW YORK

Image Books edition 1969
by special arrangement with
Eyre & Spottiswoode (Publishers) Ltd.

Image Books edition published December 1969

CONTENTS

INTRODUCTION   11

EDITORIAL NOTE   35

FOREWORD   39

Question 1. What sort of teaching Christian theology is and what it covers   41

    Article   1. Is another teaching required apart from philosophical studies?   41

    Article   2. Is Christian theology a science?   43

    Article   3. Is Christian theology a single science?   45

    Article   4. Is Christian theology a practical science?   46

    Article   5. Is Christian theology more valuable than the other sciences?   47

    Article   6. Is this teaching wisdom?   49

    Article   7. Is God the subject of this science?   52

    Article   8. Is this teaching probative?   53

    Article   9. Should holy teaching employ metaphorical or symbolical language?   56

    Article 10. Can one passage of holy Scripture bear several senses?   58

Question 2. Whether there is a God   62

    Article   1. Is it self-evident that there is a God?   63

    Article   2. Can it be made evident?   65

    Article   3. Is there a God?   67

Question 3. God's simpleness   71

    Article   1. Is God a body composed of extended parts?   72

    Article   2. Is God composed of 'form' and 'matter'?   74

    Article   3. Is God to be identified with his own es-

sence or nature, with that which makes
him what he is?   76

Article   4. Can one distinguish in God nature and
existence?   78

Article   5. Can one distinguish in God genus and
difference?   80

Article   6. Is God composed of substance and accidents?   82

Article   7. Is there any way in which God is composite, or is he altogether simple?   84

Article   8. Does God enter into composition with
other things?   86

Question 4. God's perfection   89

Article   1. Is God perfect?   89

Article   2. Is God's perfection all-embracing, containing, so to say, the perfection of
everything else?   91

Article   3. Can creatures be said to resemble God? 93

Question 5. The general notion of good   96

Article   1. Is being good really the same thing as
existing?   96

Article   2. If one assumes that being good and existing differ merely as ideas, which idea
is the more fundamental?   98

Article   3. If one assumes that existing is more fundamental, is everything that exists good?   101

Article   4. What kind of causality is implicit in the
notion of goodness?   102

Article   5. Is goodness a matter of being in condition, form and order?   104

Article   6. The division of good into the worthy,
the useful and the delightful.   107

Question 6. The goodness of God   110

    Article   1. *Can one associate goodness with God?*   110

    Article   2. *Is God supremely good?*   111

    Article   3. *Is God alone good by nature?*   113

    Article   4. *Does God's goodness make everything good?*   115

Question 7. God's limitlessness   117

    Article   1. *Is God unlimited?*   117

    Article   2. *Is anything other than God unlimited in being?*   119

    Article   3. *Can anything be unlimited in size?*   121

    Article   4. *Can there exist an unlimited number of things?*   124

Question 8. God's existence in things   127

    Article   1. *Does God exist in everything?*   127

    Article   2. *Is God everywhere?*   129

    Article   3. *Is God everywhere in substance, power and presence?*   131

    Article   4. *Is being everywhere something that belongs to God alone?*   134

Question 9. God's unchangeableness   137

    Article   1. *Is God altogether unchangeable?*   137

    Article   2. *Is only God unchangeable?*   139

Question 10. The eternity of God   143

    Article   1. *What is eternity?*   143

    Article   2. *Is God eternal?*   145

    Article   3. *Does eternity belong to God alone?*   147

    Article   4. *Is eternity different from the æon and time?*   149

    Article   5. *The difference between the æon and time.*   151

Article   6. *Is there only one æon, as there is one*
            time and one eternity?   155

Question 11. The oneness of God   158

Article   1. *Does being one add anything to existing?*   158
Article   2. *Is being one the opposite of being many?*   160
Article   3. *Is there one God?*   163
Article   4. *Is God supremely one?*   164

Question 12. How God is known by his creatures   166

Article   1. *Can any created mind see the essence of*
               God?   166
Article   2. *Does the mind see the essence of God*
               by means of any created likeness?   169
Article   3. *Can we see the essence of God with our*
               bodily eyes?   171
Article   4. *Can any created intellect see the essence*
               of God by its own natural powers?   173
Article   5. *Does the created mind need a created*
               light in order to see the essence of God?   176
Article   6. *Is the essence of God seen more perfectly*
               by one than by another?   178
Article   7. *Can a created mind comprehend the es-*
               sence of God?   180
Article   8. *Does it in seeing the essence of God see*
               all things?   183
Article   9. *Is it by means of any likeness that it*
               knows what it sees there?   185
Article 10. *Is all that is seen in God seen together?*   187
Article 11. *Can any man in this life see the essence*
               of God?   188
Article 12. *Can we know God by our natural reason*
               in this life?   191

Article 13. Besides the knowledge we have of God by natural reason is there in this life a deeper knowledge that we have through grace? 192

Question 13. Theological language 195

Article 1. Can we use any words to refer to God? 195

Article 2. Do any of the words we use express something that he is? 198

Article 3. Can we say anything literally about God or must we always speak metaphorically? 202

Article 4. Are all the words predicated of God synonymous? 204

Article 5. Are words used both of God and of creatures used univocally or equivocally? 205

Article 6. Given that they are in fact used analogically, are they predicated primarily of God or of creatures? 209

Article 7. In speaking of God can we use words that imply temporal succession? 212

Article 8. Does 'God' mean a thing of a certain kind or a thing having a certain operation? 217

Article 9. Is the name 'God' peculiar to God or not? 219

Article 10. When it is used of God, of what shares in divinity and of what is merely supposed to do so, is it used univocally or equivocally? 222

Article 11. Is 'He who is' the most appropriate name for God? 225

Article 12. Can affirmative statements correctly be made about God? 227

APPENDICES

1. The *Summa* and the Bible   231
2. The Dialectic of Love in the *Summa*   242
3. Natural and Supernatural   255
4. The Meaning of the Word 'God'   259
5. The Five Ways   262
6. Analogy   293

GLOSSARY   295
INDEX   303

INTRODUCTION

ST THOMAS AQUINAS stands for a body of thought which for
seven centuries has moved at the centre of Western Catholicism. Yet having said that, some reservations should at once
be drawn, lest what follows be set down to the partisanship
of a Dominican or as a crass identification of the faith with an
intellectual system.

First, seven centuries are not such a long stretch in the life
of the Church, which was already effectively bearing witness
to the truths of Revelation before they were set in the frame-
work of one single and extensive philosophy. Second, even
during that period its central position has been lost to view,
or not seen to count, as the Church's engagement with human
thoughts and affections has swirled elsewhere. Third, and
most important, we refer to philosophical theology, not directly to Christian belief, from which indeed it may flow,
yet not in such a way that acceptance of the principles of
faith commits a person to this or that rational development.
Fourth, and connected, a religious philosophy which proves
well adapted to bring out the meanings, relations, and consequences of the truths of faith not unnaturally will receive
official endorsement and perhaps inevitably incur the danger
of becoming a party-line for administrators of the establishment more accustomed to disciplinary and legal than to more
contemplative forms of thought. And fifth, if we speak of
St Thomas occupying a position, this should be regarded, not
as dug in and defensive, but rather as a commanding height
from which to range with confidence and ease.

Whether the force of manoeuvre has always been maintained is another matter: there have been times when his followers have been like poor Bazaine who immobilized his field-
army behind the fortifications of Metz. For here is a body of
thought which is more versatile, and therefore more authentically itself, when working as a minority and not a majority movement, or when not being paraded under anti-

Modernist drill-sergeants with their manuals of standardized mechanization.

Only with such provisoes can we assess the true importance of the *Summa Theologiae* in the history of human thought, sacred and profane. It represents the first completed attempt to establish Christian theology as a scientific discipline, and students who start from inside the Christian tradition recognize that it is among the few masterpieces of its kind, though not all would agree that it is the kind of thing that should be done. Nevertheless St Thomas's appeal to those who look at Christianity from outside, who have come to respect his influence in psychological, metaphysical, and social philosophy, and who may rank him among Plato, Aristotle, Spinoza, Kant, and Marx, appears even more significant, and paradoxically for theological reasons, which will become clearer as God's saving truths are more openly acknowledged to transcend 'confessional' formulation, and the consequent ecumenism is extended beyond the frontiers set by terms historically and technically Christian.

Let me elaborate, though I fear that I shall have to be so compressed that nothing will escape save a few hints. Singleness in variety strikes the keynote of his thought, the unity of human and religious experience and the continuity between all the parts of creation. Indeed all comes back to his doctrine of creation, perhaps his chief title to fame as an original thinker, where, going far beyond Aristotle, he takes his criticism of monism from the order of being itself and establishes the metaphysical status of creatures, or many beings.[1] This pluralism reinforces his conviction that all truth, by whomsoever it is uttered, is from the Holy Spirit: it runs throughout his discourse. And so he cherishes creatures at once for themselves and because of the transcendent goodness of God, and affirms the value of nature because of grace, of reason because of faith, of flesh because of spirit. Values are seen in subordination, yet not thereby in subjection. For as things are in

---

[1] *Summa Theologiae*, 1a. 44–49. Vol. 8. Creation, Distinction, Variety. ed. T. Gilby. London, New York, 1969.

themselves so they act and attract in themselves; they may be secondary yet still be principal and not just instrumental, penultimate ends and not just means to an end. Consequently each value can be respected in itself and discussed in the purity of its own proper medium; philosophy can flourish because of theology, yet not be used to grind a theological axe. Indeed it may be recalled that St Thomas's philosophy has sometimes been excised from his theology, to stand no more incomplete than other purely rational systems of humanism or theism. His theology, however, cannot be excised from his philosophy—any more than God's grace from our nature.

He is not sectarian, then, nor are his preoccupations ecclesiastical in the 'churchy' sense of the term. In fact during his lifetime he was more warmly regarded by the lay philosophers and *artistae* than by the divines, certainly by those who secured his condemnation three years after his death. Although this was quashed afterwards and his followers gained for him a position of theological privilege, the suspicions of some religious thinkers were not allayed, and if anything have been heightened in recent years: that he was a saint in his life is not denied, but they look askance at the naturalism, rationalism, or this-worldliness of much of his writings.

The times in which he lived made both for his weakness and his strength. The decline of calligraphy ran parallel to that in the style of theological writing compared with the century before; technical terms and phrases may have sharpened analysis, but did not contribute to the warmth and grace of communication. His expository writings seem to us crabbed and repetitious, and particularly uncongenial in a literal translation. As you follow his argument you have the impression of watching with a workman chiselling away flakes of stone; the strokes are exact enough, but the effect is not of something elegant and finely chiselled: we shall have more to say on this point later on.

His strength is that he took the foremost part in what was no provincial episode in the history of thought. Philosophy entered the world in the fourth century B.C.; it entered the Christian world in the thirteenth century; the results were no less far-reaching and dramatic. The wisdom of the children of God and the wisdom of the children of this world, and both at full strength (so far as this could be when each was apart), were coming together on collision courses. One seemed to carry the whole weight of a sacred tradition, the other that of a secular experience which was to be increasingly accepted in the West.

Humanly speaking it was St Thomas and his group who averted the crash, though it was not in their mind that each should go on its own separate way henceforth. Such was his decisive intervention in the history of religious thought, marked by his opposition to the 'double-truth' theory, that what was true to faith could be false to reason, and what was false to faith could be true to reason. This has long survived its medieval setting, and it is a certain perennial quality in the questions St Thomas met and the answers he gave that give him contemporary relevance nowadays. His school has outlasted the flowering and decay of the high Middle Ages, the triumphs and crumbling plaster of the Baroque, and though curiously lethargic under the Enlightenment was as curiously reinvigorated by the rationalism and materialism of the nineteenth century.

What was he like, this man for many seasons? Tall, large, and fair, normally rather tranquil, with an abstracted air, yet courteous in his manner, patient and rather patrician in debate. He was born in 1225, at the Castle of Rocca Secca above Aquino, in the country fought over by the Allies in their advance from Naples to Rome. He was of mixed Lombard, Norman, and possibly Swabian stock; his family was related by kinship and service to the Emperor Frederick II, and was to suffer tragically when the Hohenstaufens were supplanted by the Angevins. Soldiers, courtiers, poets, they belonged to the glittering culture of Sicily, the first medieval kingdom to become a State as a formal and legal polity. A child oblate at the neighbouring Abbey of Monte Cassino, he left there to enter the University of Naples; founded by the Emperor, it was the first of what would now be called the State Universities. There, to the energetic displeasure of his family, he joined the Dominicans, a licenced but unbeneficed body of wandering preachers, teachers, and scholars, with little standing in the world of feudal securities. Both moves are significant, the first when he left the patriarchal community of monasticism, the second when he left the official establishment for a more open society.

Sent to Paris and Cologne for his studies, mainly under the celebrated Master Albert—called 'the Great', and already legendary for his researches and experiments in the field of natural science, yet also an advanced philosopher open to the speculations of Avicenna, and one of the most considerable theologians of the century—his own teaching and writing career falls into four periods. First, as lecturer and afterwards professor at the University of Paris; second, as theologian to the Papal Court; third, of his recall to Paris; and fourth, the final years when he returned to his native land, charged to organize Dominican studies in Naples. Called to the General Council of Lyons, he died on his way there in 1274 at the Abbey of Fossanova, not far away from his birthplace. The second and third periods are those of his maturity, when he was freeing himself from some of the strains of Augustinianism and Platonism, and recovering with the aid of his friends an Aristotle more Hellenic than was presented by the Arabs.* It was then that he wrote his greatest work, the *Summa Theologiae*, to which we now turn.

Structure

1. BEFORE ANATOMIZING the *Summa* be advised that it composes a living whole pressing forward in a continuous movement which, except for purposes of schematization, should

---

* For a study of St Thomas's thought see E. Gilson, *The Christian Philosophy of St. Thomas Aquinas*, London-New York, 1957. For its setting in history, E. Gilson, *History of Christian Philosophy in the Middle Ages*, London-New York, 1955. For compendiums, T. Gilby, St Thomas Aquinas, *Philosophical Texts*, Oxford-New York, 1951, and Galaxy paperback; *Theological Texts*, Oxford-New York, 1955. For a massive introduction, A. C. Pegis, *Basic Writings of St. Thomas Aquinas*, New York, 1945.

not be arrested in sets of scholastic 'stills'. Charts have been traced to show its divisions and subdivisions ramifying with all the complication and more of the logic of a genealogical tree: such fixed and flat reproductions are convenient for reference, though they fail to convey the motion and fuller dimensions in which human ideas and lives are begotten.

Moreover its arguments are less like a progressive series of theorems than like waves merged in the ebb and flow of the tide, the grand Platonic sweep of the whole work which follows the *exitus* and *reditus* of Creation—the going forth of things from God and their coming back to him, the setting out and returning home, the first birth in which we are possessed by God and the second birth from which he is possessed by us. For the *Summa* is more than a great monument to theism: it is the orchestration of the Christian mysteries in perennial reason, in which the God of the philosophers is not pitted against the God of Abraham, Isaac, and Jacob, or against the Father revealed in Christ.

On the surface it may seem a mixture, of passages, sometimes long sustained, of pure rationalism and of Scriptural exegesis, of severe demonstration from the necessity in things and of recommendation from a vivid sense, quaint sometimes to modern tastes, of the analogies running through the whole universe and kingdom of God;[2] topics of no direct religious interest appear to engross large sections. Penetrate more deeply, however, and all parts are seen to be combined and charged with one common purpose, namely to show God's own truth, not in its proper terms, for that is not possible even were it called for,[3] not even in poetic terms to evoke its secret glance, but more plainly in the terms of sacred history and of a universal and communicable human philosophy.[4] Autobiographical touches are notably absent, and the work is

---

[2] An argument from strict necessity, often beginning *necesse est*, is clearly distinguished from an argument from probability, *oportet* or *conveniens est*. See 1a. 32, 1; 3a. 1, 1–2. Also Blackfriars *Summa*, Vol. 1, Appendix 6, *Theology as Science*.

[3] ibid, Appendix 7, *Revelation* 6

[4] ibid, Appendix 9, *Doctrinal Development*

less the profession of a private faith than the objective exposition of how God's public revelation can be lodged in the reasonable discourse of men together. The *Summa* is a period piece only in that the technical terms and the turns of phrase are those of a western and medieval vogue.

2. There are three *parts*. consisting of *questions* divided into *articles*.

The first part, *Prima Pars* (1a), is about God and his creatures streaming forth from him. The second part, on the return of intelligent beings to their source, is taken in two movements, the *Prima Secundæ* (1a2æ) on human acts, morality, law, and grace, and the lengthy *Secunda Secundæ* (2a2æ) which repeats the movement on the virtues in greater detail. Thirdly the *Tertia Pars* (3a) considers Christ 'who as man is the way of our striving for God'.[5]

3. The questions fall into groups customarily called treatises, in which they may again be arranged into smaller groups, on a principle of division clearly noted at the appropriate place, the preface to a question. For instance, after a preliminary question on the nature of Christian theology, St Thomas announces his plan for the *Prima Pars*, 'our examination concerning God is threefold, for we shall ponder on truths relating first, to his nature, second, to the distinction of divine persons, third, to the coming forth of creatures from him. Thus with respect to the divine nature we must consider first, whether there is a God, second, what he is, or rather how he is not, third, the qualities of his activity, namely of knowledge, will, and might.'[6] Later, as occasion arises, he will distribute his subject-matter more particularly, and always with scrupulous regard for the logic of division.

The titles and cross-headings introduced in printed editions and adopted in this series to mark the volumes and arrange them within themselves are not, as such, St Thomas's own but adapted from his prefaces to a group of questions. The student is helped when the work is broken up in sections, yet he should not be tempted to mistake a cursive for an uncial

---

[5] 1a. 2 Prol.   [6] ibid

style of thought; and so, though the volumes will be made as self-contained as the needs of their topic require, they are still to be treated like members of an organic acting whole, like eyes and hands, to be properly appreciated only there, and not when they are disjected. St Thomas's frequent use of cross-references is dictated not merely by the tidy treatment of a subject; it is a reminder that the spirit of his thought is like the human soul, entire in every part of the body.[7] It manifests, too, his response to the analogies running from top to bottom of reality; nothing stands isolated and sealed up, each is open to another, and the coherence and continuity are such that it is without strain or abruptness that he looks to the biology of worms for a clue to the living process of Persons within the Godhead,[8] and to the mysteries there for illustrations of the workings of human psychology.[9]

4. A question, *quæstio* (from *quæro*, to search for), represents an inquiry rather than an interrogation, or rather, in the *Summa*, a group of points of inquiry or subjects for discussion. Its title printed as a cross-heading is taken from the introductory summary to a section in the text; in some editions the wording is not his, and the position and prominence are such as to interrupt the flow of his discourse. He himself writes, 'having considered what God is like in himself we now go on to consider what he is like in our knowledge, and here thirteen points of inquiry arise'.[10] Or again, 'having considered the production of creatures in being and their distinctness, now let us consider this more closely, and first the distinction between good and evil, and then the distinction between spiritual and bodily creatures. As for the first, let us inspect evil and the cause of evil. As for evil, six points of inquiry arise'.[11]

5. The points of inquiry comprising a question are treated in articles: *articulus*, a small joint or member (a diminutive of *artus*, *arthron*, a socket or, in the plural, limbs), applied to a division or part of speech, or a turning-point of stage in a

---

[7] 1a. 76, 8   [8] 1a. 27, 2   [9] 1a. 93, 7
[10] 1a. 12 Prol.   [11] 1a. 48 Prol.

process. Here again it should be observed that any typographical emphasis laid on an article-title, though useful for quick reference, should not pin down the movement of his thought or suggest that he is working on a cell enclosed in a shell. He himself merely enumerates the articles at the opening of the question; thus, here there are such and such a number of points of inquiry, namely, first, whether this be that, second, whether that be that, third and so forth. Then as he reaches each in turn, he turns to them without flourish, this first, or second, or third point of inquiry is approached as follows, it seems that this is not that, or that that is that, and so forth. That an article should not be taken in isolation is clearly indicated when discussing how faith articulates in the complexity of our reason the single and simple divine reality; 'the very term *article* signifies a fitting together of distinct parts within the integral whole; in this sense physiology treats of the joints of limbs, so Greek grammar uses the article to mark gender, number, and case and rhetoric decides the beat of a sentence'.[12]

Nevertheless an article in the *Summa* juts out as a task which is proposed, *problēma*; it is the unit of investigation, *zētēma*, and therefore its typical structure calls for description. It is built up in five stages: *a*. the title, *b*. the opening arguments for a position opposed to the one he will take up, *c*. a brief countering statement, *d*. the exposition and settlement of the issue, *e*. the replies to the opening arguments.

a. The wording of the title appears in the outline traced at the beginning of the question. Usually it begins *utrum*, whether, the interrogative adverb introducing alternatives, the neuter of *uter*, which of the two? St Thomas confines his use of the term to occasions when the alternatives are opposed by force of their meaning and not because of a contingent supposition. The title announces in effect that here is no thesis to be defended, in the manner of later Scholasticism, but an open question to be discussed.

b. The answer is not immediately resolved for a debate,

---

[12] 2a2æ. 1, 2 & 6

dialeksis, is opened with arguments, commonly called the objections, though nowadays this is too hostile a word. They do not oppose a conclusion, for this has yet to be drawn; *objicere* meant to throw out suggestions or reasons for one or the other side of a question not yet settled. They are brief and comprehensive, not made up by St Thomas but edited from things men had said or were saying; they are always respected and usually express doubts and half-truths that should be taken into account, and as such are not blankly denied, but sorted out by drawing a distinction.[13]

c. Normally the third phase beginning 'on the other hand', *sed contra*, is not a rebuttal of the arguments but rather a gesture towards an alternative position recommended by approved authorities or by reason.

d. This introduces St Thomas's own exposition and settlement of the issue, *determinatio, dusis*, in what is called the body of the article, *corpus articuli*. Printed editions begin, *Respondeo dicendum quod*, 'My answer is that'. Our edition, however, prefers the simple *Responsio*, 'Reply', as more authentic by manuscript evidence and more in keeping with the author's impersonal style: only here and there does he use the first person singular, and the effect is all the more pungent in consequence.

e. Finally, the replies to the opening arguments, which are often qualified in the light of the exposition or taken as opportunities for its further development. They display two of St Thomas's characteristics, modesty and control, for he keeps to the limits and has clearly mastered the evidence of the case.

6. This shape shows that an article is a debate in miniature. It was composed, not as an artifice of fiction or imaginary conversation with a didactic purpose, but to record the living conflict of ideas in St Thomas's day; the names may have changed yet many of the causes are still contemporary.

---

[13] *Commentary on the Metaphysics* III, *lect.* 1, 'those who look for truth without first considering their doubts are like people who do not look where they are going'.

To appreciate where he stands the entire article must be read; it is not enough to abstract the conclusion from the *corpus*. Sometimes the *sed contra* is omitted or swings too far to one extreme, in which case it is corrected by a reply; indeed in the ampler situation of debate in the Disputed Questions it extends to a series of arguments diametrically opposed to the opening series, both of which have to be brought into perspective by his exposition.

Method

1. SCHOLASTIC DISPUTATION, which the *Summa* reproduces in a compressed form, can be represented as an occupation sometimes idle sometimes serious, yet always extrinsic and interiorly unrelated to the life of religion, almost as a piece of theatre before a curtain which has to be raised before the real drama of Everyman can be seen, or as a diversion when the medievals exercised their logical skill in finding reasons for the phenomena they registered, in discussing data uncritically accepted from Aristotle, and in embroidering on the doctrine and discipline of the Church. On the contrary it should be emphasized that the debate as it proceeds in the *Summa* develops from and is all one of a piece with cleaving to God who reveals himself to us.

Certainly a purely rational philosophy and theology can be lifted out of its pages, and this can stand on its own not only as an archæological fragment but also as a present cause, namely secular Thomism—so far as is possible for such a system. Certainly there are long passages on metaphysics, theism, psychology and natural philosophy, individual, social, and political morality which appeal to no evidence higher than reason and ordinary experience can find. Nevertheless these, as existing in the *Summa*, are assimilated into a Christian discourse so that they become truths of a different kind. Their own proper character is not lost, but they are now taken into a new dimension, much as the senses, though they can be treated as generically common to animals and human beings, when brought into the life of reason become different in kind, and open to us a world the beasts do not touch. Nor

are they accretions on the deposit of faith, for the development of doctrine is not a process of growth by the addition of
external matter or the adhesion of particles from outside; it
is homogeneous, that is to say neither evolving from heterogeneous sources nor still less acting like a mixture of incongruous elements. Only on the surface can the *Summa* be
viewed as a hybrid of faith and reason; even so then not without pride of ancestry or hope of posterity. For both parents
spring from the same single and simple truth of God and are
conjoined in the regeneration of man's single substance as a
child of God.

Grace and nature are not separate things though their concepts are distinct.[14] The activity of grace goes far beyond the
resources of nature, yet presupposes the activity of nature
which it enlarges. Texts may be quoted in support, but if
you seek a reminder, then enter the whole *Summa* and look
around you. With particular reference to the interpenetration of faith and reason, the opening question states the
theme which will be constantly repeated with variations.
Christian theology derives from faith yet is truly science; its
interest is the world as seen in the fresh light of revelation
and as related to God as he is in himself; faith gathers in reason as unforcedly as liking yields to loving.

2. The first principles of this *sacra doctrina* are neither self-
evident nor are they assented to because their terms can be
shown to be held together by an inner necessity. They are
about things beyond the reach of reason, which things, to the
extent that they are manifested to us in this world, all cluster
round what philosophical theory must regard as a contingent
event, namely the Christian Fact, the entrance into human
history of God's might and saving mercy, not because of any
emanative determinism of his mind but in the perfect freedom of his will. We may gratefully reflect, how right that it
was and is so, and indeed one office of theology will be to
sound all the rational resonances to the mystery of God's presence among us, but we cannot declare that it had to be so.

---

[14] cf Appendix 3, *Natural and Supernatural*

The very first article of the *Summa* indicates this approach, of which the classical example occurs in the first question of the *Tertia Pars* on the reasons for the Incarnation. There the rule is laid down, 'the blessings that come to us by God's freewill above all that is owing to creatures cannot become known to us except in so far as they are delivered in Holy Scripture, through which the divine will is signified to us'.[15]

The discourse of Christian theology is carried throughout on our assent to this declaration of God's will, and on our acceptance of a power we cannot postulate from reasoning and a mercy we cannot earn. Though in the human sciences the argument from authority is weakest, here no other course is open to us. Hence Christian theology differs in kind from philosophical theology; its subject is more than the God of the philosophers who can be inferred as the integrator of the universe about us, but God himself, the Father revealed in the Son, the Father to whom we are born by the Spirit, the blessed Trinity of Persons whose life we are called to share.

Faith itself is based on nothing else but God's own truth. Christian theology, however, is not naked faith, but faith invested by grace with reason and imagination, and its direct and immediate authority is God's revelation as embodied in the living Scriptures, that is to say, the living Church.[16] That is the source of its cogent arguments, so much so that the first question of the *Summa* uses *sacra doctrina* and *sacra scriptura* as interchangeable terms. Holy teaching is committed to God's word as delivered to the Prophets and Apostles, not to any divine disclosure that may have been made to others. The writings of the Fathers and Doctors of the Church are in the mainstream of public revelation; they belong to the mind of the Church, and therefore are treated as inside authorities, although arguments based on their witness lack the force, *robur*, of Scripture. Pagan poets and philosophers, however, are treated as outside authorities, although their teaching may serve to recommend or confirm the mysteries of faith.

3. The theological arguments of the *Summa* start by ac-

---

[15] 3a. 1, 3.   [16] Appendix 1, *The Summa and the Bible*

cepting what is declared by the living tradition of the Church, and respect for this authority is maintained throughout. The sense of the word had not then hardened to signify an imposed or authoritarian prerogative, but still kept its early sense of begetting and cherishing, of being a source, *auctoritas et fontalitas*: to be authoritative was to be authentically in the tradition, and the tribute was paid less to the writer as a person than to the esteem in which his writing was held by the Church. *Auctoritates* are quasi-axiomatic and rank high in worth, *dignitates* Boethius calls them, *axiōma*; they offer a standing, *locus, topos*, for argument. St Thomas is critically reluctant to enlarge their force, yet his reverence continues even when scaled down to the lesser witness of theologians, as when he speaks of Hugh of St Victor's teaching being magistral but not authoritative.[17] He shows a similar regard for writings from outside and in parts hostile to his tradition, by Avicenna, Averroes, Maimonides and others.

4. Meditation on the Scriptures and the Fathers, above all on St Augustine, was common form with the divines who were his predecessors and contemporaries. His singular contribution was to meet the occasion when Aristotle was no longer just the great logician, but The Philosopher, *Philosophus*: let Aristotle stand as a symbol for ambitious and confident rationalism. Before this St Thomas neither stood on the defensive nor beat a retreat; it was no threat but a promise, and one very much to his liking. The *sacra doctrina* of divine revelation was not to be held withdrawn in a special area of religious conviction and feeling, but was to advance into the whole world of human experience, and in particular of reasoned experience. The mystery was not to be reduced to human concepts or framed in a system; all the same it could and should be shown forth to men glinting with reasons. What was new was not so much the attempt nor even the success, but rather that the effort was sustained so imperturbably and in a manner so matter-of-fact and unapologetical.

---

[17] 2a2æ. 5, 1 ad 1.

This sprang from his clear recognition of the distinction yet combination of grace and nature in the Christian universe, and of spiritual and material in the physical universe. They were not set against one another as though they stood on opposite or even parallel courses which never met, nor were they different things which at best could be juxtaposed with tolerable harmony; they were two in one flesh, real only in a single substance, married by the Word made flesh, the son of God and the son of man. As sense and passion could be taken into intelligence and will and remain perfect sense and passion, and indeed become heightened sense and passion, so reason could be taken into faith.

The Christian man is the whole man, sensing, feeling, thinking, willing and all. He is not composed of two layers, the lower of which, having served its purpose of supporting the higher, will one day be removed, for that too is penetrated by divine revelation—*the word piercing to the joints and marrow*.[18] Nor is there some mysterious apex of his soul away from the rest of him, where alone he can communicate with divinity. The promises made to Abraham and his seed have been inherited by the Church, and God still speaks to his people—no longer just a tribe but also a polity enjoying the decencies of *civilis conversatio* under reasonable law—and in the medium of shared human experience, that is of meaning and choice. It is this public revelation, not private mysticism, that opens to us the way of salvation, and though it anticipates a vision and love beyond the chatter of thought, *volubiles cogitationes*, its communications are conducted through human channels and therefore have to be talked about. Faith comes by hearing, and revelation reaches us through our environment, and then when accepted impregnates our thinking and imagining. From this stems a theology which is truly a science, indeed the noblest of the sciences. There is, as it were, a patch where the light of reason shines in the darkness of faith, and through the mist of doubts that may arise. Reason itself is not an authority in the sense al-

---

[18] *Hebrews* 4:12

ready indicated, for it proposes a truth not to be taken on trust but to be seen by its own evidence, either immediate or mediate through proof. Faith is not this sort of knowledge, for its articles, which are the principles of theology, neither carry their own evidence nor can they be demonstrated. Assent to them, however, and reason comes into much more than its own. This, then, is the rôle of theology as science, to enlarge the truths of faith in our minds, to develop and relate their implications, and to disclose riches hitherto unsuspected.

5. Often the process has the severity of demonstration, where one truth is inferred from another and with certainty in the light of causality, this being taken in its widest sense to include efficient, formal, exemplar, and final causes. To that extent theology can be a system displaying within itself the strictest logical necessity. The demonstration may proceed through effect to cause, as in the proofs for the existence of God, or from cause to effect, as when his eternity is inferred from his pure actuality; the first, which shows that a thing is so, is called by St Thomas a *demonstratio quia, hoti*, the second, which shows the reason why it is so, is called a *demonstratio propter quid, dioti*: they correspond closely enough to *a posteriori* and *a priori* deduction respectively.[19]

6. The dialectic, however, is wider than a strict syllogistic, for other reasonings abound, not to be mistaken for demonstrations, though at first sight sometimes they may look dressed like them. They are recommendations of a conclusion, arguments for its probability, *ex convenientia*, pointers that it should be so, confirmations that it fits in with the rest of our experience. St Thomas, distinguishing them from proofs which provide evidence enough or adequate reason, *ratio sufficiens*, for a conclusion, observes that they do not reach to the root of the matter and explain it, but, like working hypotheses, show the congruity of positing it, so enabling the appearances to be preserved, *salvari apparentia*, for him an important function, since he regarded phenomena as manifesting not veiling reality.

---

[19] 1a. 2, 2

They make out a case of varying force, and range from those with universal appeal, thus the application of human concepts of knowing and loving to the mystery of the Trinity, and of generosity, courtesy, mercy, and 'sharing' to the motives why God became man for us and died on the cross,[20] to those with a more limited appeal, thus reasons from the logic of division in favour of seven gifts of the Spirit and seven sacraments,[21] from cosmology to show the necessity of faith[22] or describe the ministry of angels,[23] from symbolism to show how the New Law is contained in the Old[24] and why Christ was tempted in the desert,[25] from external finality to suggest that men were not meant to walk on all-fours for if they did they would pick up their food by the mouth and their lips would stretch and become tough and gross,[26] and from a medieval humour that now may sometimes fall rather flat, as when he probes elements worse in Eve's sin than in Adam's.[27]

Such arguments have to be taken with discretion and a sense of proportion. Analysis may be substituted for understanding when they are isolated and taken apart, and then to be underestimated, or perhaps overestimated. For it is in the whole, in the singleness of faith and a unified world-view, that they converge and have a cumulative force, and it is only there that some of them will be found endearing yet not calling for too solemn treatment. St Thomas defended the employment of metaphorical and symbolical language for the communication of revealed truth, and recognized the wealth of allegory, morality, and eschatology beneath the literal sense of its statement; he also admitted the value of bathos, the benign come-down that makes authentic theology so much more than fine writing and uplift.[28] He commanded a poet's technique and his poems are full of doctrine, yet he did not think of poetry as the best method of teaching and, though

---

[20] 1a. 27, 3, 4; 32, 1; 34, 1; 36, 1. 3a. 1, 1, 2; 46, 1–4
[21] 1a2æ. 68, 4. 3a. 65, 1   [22] 2a2æ. 2, 3   [23] 1a. 112, 1
[24] 1a2æ. 107, 3   [25] 3a. 41, 2   [26] 1a. 91, 3 ad 3
[27] 2a2æ. 163, 4   [28] 1a. 1, 9 ad 3

at moments you feel he can scarcely prevent himself from soaring, he sticks to the level he has chosen in the *Summa*, and plods through the arguments.

7. Compare the sequences, the *Lauda Sion* of St Thomas with the contemporary *Stabat Mater*, or even the *Dies Iræ*, and at once you are struck by the non-subjective and non-emotional quality of his tone. This is even more marked in his prose. Passages of fine writing are rare, and these tease you with the feeling that elsewhere he was humdrum by choice. Did you not know it for a fact you would suspect that much was dictated. The pace seldom quickens from a steady jog-trot, the movement is not lissom, the syntax not versatile, the vocabulary is more spare than the ideology. There is no ornamentation, no attempt at elegant variation, no subtlety of tint; the sentences as they stand are like a scientist's jottings in basic English. Treat the *Summa* as the lexicon for a philosophy of religion, and it will not be surprising if the ideas delivered straight from it taste like food from a deep-freeze. How then does its discovery communicate an excitement that for many on rereading never palls?

The answer in one word is analogy. The same term repeated over again does not always bear the same fixed sense, but receives an interior movement and modulation according as its position varies in the whole. Such terms are like living cells, not like bits of a mosaic; they are open and respond to one another, and while ever keeping their proper likeness and form can be shotted and shimmering with differences. They are not given the same name by the accident of the poverty of language, for that is mere equivocation (*æquivocum purum, a casu*) which is the occasion of fallacy, but in order to manifest mobile inner relationships by a designed equivocation (*æquivocum a consilio*, or *analogum*).[29] Thus, to take some stock instances, such terms as *natura, ratio, forma, species, causa*, and *scientia* are variously inflected from

---

[29] For analogy in general see 1a. 13 below. Appendix 6.

their context; similarly such terms as *mens, intellectus, spiritus, anima, corpus,* and *concupiscentia* should be read against a background that changes from Aristotle to St Paul, and from Dionysius to St Augustine.

8. Nevertheless St Thomas's style remains an instrument of precision once you appreciate that he was not writing a mathematical treatise or a legal document where single terms can be treated as atoms of discourse or analysed into their fixed univocal sense: misapprehensions on this point have brought him into false credit and discredit. He was renewing Aristotle's achievement of a synthesis beyond the static world of Parmenides and the fluid world of Heraclitus without, like Plato, finding meaning by forsaking the material world about us; he was addressing himself as a philosopher to existing things first shown us through the senses and not to disembodied essences, and as a theologian to the works of God in history, from which he suffered even less temptation to escape. He had to render things that were at once dark and shimmering, deep and on the surface, single and complex, firm and supple, irreducibly individual yet sharing in the common whole; and he paid them the compliment of attempting to do so without breaking into poetry. How far he surpassed Aristotle appears from his key-passages on the metaphysics of analogy, relation, and creation.[30]

9. It is not in metaphysics alone that he is so free from monotony at depth. The *Summa* throngs with ideas from many different traditions, of the Scriptures, of the Fathers and notably of St Augustine, of western and oriental Platonism, of two Aristoteleanisms, one from the Greeks and the other from the Arabs (a comprehensive term for writers ranging from Turkestan in the east to Spain in the west), of the Latin Stoics and of the Roman Law, of the freedom, feudalism and chivalry which were the heritage of his Norman and Lombard blood. If this richness is to be recaptured, or even suggested, then a translation must use the resources of Eng-

---

[30] 1a. 13, 4, 5; 28, 1, 2; 44, 1; 45, 1, 3, 4; 47, 1–2

lish; it is probably better to risk some inconsistency than to
stick to a small number of equivalent terms.

To say that St Thomas wrote in Latin but thought in
Greek would unduly tax historical judgment, yet it brings out
the delicacy and biological movement of his argument, so
misrepresented as the shuttling of counters into place. He
himself used a language of translation, in the sense that he
did not write in the Latin of Cicero or of the Fathers or of
humanists of Chartres; it was neither the Latin of the lawyers
nor of the liturgy, nor yet the vernacular. It was a scholastic
language, the technique of a school devoted to a special task.
If years later it was heard only in the atmosphere of schools
grown rather fusty, employing tricks of communication as peculiar as Winchester notions, in his day it was the product of
an exacting effort to forge from the non-metaphysical language of Latin a weapon that could engage with the subtle
play of the Greek: certainly the debates at the Council of
Florence left the Latins who used it with no feeling of in-
feriority, and some of the acutest of the Byzantines turned it
back into their own language.

The effort was all the more exacting because in stripping
everything down to the essentials of meaning, he still had to
preserve the truth that when all is said and done all reality
comes back to subsisting things in the round. If his means
were abstract his ends were concrete. So he could dispense
with the interest of figures of speech, discipline the imagination with an austerity diet, be content with a grammar that
many might consider schoolboyish, neglect mere stylistic
polish, but he could not rest with a thin philosophism of
pure essences. How well he fulfilled the saying, *verba phi-
losophorum sunt formalia*—the terms of philosophical discourse are to be taken according to their central and definitive
meaning apart from their material subject and any interest on
their fringes—yet all the same the asceticism of the logical and
notional purity he achieved was for him a part of the apos-
tolate and only a stage towards the vision of the living God.

OUTLINE OF THE SUMMA

INTRODUCTION: the nature and scope of Christian theology (1a. 1)

PART 1. GOD

1. THE NATURE OF GOD
   1. The Existence of God (1a. 2)
   2. The Mode of God's Existence (1a. 3–13)
   3. God's Activity (1a. 14–26)

2. THE THREE PERSONS IN GOD
   1. Origination within God (1a. 27)
   2. Relation within God (1a. 28)
   3. The Divine Persons
      1. Absolutely Considered
         1. Together (1a. 29–32)
         2. Singly (1a. 33–8)
      2. Relatively Considered (1a. 39–43)

3. THE COMING FORTH OF THINGS FROM GOD
   1. The Production of Creatures (1a. 44–6)
   2. The Distinction of Creatures
      1. In General (1a. 47)
      2. Good and Evil (1a. 48–9)
      3. Spiritual and Material (1a. 50–102)
   3. The Governance of Creatures (1a. 103–19)

PART 2. MAN'S JOURNEY TO GOD

1. THE ULTIMATE GOAL OF HUMAN LIFE (1a2æ. 1–5)

2. MAN'S ACTIVITY IN RELATION TO HIS GOAL
   1. General Considerations
      1. Human Activity
         1. The Psychology of Freedom (1a2æ. 6–17)
         2. Morality (1a2æ. 18–21)
         3. The Emotions (1a2æ. 22–48)

  2. Principles of Human Activity
    1. Intrinsic
      1. Virtue (1a2æ. 49–70)
      2. Vice (1a2æ. 71–89)
    2. Extrinsic
      1. Law (1a2æ. 90–105)
      2. Grace (1a2æ. 106–14)
2. Special Considerations
  1. For All Walks of Life
    1. Theological Virtues
      1. Faith (2a2æ. 1–16)
      2. Hope (2a2æ. 17–22)
      3. Friendship (2a2æ. 23–46)
    2. Cardinal Virtues
      1. Prudence (2a2æ. 47–56)
      2. Justice (2a2æ. 57–122)
      3. Courage (2a2æ. 123–40)
      4. Moderation (2a2æ. 141–70)
  2. For Particular Callings
    1. Charismatic Gifts (2a2æ. 171–8)
    2. Action and Contemplation (2a2æ. 179–82)
    3. Office and Status (2a2æ. 183–9)

PART 3. CHRIST, MAN'S ROAD TO GOD

1. THE SAVIOUR
  1. The Mystery of the Incarnation (3a. 1–26)
  2. The Life, Death, and Resurrection of Christ (3a. 27–59)

2. THE SACRAMENTS OF SALVATION
  1. In General (3a. 60–5)
  2. In Particular (3a. 66–90. *Supplementum* 1–68)

3. RESURRECTION AND ETERNAL LIFE (*Supplementum* 69–99[101])

THE PRESENT VOLUME contains the first thirteen Questions of the First Part and together with its companion volume, which follows, completes the treatise 'on the One God', or 'on the divine nature' (1a. 1–26), which prepares for the studies on the Blessed Trinity.

They open with discussions about what Christian theology is (Q. 1). On the one hand it is not the theological virtue of faith, by which we commit ourselves to God beyond all the evidences at present apparent to us; on the other it is not just a purely rational philosophy of religion, which may discuss natural effects of supernatural reality while always, as it were, looking at the truths of grace from outside. At once believing and scientific, it lies between; an effort from within faith to extend its principles into conclusions. St Anselm speaks of faith seeking understanding; it is based on the knowledge the blessed have, the *scientia beatorum*, and will eventually be brought to their vision and comprehension; in the meantime it seeks that half-understanding which may come from the play of wit and imagination. For God reveals himself to the whole man, compact of spirit and sense, rational, affective, social, not to an isolated *apex animae*. Hence the descensive continuity from faith to a theology, which presents to the world a coherent body of doctrine. *Sacra doctrina* gives reasons, strikes harmonies, and uses figures of speech which touch at so many points our human condition. The Word Made Flesh, that union is the mystery of faith; it is not enough to exalt the first, but, as Karl Barth came to see, there must also be tender regard for the second. And so for St Thomas theology is the words of God made flesh.

Next is discussed the existence of God (Q. 2). Of course people know that God is there before they look for the clues, but the *Summa* is not tracing the biography of a believer, but the stages of a theological passage, to which at the start it is not self-evident that God exists. No proof, however, can be expected on the mathematical model, for there is nothing behind God to prove him by. Accordingly we must look for another type of demonstration, which begins from the world about us and shows that it makes some sort of sense only if there is a ground of reality beyond it. It is conducted along the famous five ways, *quinque viae*, all of which reach an object 'which we call God'.

They are shown to converge in the following Questions (2–11), which tell us about the one God by showing us how he is not. Can we ever know him just as he is? Q. 12 argues we are promised more than theophanies. Q. 13, one of the most important in the *Summa*, returns to our present knowledge. It steers a careful course between anthropomorphism and agnosticism. It allows the proper use of metaphor in our talk about God, but claims that theological language can go further without being required to lapse into the reverent silence of the negative theology of a long mystical tradition.

EDITORIAL NOTE

This edition presents the English translation, slightly modified here and there, matching the Latin text of the volumes of the *Summa Theologiae*, published by Blackfriars in conjunction with Eyre and Spottiswoode, Her Majesty's Printers, London, and the McGraw-Hill Book Company, New York. St Thomas's own references have been kept, but for the rest the apparatus of explanatory footnotes has been reduced, together with the appendices. The glossary is a reconstruction; some old entries have been expanded, others omitted, new ones added. An index has been compiled for the convenience of students.

Variations in manuscripts and printed editions are not such as to call for note here. The readings were consulted, but in principle each translator was left to make the working text of his choice, instructed as often as not by his own teaching experience. Usually it turned out to be either the *Piana* or the *Leonina*, so named after the noble folios published under the patronage of Pius v and Leo xiii respectively, but sometimes it was the text used by the Dominicans of Paris in the edition of the *Revue des Jeunes*, or that published by B. Geyer of Münster, or that corrected by T. Pègues of the Toulouse Dominicans.

The translators did not attempt a constant word for word rendering, for that would have produced a flat betrayal of the inner spring and variety of the thought, but a version in running English faithful to the meaning and order of the Latin. Where the reader experiences difficulty with a technical term and does not find an explanatory footnote, he is referred to the glossary or to the index. Those footnotes indicated by a number are the reference given by St Thomas those indicated by a letter are editorial references and explanatory remarks.

Scriptural references are to the Vulgate. *Summa* cross-references are given without title; thus 1a. 3, 4 ad 1 indicates Part One, Question 3, article 1, reply to the first objection.

The Migne notation, *Patrologiae Latinae cursus completus* (PL) and *Patrologiae Graecae cursus completus* (PG), is given for patristic works; the Bekker, *Aristotelis Opera*, for works of Aristotle.

The *Summa* is divided into three parts: Part One (1a), on God and the streaming forth of creatures from him; Part Two (subdivided into the 1a2æ and the 2a2æ), on their returning to him; and Part Three (3a), on Christ, who is the way, the truth, and the life. Each part is composed of treatises, which are usually broken up into general headings or 'Questions', which in their turn are broken up into discussions on particular points of inquiry, or 'articles'. These are cast in the following form: arguments for a plain yes or no to the query raised, declaration of the author's own position, his explanation and qualifications, followed by his reply to the difficulties. The strictly logical ramification of the whole work can be traced from the introductory text to treatises and Questions.

Of the Blackfriars series this book contains Vol. 1, *Christian Theology* (1a. 1), edited and translated by Thomas Gilby, O.P.; Vol. 2, *Existence and Nature of God* (1a. 2–11), edited and translated by Timothy McDermott, O.P.; and Vol. 3, *Knowing and Naming God* (1a. 12–13), edited and translated by Herbert McCabe, O.P. Of the appendices in this volume, Appendix 4 was written by Fr McDermott. Appendix 6 by Fr McCabe, the rest, together with the Introduction, by the General Editor.

SUMMA THEOLOGIAE

VOLUME I
The Existence of God

Part One: Question 1   THOMAS GILBY, O.P.
Part One: Questions 2–11   TIMOTHY MC DERMOTT, O.P.
Part One: Questions 12–13   HERBERT MC CABE, O.P.

FOREWORD

Since the teacher of Catholic truth has not only to develop advanced students but also to shape those who are making a start, according to St Paul, *Even as unto babes in Christ I have fed you with milk and not meat*,[1] we propose in this work to convey the truths which are part of the Christian religion in a style serviceable for the training of beginners.

For we have in mind how much newcomers to this teaching are hindered by various writings about it, partly by a swarm of pointless questions, articles, and arguments, partly because essential points are treated according to the requirements of textual commentary or of academic debate, not to those of a sound educational method, partly because repetitiousness breeds boredom and muddle in their minds.

Eager, therefore, to avoid these and other like drawbacks, and trusting in God's help, we shall try to pursue the truths of Christian theology, and, so far as the subject permits, to be concise and clear in the process.

---

[1] *1 Corinthians* 3:1

Question 1. What sort of teaching Christian theology is and what it covers

In order to keep our efforts within definite bounds we must first investigate this holy teaching[a] and find out what it is like and how far it goes. Here there are ten points of inquiry:

1. about its need;
2. whether it be science;
3. whether it be single or several;
4. whether it be theoretical or practical;
5. how it compares with other sciences;
6. whether it be wisdom;
7. what is its subject;
8. whether it sets out to prove anything;
9. whether it should employ metaphorical or symbolical language;
10. whether its sacred writings are to be interpreted in several senses.

Article 1. Is another teaching required apart from philosophical studies?

THE FIRST POINT: 1. Any other teaching beyond that of science and philosophy seems needless. For man ought not to venture into realms beyond his reason; according to Scripture, *Be not curious about things far above thee.*[1] Now the things lying within range of reason yield well enough to scientific and philosophical treatment. Additional teaching, therefore, seems superfluous.

2. Besides, we can be educated only about what is real; for nothing can be known for certain save what is true, and what

---

[a] *sacra doctrina*, sacred doctrine. This introductory Question is going to vindicate the special place of Christian theology among the sciences and to discuss its method.

[1] *Ecclesiasticus* 3:22

is true is identical with what really is. Yet the philosophical sciences deal with all parts of reality, even with God; hence Aristotle refers to one department of philosophy as theology or the divine science.[2] That being the case, no need arises for another kind of education to be admitted or entertained.

ON THE OTHER HAND St Paul says, *All Scripture inspired of God is profitable to teach, to reprove, to correct, to instruct in righteousness.*[3] Divinely inspired Scripture, however, is no part of the branches of philosophy traced by reasoning. Accordingly it is expedient to have another body of sure knowledge inspired by God.

REPLY: It should be urged that human well-being has called for schooling in what God has revealed, in addition to the philosophical researches pursued by human reasoning.

Above all because God destines us for an end beyond the grasp of reason; according to Isaiah, *Eye hath not seen, O God, without thee what thou hast prepared for them that love thee.*[4] Now we have to recognize an end before we can stretch out and exert ourselves for it. Hence the necessity for our welfare that divine truths surpassing reason should be signified to us through divine revelation.

We also stand in need of being instructed by divine revelation even in religious matters the human reason is able to investigate. For the rational truth about God would be reached only by few, and even so after a long time and mixed with many mistakes; whereas on knowing this depends our whole welfare, which is in God.[b] In these circumstances, then, it was to prosper the salvation of human beings, and the more widely and less anxiously, that they were provided for by divine revelation about divine things.

These then are the grounds of holding the sacred doctrine

---

[2] *Metaphysics* VI, 1. 1026a19   [3] II *Timothy* 3:16

[4] *Isaiah* 64:4

[b] St Thomas pursues the argument at greater length in the *Summa contra gentiles* I, 4. Image Books D 26, pp. 66–68.

which has come to us through revelation beyond the discoveries of the rational sciences.

Hence: 1. Admittedly the reason should not pry into things too high for human knowledge, nevertheless when they are revealed by God they should be welcomed by faith: indeed the passage goes on to say, *Many things are shown thee above the understanding of men.*[5] And on them Christian teaching rests.

2. The diversification of the sciences is brought about by the diversity of aspects under which things can be known. Both an astronomer and a physical scientist may demonstrate the same conclusion, for instance that the earth is spherical; the first, however, works in a mathematical medium prescinding from material qualities, while for the second his medium is the observation of material bodies through the senses. Accordingly there is nothing to stop the same things from being treated by the philosophical sciences when they can be looked at in the light of natural reason and by another science when they are looked at in the light of divine revelation. Consequently the theology of holy teaching differs in kind from that theology which is ranked as a part of philosophy.[c]

Article 2. Is Christian theology a science?

THE SECOND POINT: 1. Christian theology does not look like science. For every science advances from self-evident principles. Yet Christian theology advances from the articles of faith and these are not self-evident, since not everybody grants them; *for not all have faith.*[1] Consequently it is not a science.

2. Besides, a science is not concerned with individual cases.[a] Sacred doctrine, however, deals with individual events

---

[5] *Ecclesiasticus* 3:25

[c] i.e. natural theology, sometimes called 'theodicy'

[1] II *Thessalonians* 3:2

[a] A science is not directly engaged with incidents in their par-

and people, for instance the doings of Abraham, Isaac, Jacob and the like. Therefore sacred doctrine is not a science.

ON THE OTHER HAND. Augustine says that *this science alone is credited with begetting, nourishing, protecting, and making robust the healthiest faith.*[2] These functions belong to no science other than holy teaching. Therefore it is a science.

REPLY: Christian theology should be pronounced to be a science. Yet bear in mind that sciences are of two kinds: some work from premises recognized in the innate light of intelligence, for instance arithmetic, geometry, and sciences of the same sort; while others work from premises recognized in the light of a higher science, for instance optics starts from principles marked out by geometry and harmony from principles indicated by arithmetic.

In this second manner is Christian theology a science, for it flows from founts recognized in the light of a higher science, namely God's very own which he shares with the blessed. Hence, rather as harmony credits its principles which are taken from arithmetic, Christian theology takes on faith its principles revealed by God.

Hence: 1. Let us repeat that the premises of any science, no matter what, are either evident in themselves or can be resolved back into what a higher science recognizes. Such, as we have observed, are the principles of Christian theology.

2. Sacred doctrine sets out individual cases, not as being preoccupied with them, but in order both to introduce them as examples for our own lives, as is the wont of moral sciences, and to proclaim the authority of the men through whom divine revelation has come down to us, which revelation is the basis of sacred Scripture or doctrine.

---

ticularity, but with the common meanings they disclose within its frame of reference.

[2] *On the Trinity* XIV, 7. PL 42, 1037

Article 3. Is Christian theology a single science?

THE THIRD POINT: 1. The holy teaching would not appear to form one science. For, according to Aristotle, *a science has unity by treating of one class of subject-matter*.[1] Now here the Creator and creatures are both treated of, yet they cannot be grouped together within the same class of subject-matter. Therefore holy teaching is not just one science.

2. Further, Christian theology discusses angels as well as bodily creatures and human conduct. These offer fields for diverse philosophical sciences. Christian theology, then, is not a single unified science.

ON THE OTHER HAND holy Scripture refers to it as being one; thus, *he gave to him the science of holy things*.[2]

REPLY: Holy teaching should be declared a single science. For you gauge the unity of a faculty and its training by its object, and this should be taken precisely according to the formal interest engaged and not according to what is materially involved; for instance the object of the sense of sight is a thing as having colour, a formal quality exhibited by men, donkeys, and stones in common. Now since holy Scripture looks at things in that they are divinely revealed, as already noted,[3] all things whatsoever that can be divinely revealed share in the same formal objective meaning. On that account they are included under holy teaching as under a single science.

Hence: 1. Holy teaching does not express judgments about God and creatures as though they were counterbalancing, but about God as principal and about creatures in relation to him, who is their origin and end. Hence its unity as science is not hampered.

2. Nothing debars the distinct subject-matters which diversify lower and more particular faculties and trainings from

---

[1] *Posterior Analytics* 1, 28. 87a38   [2] *Wisdom* 10:10
[3] art. 1 above

being treated in common by a higher and more general faculty and training; this is because the latter envisages an object in a wider formal scene. Take for instance our central internal sense;[b] visual and audible phenomena are both included in its object, namely a thing the senses can perceive, and while gathering in all the objects of the five external senses it yet remains a single unified faculty. Likewise different classes of object separately treated by the diverse philosophical sciences can be combined by Christian theology which keeps its unity when all of them are brought into the same focus and pictured in the field of divine revelation: thus in effect it is like an imprint on us of God's own knowledge, which is the single and simple vision of everything.

Article 4. Is Christian theology a practical science?

THE FOURTH POINT: 1. Christian theology appears to be a practical science.[a] For Aristotle says that *a practical science is that which ends in action.*[1] But Christian theology is for action, according to Scripture, *Be ye doers of the word and not hearers only.*[2] Therefore Christian theology is a practical science.

2. Moreover, sacred doctrine is divided into the Old Law and the New Law. Now law is part of moral science, which is a practical science. Therefore sacred doctrine is a practical science.

ON THE OTHER HAND, every practical science is concerned with what men can do and make, thus ethics is about human acts and architecture about building. Christian theology, however,

---

[b] *sensus communis*, one of the internal senses of Aristotelean psychology. It acts as the central clearing house for the data of the other senses.

[a] practical science, directed to doing or making something. Contrast with theoretical science, concerned with knowing what is the truth.

[1] *Metaphysics* II, 1. 993b21   [2] *James* 1:22

is about God, who makes men and is not made by them. It is therefore more contemplative than practical.

REPLY: As already remarked,[3] the holy teaching while remaining single nevertheless embraces things belonging to the different philosophical sciences because of the one formal meaning which is its interest in all manner of things, namely the truth they bear in the light of God. Whereas some among the philosophical sciences are theoretical and others are practical, sacred doctrine takes over both functions, in this being like the single knowledge whereby God knows himself and the things he makes.

All the same it is more theoretical than practical, since it is mainly concerned with the divine things which are, rather than with things men do; it deals with human acts only in so far as they prepare men for that achieved knowledge of God on which their eternal bliss reposes.

This leaves the way open for the answer to the difficulties.

Article 5. Is Christian theology more valuable than the other sciences?

THE FIFTH POINT: 1. It would seem that Christian theology is not more valuable than the other sciences. For certainty is part of a science's value. Now the other sciences, the premises of which are indubitable, look more assured and certain than Christian theology, of which the premises, namely the articles of faith, are open to doubt. Accordingly these other sciences seem more valuable.

2. Again, a lower science draws on a higher, like the musician on the arithmetician. Holy teaching, however, draws on philosophical learning; for St Jerome allows that *the ancient writers so filled their books with the theories and verdicts of philosophers that at first you are at a loss which to admire more, their secular erudition or their skill in the Scriptures.*[1] Holy teaching, then, has a lower standing than other sciences.

---

[3] art. 4 above   [1] *Epistle* 70. PL 22, 668

ON THE OTHER HAND the Bible describes the other sciences as its maidservants: *She hath sent her handmaids to invite to the tower.*[2]

REPLY: Having noticed that this science is theoretical in one respect and practical in another we now go on to observe how it ranks above all the other sciences, theoretical and practical alike.

Among the theoretical sciences one is reckoned more important than another, first because of the certitude it brings, and next because of the worth of its subject. On both counts sacred doctrine surpasses the others. As to certitude, because theirs comes from the natural light of human reason which can make mistakes, whereas sacred doctrine's is held in the light of divine knowledge which cannot falter. As to worth of subject, because their business is only with things underneath reason, whereas sacred science leads to heights the reason cannot climb.

Then among the practical sciences, that stands higher which has the further purpose, for instance statesmanship commands military art because the efficiency of the fighting services subserves the good of the commonwealth. Now in so far as sacred doctrine is a practical science, its aim is eternal happiness, and this is the final end governing the ends of all the practical sciences.

Hence it is clear that from every standpoint sacred doctrine excels all other sciences.

Hence: 1. There is nothing to stop a thing that is objectively more certain by its nature from being subjectively less certain to us because of the disability of our minds, which, as Aristotle notes, *blink at the most evident things like bats in the sunshine.*[3] Doubt about the articles of faith, which falls to the lot of some, is not because the reality is at all uncertain, but because the human understanding is feeble. Nevertheless, as Aristotle also points out, the slenderest acquaintance

---

[2] *Proverbs* 9:3   [3] *Metaphysics* II, 1. 993b10

we can form with heavenly things is more desirable than a thorough grasp of mundane matters.[4]

2. Holy teaching can borrow from the other sciences, not from any need to beg from them, but for the greater clarification of the things it conveys. For it takes its principles directly from God through revelation, not from the other sciences. On that account it does not rely on them as though they were in control, for their rôle is subsidiary and ancillary; so an architect makes use of tradesmen as a statesman employs soldiers. That it turns to them in this way is not from any lack or insufficiency within itself, but because our understanding is wanting; it is the more readily guided into the world above reason, set forth in holy teaching, through the world of natural reason from which the other sciences take their course.

Article 6. Is this teaching wisdom?

THE SIXTH POINT: 1. Apparently it is not wisdom.[a] For no teaching which assumes its principles from elsewhere deserves the name of wisdom, since, as Aristotle remarks, *the office of the wise is to govern others, not to be governed by them*.[1] Now the principles of this teaching are suppositions from another place, as noted earlier on.[2] Therefore it is not wisdom.

2. Further, one charge on wisdom is to prove the premises of the other sciences; that is why Aristotle calls it *the chief of the sciences*.[3] But theological teaching does not prove the premises of the other sciences, and therefore it is not wisdom.

3. Besides, this teaching is acquired by study. Wisdom, however, is received from the outpouring of the Spirit, and

---

[4] *De partibus animalium* 1, 5. 644b31

[a] wisdom: the knowing of things in their ultimate causes. Contrasted with specialist science: the knowing of things in their proximate causes.

[1] *Metaphysics* I, 2. 982a18   [2] art. 2 above

[3] *Ethics* VI, 7. 1141a16

as such is numbered among the seven Gifts of the Holy Spirit, set forth by Isaiah.[4] This teaching, then, is not wisdom.

ON THE OTHER HAND *Deuteronomy* says early on, before setting down the ten commandments, *This is our wisdom and understanding in the presence of the people*.[5]

REPLY: Holy teaching should be declared to be wisdom highest above all human wisdoms, not indeed in some special department but unconditionally.

To govern and judge belongs to the wise person, and since judgment in the light of the higher cause also holds judgment in the light of lower causes, that person is called wise about any matter who there maturely considers the highest cause. Take architecture for example: you apply the terms 'wise' and 'master-builder' to the artist who plans the whole structure, and not the artisans under him who cut the stones and mix the mortar; thus St Paul says, *As a wise architect I have laid the foundations*.[6] Then again, in relation to the whole of life you call that person wise when he directs human acts to their due end for good and all; hence the text, *Wisdom is prudence to a man*.[7] That person, therefore, who considers maturely and without qualification the first and final cause of the entire universe, namely God, is to be called supremely wise; and so St Augustine treats wisdom as knowledge of divine things.[8]

Now holy teaching goes to God most personally as deepest origin and highest end, and that not only because of what can be gathered about him from creatures (which philosophers have recognized, according to the epistle, *What was known of God is manifest in them*[9]) but also because of what he alone knows about himself and yet discloses for others to share. Consequently holy teaching is called wisdom in the highest degree.

---

[4] *Isaiah* 11:2   [5] *Deuteronomy* 4:6   [6] 1 *Corinthians* 3:10

[7] *Proverbs* 10:23   [8] *On the Trinity* 12, 14. PL 42, 1009

[9] *Romans* 1:19

Hence: 1. Holy teaching assumes its principles from no human science, but from divine science, by which as by supreme wisdom all our knowledge is governed.

2. The premises of other sciences are either self-evident, in which case they cannot be proved, or they are proved through some natural evidence in some other science. What is exclusive to this science's knowledge is that it is about truth which comes through revelation, not through natural reasoning. On this account establishing the premises of other sciences is none of its business, though it may well be critical of them. For whatsoever is encountered in the other sciences which is incompatible with its truth should be completely condemned as false: accordingly St Paul refers to the pulling down of ramparts, destroying counsels, and every height that rears itself against the knowledge of God.[10]

3. Since having a formed judgment characterizes the wise person, so there are two kinds of wisdom according to the two ways of passing judgment. This may be arrived at from a bent that way, as when a person who possesses the habit of a virtue rightly commits himself to what should be done in consonance with it, because he is already in sympathy with it; hence Aristotle remarks that the virtuous man himself sets the measure and standard for human acts.[11] Alternatively the judgment may be arrived at through a cognitive process, as when a person soundly instructed in moral science can appreciate the activity of virtues he does not himself possess.[b]

The first way of judging divine things belongs to that wisdom which is classed among the Gifts of the Holy Ghost; so St Paul says, *The spiritual man judges all things*,[12] and Dionysius speaks about *Hierotheus being taught by the experience of undergoing divine things, not only by learning about them*.[13] The second way of judging is taken by sacred

---

[10] II *Corinthians* 10:4–5   [11] *Ethics* x, 5. 1176a17

[b] The distinction between real and notional knowledge, cognate to that between affective and abstract knowledge. There is a difference between experiencing what we are in love or hate with, and assenting to what we have read about.

[12] I *Corinthians* 2:15   [13] *Divine names* II, 9. PG 3, 648

doctrine to the extent that it can be gained by study; even so the premises are held from revelation.

Article 7. Is God the subject of this science?

THE SEVENTH POINT: 1. God would not seem to be the subject of this science. For, according to Aristotle, every science should begin by presupposing what its subject is.[1] This science, however, does not start by making the assumption of defining God; as St John Damascene remarks, *In God we cannot say what he is.*[2][a] It follows that God is not the subject of this science.

2. Besides, all matters about which a science reaches settled conclusions enter into its subject. Now sacred Scripture treats many things other than God, for instance about creatures and human conduct. Therefore its subject is not purely God.

ON THE OTHER HAND, what a science discusses is its subject. In this case the discussion is about God; for it is called theology, as it were, talk about God. Therefore he is the subject of this science.

REPLY: That God is the subject of this science should be maintained. For a subject is to a science as an object to a psychological power or training. Now that properly is designated the object which expresses the special term why anything is related to the power or training in question; thus a man or a stone is related to eyesight in that both are coloured, and so being coloured is the proper object of the sense of sight. Now all things are dealt with in holy teaching in terms of God, either because they are God himself or because they are relative to him as their origin and end. Therefore God is truly the object of this science.

---

[1] *Posterior Analytics* 1, 4. 71a13
[2] *Orthodox faith* 1, 4. PG 94, 797
[a] cf Question 13 which concludes this volume

This also is clear from the fact that the first principles of this science are the articles of faith, and faith is about God. Now the subject of a science's first principles and of its entire development is identical, since the whole of a science is virtually contained in its principles.

Some writers, however, preoccupied with the things treated of by sacred doctrine rather than with the formal interest engaged, have indicated its subject-matter otherwise, apportioning it between the reality and its symbols, or regarding it as the works of redemption, or the whole Christ, namely head and members.[b] All these indeed are dwelt on by this science, yet as held in their relationship to God.

Hence: 1. Though we cannot know what God is, nevertheless this teaching employs some effect of his, of nature or of grace, in place of a definition, and by this means discusses truths about him. Some of the philosophical sciences adopt a similar method, of grounding the argument on the effect, not on the definition, of the cause when demonstrating something about a cause through its effect.

2. All other things that are settled in holy Scripture are embraced in God, not that they are parts of him—such as essential components or accidents—but because they are somehow related to him.

Article 8. Is this teaching probative?

THE EIGHTH POINT: 1. This teaching does not seem to be probative. For St Ambrose says, *Away with arguments where faith is at stake*.[1] Now faith is the principal quest of this teaching, according to St John, *These things are written that you may believe*.[2] Therefore it is not probative.

2. Again, were it to advance arguments, they would be either from authority or from the evidence of reason. If from

---

[b] Thus Peter Lombard for the first, Hugh of St Victor for the second, Robert Grosseteste for the third—theologians held in great respect by St Thomas.

[1] *On the Catholic faith* I, 13. PL 16, 570   [2] John 20:31

authority, then the process would be unbefitting the dignity of this teaching, for, according to Boethius,[3] authority is the weakest ground of proof. If from the evidence of reason, then the process would not correspond with its purpose, for according to St Gregory, *Faith has no merit where the reason presents actual proof from experience.*[4] Well then, holy teaching does not attempt proofs.

ON THE OTHER HAND St Paul requires of a bishop that he should *embrace the faithful word which is according to doctrine that he may be able to exhort in sound doctrine and convince the gainsayers.*[5]

REPLY: As the other sciences do not argue to prove their premises, but work from them to bring out other things in their field of inquiry, so this teaching does not argue to establish its premises, which are the articles of faith, but advances from them to make something known, as when St Paul adduces the resurrection of Christ to prove the resurrection of us all.[6]

Then bear in mind that among the philosophical sciences subordinate sciences neither prove their premises nor controvert those who deny them; these functions they leave to a superior science. The supreme science among them, namely metaphysics, contests the denial of its principles with an opponent who will grant something; if nothing, then debate is impossible, though his reasonings may be demolished.

So sacred Scripture, which has no superior science over it, disputes the denial of its principles; it argues on the basis of those truths held by revelation which an opponent admits, as when, debating with heretics, it appeals to received authoritative texts of Christian theology, and uses one article against those who reject another. If, however, an opponent believes nothing of what has been divinely revealed, then no

---

[3] *On the Topics of Cicero* I. PL 64, 1166
[4] *On the Gospels* II, 26. PL 76, 1197   [5] *Titus* 1:9
[6] I *Corinthians* 15:12

way lies open for making the articles of faith reasonably credible; all that can be done is to solve the difficulties against faith he may bring up. For since faith rests on unfailing truth, and the contrary of truth cannot really be demonstrated, it is clear that alleged proofs against faith are not demonstrations, but charges that can be refuted.

Hence: 1. Though arguments of human reason reach no position to prove the things of faith, nevertheless, as noted above, holy teaching does work from the articles of faith to infer other things.

2. Argument from authority is the method most appropriate to this teaching in that its premises are held through revelation; consequently it has to accept the authority of those to whom revelation was made. Nor does this derogate from its dignity, for though weakest when based on what human beings have held, the argument from authority is most forcible when based on what God has disclosed.

All the same Christian theology also uses human reasoning, not indeed to prove the faith, for that would take away from the merit of believing, but to make manifest some implications of its message. Since grace does not scrap nature but brings it to perfection, so also natural reason should assist faith as the natural loving bent of the will ministers to charity. St Paul speaks of *bringing into captivity every understanding unto the service of Christ*.[7] Hence holy teaching uses the authority of philosophers who have been able to perceive the truth by natural reasoning, for instance when St Paul quotes the saying of Aratus, *As some of your poets have said, we are of the race of God*.[8]

Yet sacred doctrine employs such authorities only in order to provide as it were extraneous arguments from probability. Its own proper authorities are those of canonical Scripture, and these it applied with convincing force. It has other proper authorities, the doctors of the Church, and these it looks to as its own, but for arguments that carry no more than probability.

---

[7] II *Corinthians* 10:5   [8] *Acts* 17:28

For our faith rests on the revelation made to the Prophets and Apostles who wrote the canonical books, not on a revelation, if such there be, made to any other teacher. In this sense St Augustine wrote to St Jerome; *Only to those books or writings which are called canonical have I learnt to pay such honour that I firmly believe that none of their authors have erred in composing them. Other authors, however, I read to such effect that, no matter what holiness and learning they display, I do not hold what they say to be true because those were their sentiments.*[9]

Article 9. Should holy teaching employ metaphorical or symbolical language?

THE NINTH POINT: 1. It seems that holy teaching should not use metaphors.[a] For what is proper to a lowly type of instruction appears ill-suited to this, which, as already observed,[1] stands on the summit. Now to carry on with various similitudes and images is proper to poetry, the most modest of all teaching methods. Therefore to make use of such similitudes is ill-suited to holy teaching.

2. Moreover, this teaching seems intended to make truth clear; and there is a reward held out to those who do so: *Those who explain me shall have life everlasting.*[2] Such symbolism, however, obscures the truth. Therefore it is not in keeping with this teaching to convey divine things under the symbolic representation of bodily things.

3. Again, the nobler the creatures the closer they approach God's likeness. If then the properties of creatures are to be read into God, then at least they should be chiefly of the more excellent not the baser sort; and this is the way frequently taken by the Scriptures.

---

[9] *Epistles* 82, 1. PL 33, 277

[a] metaphor: literally 'to carry from place to place', a figure of speech which transfers a meaning proper to one subject to another subject because of some likeness. For a careful discussion of such usage in theology cf Question 13, art. 9 below.

[1] art. 5 above   [2] *Ecclesiasticus* 24:31

ON THE OTHER HAND the Lord says, *I have multiplied visions and I have used similitudes by the ministry of the prophets.*[3] To put something across under imagery is metaphorical usage. Therefore sacred doctrine avails itself of metaphors.

REPLY: Holy Scripture fittingly delivers divine and spiritual realities under bodily guises. For God provides for all things according to the kind of things they are. Now we are of the kind to reach the world of intelligence through the world of sense, since all our knowledge takes its rise from sensation. Congenially, then, holy Scripture delivers spiritual things to us beneath metaphors taken from bodily things. Dionysius agrees, *The divine rays cannot enlighten us except wrapped up in many sacred veils.*[4]

Then also holy Scripture is intended for all of us in common without distinction of persons, as is said in the epistle, *To the wise and the foolish I am a debtor,*[5] and fitly puts forward spiritual things under bodily likenesses; at all events the uneducated may then lay hold of them, those, that is to say, who are not ready to take intellectual truths neat with nothing else.

Hence: 1. Poetry employs metaphors for the sake of representation, in which we are born to take delight. Holy teaching, on the other hand, adopts them for their indispensable usefulness, as just explained.

2. Dionysius teaches in the same place that the beam of divine revelation is not extinguished by the sense imagery that veils it, and its truth does not flicker out, since the minds of those given the revelation are not allowed to remain arrested with the images but are lifted up to their meaning; moreover, they are so enabled to instruct others. In fact truths expressed metaphorically in one passage of Scripture are more expressly explained elsewhere. Yet even the figurative disguising serves a purpose, both as a challenge to those eager to find out the truth and as a defence against unbelievers ready to ridicule;

---

[3] *Hosea* 12:10   [4] *Heavenly hierarchy* I, 2. PG 3, 121
[5] *Romans* 1:14

to these the text refers, *Give not that which is holy to the dogs.*[6]

3. Dionysius also tells us that in the Scriptures the figures of base bodies rather than those of fine bodies more happily serve the purpose of conveying divine things to us.[7] And this for three reasons. First, because thereby human thinking is the more exempt from error, for the expressions obviously cannot be taken in the proper sense of their words and be crudely ascribed to divine things; this might be more open to doubt were sublime figures evoked, especially for those people who can summon up nothing more splendid than physical beauty. Secondly, because understatement is more to the point with our present knowledge of God. For in this life what he is not is clearer to us than what he is; and therefore from the likenesses of things farthest removed from him we can more fairly estimate how far above our speech and thought he is. Thirdly, because thereby divine matters are more effectively screened against those unworthy of them.

Article 10. *Can one passage of holy Scripture bear several senses?*

THE TENTH POINT: 1. It would seem that the same text of holy Scripture does not bear several senses, namely the historical or literal, the allegorical, the tropological or moral, and the anagogical. Allow a variety of readings to one passage, and you produce confusion and deception, and sap the foundations of argument; examples of the stock fallacies, not reasoned discourse, follow from the medley of meanings. Holy Scripture, however, should effectively display the truth without fallacy of any sort. One text, therefore, should not offer various meanings.

2. Besides, St Augustine holds that *Scripture which is entitled the Old Testament has a fourfold meaning, namely according to history, to etiology, to analogy, and to allegory.*[1]

---

[6] *Matthew* 7:6   [7] op. cit. II, 2. PG 3, 136
[1] *On the usefulness of believing* 3. PL 42, 68

Now these four appear inconsistent with the four mentioned above; which therefore appear awkward headings for interpreting a passage of Scripture.

3. Further, there is also a parabolic sense, not included among them.[a]

ON THE OTHER HAND, St Gregory declares that *holy Scripture transcends all other sciences by its very style of expression, in that one and the same discourse, while narrating an event, transmits a mystery as well.*[2]

REPLY: That God is the author of holy Scripture should be acknowledged, and he has the power, not only of adapting words to convey meanings (which men also can do), but also of adapting things themselves. In every branch of knowledge words have meaning, but what is special here is that the things meant by the words also themselves mean something. That first meaning whereby the words signify things belongs to the sense first-mentioned, namely the historical or literal. That meaning, however, whereby the things signified by the words in their turn also signify other things is called the spiritual sense; it is based on and presupposes the literal sense.

Now this spiritual sense is divided into three. For, as St Paul says, *The Old Law is the figure of the New,*[3] and the New Law itself, as Dionysius says, *is the figure of the glory to come.*[4] Then again, under the New Law the deeds wrought by our Head are signs also of what we ourselves ought to do.

Well then, the allegorical sense is brought into play when the things of the Old Law signify the things of the New Law; the moral sense when the things done in Christ and in those

---

[a] allegory: description of one subject under guise of another, extended metaphor. Tropology: the use of tropes or figures of speech, and especially in moral discourse Anagogy: pointing the way from lower to higher Etiology: the assignment of a cause. Analogy: a likeness of attributes or relations. Parable: a comparison of situations.

[2] *Morals* xx, 1. PL 76, 135   [3] *Hebrews* 7:19

[4] *Ecclesiastical hierarchy* v, 2. PG 3, 501

who prefigured him are signs of what we should carry out; and the anagogical sense when the things that lie ahead in eternal glory are signified.

Now because the literal sense is that which the author intends, and the author of holy Scripture is God who comprehends everything all at once in his understanding, it comes not amiss, as St Augustine observes, if many meanings are present even in the literal sense of one passage of Scripture.[5]

Hence: 1. These various readings do not set up ambiguity or any other kind of mixture of meanings, because, as we have explained, they are many, not because one term may signify many things, but because the things signified by the terms can themselves be the signs of other things. Consequently holy Scripture sets up no confusion, since all meanings are based on one, namely the literal sense. From this alone can arguments be drawn, and not, as St Augustine remarks in his letter to Vincent the Donatist, from the things said by allegory.[6] Nor does this undo the effect of holy Scripture, for nothing necessary for faith is contained under the spiritual sense that is not openly conveyed through the literal sense elsewhere.

2. These three, history, etiology, and analogy, are grouped under the one general heading of the literal sense. For as St Augustine explains in the same place, you have history when any matter is straightforwardly recorded; etiology when its cause is indicated, as when our Lord pointed to men's hardness of heart as the reason why Moses allowed them to set aside their wives;[7] analogy when the truth of one Scriptural passage is shown not to clash with the truth of another. Of the four senses enumerated in the argument, allegory stands alone for the three spiritual senses of our exposition. For instance Hugh of St Victor included the anagogical sense under the allegorical, and enumerated just three senses, namely the historical, the allegorical, and the tropological.[8]

---

[5] *Confessions* XII, 31. PL 32, 844
[6] *Epistles* XCIII, 8. PL 33, 334   [7] *Matthew* 19:8
[8] *On the sacraments* I, foreword 4. PL 176, 184

3. The parabolical sense is contained in the literal sense, for words can signify something properly and something figuratively; in the last case the literal sense is not the figure of speech itself, but the object it figures. When Scripture speaks of the arm of God, the literal sense is not that he has a physical limb, but that he has what it signifies, namely the power of doing and making. This example brings out how nothing false can underlie the literal sense of Scripture.

so BECAUSE, as we have seen,[1] the fundamental aim of holy teaching is to make God known, not only as he is in himself, but as the beginning and end of all things and of reasoning creatures especially, we now intend to set forth this divine teaching by treating,

first, of God,
secondly, of the journey to God of reasoning creatures,
thirdly, of Christ, who, as man, is our road to God.

The treatment of God will fall into three parts:
first, his nature,
secondly, the distinction of persons in God,
thirdly, the coming forth from him of creatures.

Concerning the nature of God we must discuss
first, whether there is a God,
secondly, what manner of being he is, or better, what manner of being he is not.
thirdly, the knowledge, will and power involved in God's activity.[a]

Question 2. Whether there is a God

Under the first of these questions there are three points of inquiry:

1. is it self-evident that there is a God?
2. can it be made evident?
3. is there a God?

---

[1] 1a. 1, 7 above

[a] The general plan of the *Summa* is here traced out. The present volume covers the first and second of the final headings. The third is treated in the following volume of this series.

Article 1. Is it self-evident that there is a God?

THE FIRST POINT: 1. It seems self-evident that there is a God. For things are said to be self-evident to us when we are innately aware of them, as, for example, first principles. Now as Damascene says when beginning his book, *the awareness that God exists is implanted by nature in everybody*.[1] That God exists is therefore self-evident.

2. Moreover, a proposition is self-evident if we perceive its truth immediately upon perceiving the meaning of its terms: a characteristic, according to Aristotle,[2] of first principles of demonstration. For example, when we know what wholes and parts are, we know at once that wholes are always bigger than their parts. Now once we understand the meaning of the word 'God' it follows that God exists. For the word means 'that than which nothing greater can be meant'. Consequently, since existence in thought and fact is greater than existence in thought alone, and since, once we understand the word 'God', he exists in thought, he must also exist in fact. It is therefore self-evident that there is a God.[a]

3. Moreover, it is self-evident that truth exists, for even denying it would admit it. Were there no such thing as truth, then it would be true that there is no truth; something then is true, and therefore there is truth. Now God is truth itself; *I am the way, the truth and the life*.[3] That there is a God, then, is self-evident.

ON THE OTHER HAND, nobody can think the opposite of a self-evident proposition, as Aristotle's discussion of first principles makes clear.[4] But the opposite of the proposition 'God exists' can be thought, for *the fool* in the psalms *said in his heart*:

---

[1] *Orthodox faith* 1, 1. PG 94, 789

[2] *Posterior Analytics* 1, 2. 72a7

[a] This is the formulation of the celebrated argument of St Anselm's *Proslogion*, the so-called 'ontological' argument.

[3] *John* 14:6   [4] *Metaphysics* IV, 3. 1005b11

There is no God.[5] That God exists is therefore not self-evident.

REPLY: A self-evident proposition, though always self-evident in itself, is sometimes self-evident to us and sometimes not. For a proposition is self-evident when the predicate forms part of what the subject means; thus it is self-evident that man is an animal, since being an animal is part of the meaning of man. If therefore it is evident to everybody what it is to be this subject and what it is to have such a predicate, the proposition itself will be self-evident to everybody. This is clearly the case with first principles of demonstration, which employ common terms evident to all, such as 'be' and 'not be', 'whole' and 'part'. But if what it is to be this subject or have such a predicate is not evident to some people, then the proposition, though self-evident in itself, will not be so to those to whom its subject and predicate are not evident. And this is why Boethius can say that *certain notions are* self-evident and *commonplaces only to the learned, as, for example, that only bodies can occupy space.*[6]

I maintain then that the proposition 'God exists' is self-evident in itself, for, as we shall see later, its subject and predicate are identical, since God is his own existence.[7] But, because what it is to be God is not evident to us, the proposition is not self-evident to us, and needs to be made evident. This is done by means of things which, though less evident in themselves, are nevertheless more evident to us, by means, namely, of God's effects.

Hence: 1. The awareness that God exists is not implanted in us by nature in any clear or specific way. Admittedly, man is by nature aware of what by nature he desires, and he desires by nature a happiness which is to be found only in God. But this is not, simply speaking, awareness that there is a God, any more than to be aware of someone approaching is to be aware of Peter, even should it be Peter approaching: many,

---

[5] *Psalms* 13:1; 52:1   [6] *De hebdomadibus.* PL 64, 1311
[7] 1a. 3, 4 below

in fact, believe the ultimate good which will make us happy to be riches, or pleasure, or some such thing.

2. Someone hearing the word 'God' may very well not understand it to mean 'that than which nothing greater can be thought', indeed, some people have believed God to be a body. And even if the meaning of the word 'God' were generally recognized to be 'that than which nothing greater can be thought', nothing thus defined would thereby be granted existence in the world of fact, but merely as thought about. Unless one is given that something in fact exists than which nothing greater can be thought—and this nobody denying the existence of God would grant—the conclusion that God in fact exists does not follow.

3. It is self-evident that there exists truth in general, but it is not self-evident to us that there exists a First Truth.

Article 2. Can it be made evident?

THE SECOND POINT: 1. That God exists cannot, it seems, be made evident. For that God exists is an article of faith, and since, as St Paul says, faith is concerned with *the unseen*,[1] its propositions cannot be demonstrated, that is made evident. It is therefore impossible to demonstrate that God exists.

2. Moreover, the central link of demonstration is a definition. But Damascene tells us that we cannot define what God is, but only what he is not.[2] Hence we cannot demonstrate that God exists.

3. Moreover, if demonstration of God's existence were possible, this could only be by arguing from his effects. Now God and his effects are incommensurable; for God is infinite and his effects finite, and the finite cannot measure the infinite. Consequently, since effects incommensurate with their cause cannot make it evident, it does not seem possible to demonstrate that God exists.

---

[1] *Hebrews* 11:1   [2] *Orthodox faith* 1, 4. PG 94, 800

ON THE OTHER HAND, St Paul tells us that *the hidden things of God can be clearly understood from the things that he has made.*[3] If so, one must be able to demonstrate that God exists from the things that he has made, for knowing whether a thing exists is the first step towards understanding it.

REPLY: There are two types of demonstration. One, showing 'why', follows the natural order of things among themselves, arguing from cause to effect; the other, showing 'that', follows the order in which we know things, arguing from effect to cause (for when an effect is more apparent to us than its cause, we come to know the cause through the effect). Now any effect of a cause demonstrates that that cause exists, in cases where the effect is better known to us, since effects are dependent upon causes, and can only occur if the causes already exist. From effects evident to us, therefore, we can demonstrate what in itself is not evident to us, namely, that God exists.[a]

Hence: 1. The truths about God which St Paul says we can know by our natural powers of reasoning—that God exists, for example[4]—are not numbered among the articles of faith, but are presupposed to them. For faith presupposes natural knowledge, just as grace does nature and all perfections that which they perfect. However, there is nothing to stop a man accepting on faith some truth which he personally cannot demonstrate, even if that truth in itself is such that demonstration could make it evident.

2. When we argue from effect to cause, the effect will take the place of a definition of the cause in the proof that the cause exists; and this especially if the cause is God. For when proving anything to exist, the central link is not what that thing is (we cannot even ask what it is until we know that it exists), but rather what we are using the name of the thing

---

[3] *Romans* 1:20

[a] The reasons for knowing the existence of an object and the 'reason' for its existence do not always coincide.

[4] *Romans* 1:19, 20

to mean. Now when demonstrating from effects that God exists, we are able to start from what the word 'God' means, for, as we shall see,[5] the names of God are derived from these effects.

3. Effects can give comprehensive knowledge of their cause only when commensurate with it: but, as we have said, any effect whatever can make it clear that a cause exists. God's effects, therefore, can serve to demonstrate that God exists, even though they cannot help us to know him comprehensively for what he is.[b]

Article 3. Is there a God?

THE THIRD POINT: 1. It seems that there is no God. For if, of two mutually exclusive things, one were to exist without limit, the other would cease to exist. But by the word 'God' is implied some limitless good. If God then existed, nobody would ever encounter evil. But evil is encountered in the world. God therefore does not exist.

2. Moreover, if a few causes fully account for some effect, one does not seek more. Now it seems that everything we observe in this world can be fully accounted for by other causes, without assuming a God. Thus natural effects are explained by natural causes, and contrived effects by human reasoning and will. There is therefore no need to suppose that a God exists.

ON THE OTHER HAND, Scripture represents God as declaring, *I am who am.*[1]

REPLY: There are five ways in which one can prove that there is a God.

---

[5] 1a. 13, 1 below

[b] The proofs are given in the following article. They will suppose an induction from empirical data, but are deductive in form. The process, however, is *a posteriori*, not *a priori*.

[1] Exodus 3:14

The first and most obvious way is based on change. Some things in the world are certainly in process of change: this we plainly see. Now anything in process of change is being changed by something else. This is so because it is characteristic of things in process of change that they do not yet have the perfection towards which they move, though able to have it; whereas it is characteristic of something causing change to have that perfection already. For to cause change is to bring into being what was previously only able to be, and this can only be done by something that already is: thus fire, which is actually hot, causes wood, which is able to be hot, to become actually hot, and in this way causes change in the wood.[a] Now the same thing cannot at the same time be both actually x and potentially x, though it can be actually x and potentially y: the actually hot cannot at the same time be potentially hot, though it can be potentially cold. Consequently, a thing in process of change cannot itself cause that same change; it cannot change itself. Of necessity therefore anything in process of change is being changed by something else. Moreover, this something else, if in process of change, is itself being changed by yet another thing; and this last by another. Now we must stop somewhere, otherwise there will be no first cause of the change, and, as a result, no subsequent causes. For it is only when acted upon by the first cause that the intermediate causes will produce the change: if the hand does not move the stick, the stick will not move anything else. Hence one is bound to arrive at some first cause of change not itself being changed by anything, and this is what everybody understands by God.

The second way is based on the nature of causation. In the observable world causes are found to be ordered in series; we never observe, nor ever could, something causing itself, for this would mean it preceded itself, and this is not possible. Such a series of causes must however stop somewhere;

---

[a] The example is not meant to support the analysis by appeal to empirical proof, but to show how such an analysis works out when applied to the interpretation of ordinary events.

for in it an earlier member causes an intermediate and the intermediate a last (whether the intermediate be one or many). Now if you eliminate a cause you also eliminate its effects, so that you cannot have a last cause, nor an intermediate one, unless you have a first. Given therefore no stop in the series of causes, and hence no first cause, there would be no intermediate causes either, and no last effect, and this would be an open mistake. One is therefore forced to suppose some first cause, to which everyone gives the name 'God'.

The third way is based on what need not be and on what must be, and runs as follows. Some of the things we come across can be but need not be, for we find them springing up and dying away, thus sometimes in being and sometimes not. Now everything cannot be like this, for a thing that need not be, once was not; and if everything need not be, once upon a time there was nothing. But if that were true there would be nothing even now, because something that does not exist can only be brought into being by something already existing. So that if nothing was in being nothing could be brought into being, and nothing would be in being now, which contradicts observation. Not everything therefore is the sort of thing that need not be; there has got to be something that must be. Now a thing that must be, may or may not owe this necessity to something else. But just as we must stop somewhere in a series of causes, so also in the series of things which must be and owe this to other things. One is forced therefore to suppose something which must be, and owes this to no other thing than itself; indeed it itself is the cause that other things must be.[b]

The fourth way is based on the gradation observed in things. Some things are found to be more good, more true, more noble, and so on, and other things less. But such comparative terms describe varying degrees of approximation to a

***

[b] The first three 'ways' raise the question of an infinite series of movers, causes, derived existents. St Thomas rules out, not an endless progression, or regression, of incidents, but an infinity of essential subordinates: see 1a. 7, 4 below. Also 1a. 46, 2.

superlative; for example, things are hotter and hotter the nearer they approach what is hottest. Something, therefore, is the truest and best and most noble of things, and hence the most fully in being; for Aristotle says that the truest things are the things most fully in being.[2] Now *when many things possess some property in common, the one most fully possessing it causes it in the others: fire, to use Aristotle's example, the hottest of all things, causes all other things to be hot.*[3] There is something therefore which causes in all other things their being, their goodness, and whatever other perfection they have. And this we call 'God'.

The fifth way is based on the guidedness of nature. An orderedness of actions to an end is observed in all bodies obeying natural laws, even when they lack awareness. For their behaviour hardly ever varies, and will practically always turn out well; which shows that they truly tend to a goal, and do not merely hit it by accident. Nothing however that lacks awareness tends to a goal, except under the direction of someone with awareness and with understanding; the arrow, for example, requires an archer. Everything in nature, therefore, is directed to its goal by someone with intelligence, and this we call 'God'.

Hence: 1. As Augustine says, *Since God is supremely good, he would not permit any evil at all in his works, unless he were sufficiently almighty and good to bring good even from evil.*[4] It is therefore a mark of the limitless goodness of God that he permits evils to exist, and draws from them good.

2. Natural causes act for definite purposes under the direction of some higher cause, so that their effects must also be referred to God as the first of all causes. In the same manner contrived effects must likewise be referred back to a higher cause than human reasoning and will, for these are changeable and can cease to be, and, as we have seen, all changeable things and things that can cease to be require some first cause which cannot change and of itself must be.

---

[2] *Metaphysics* 11, 1. 993b30   [3] ibid, 993b25
[4] *Enchiridion* 11. PL 40, 236

HAVING RECOGNIZED that a certain thing exists, we have still to investigate the way in which it exists, that we may come to understand what it is that exists. Now we cannot know how God is, but only how he is not; we must therefore consider the ways in which God does not exist, rather than the ways in which he does. We treat then

first, of the ways in which God does not exist,
secondly, of the ways in which we know him,
thirdly, of the ways in which we describe him.

The ways in which God does not exist will become apparent if we rule out from him everything inappropriate, such as compositeness, change and the like. Let us inquire then
first, about God's simpleness, thus ruling out compositeness. And then, because in the material world simpleness implies imperfection and incompleteness, let us ask
secondly, about God's perfection,
thirdly, about his limitlessness,
fourthly, about his unchangeableness,
fifthly, about his oneness.

Question 3. God's simpleness

About the first of these questions there are eight points of inquiry:

1. is God a body? Is he, that is to say, composed of extended parts?
2. is he composed of 'form' and 'matter'?
3. is God to be identified with his own essence or nature, with that which makes him what he is?
4. can one distinguish in God nature and existence?

5. can one distinguish in him genus and difference?
6. is he composed of substance and accidents?
7. is there any way in which he is composite, or is he altogether simple?
8. does he enter into composition with other things?

Article 1. Is God a body composed of extended parts?

THE FIRST POINT: 1. God, it would seem, is a body. For anything having three dimensions is a body, and the Scriptures ascribe three dimensions to God: *He is higher than the heaven and what wilt thou do? he is deeper than hell and how wilt thou know? the measure of him is longer than the earth and broader than the sea.*[1] God then is a body.

2. Moreover, only bodies have shape, for shape is characteristic of extended things as such. God however seems to have a shape, for in *Genesis* we read: *Let us make man to our image and likeness,*[2] where image means figure or shape as in *Hebrews: who being the brightness of his glory, and the figure* (that is to say, image) *of his substance.*[3] Therefore God is a body.

3. Moreover, the parts of the body can belong only to a body. But Scripture ascribes parts of the body to God, saying in *Job, Have you an arm like God?*[4] and in the *Psalms, The eyes of the Lord are toward the righteous,*[5] and *the right hand of the Lord does valiantly.*[6] Therefore God is a body.

4. Only bodies can assume postures. But Scripture ascribes certain postures to God: thus Isaiah *saw the Lord sitting,*[7] and says that *the Lord stands to judge.*[8] Therefore God is a body.

5. Moreover, nothing can act as starting-point or finishing-point of a movement unless it be body or bodily. Now God is referred to in Scripture as the finishing-point of a move-

---

[1] *Job* 11:8–9   [2] *Genesis* 1:26   [3] *Hebrews* 1:3
[4] *Job* 40:4   [5] *Psalms* 33:16   [6] *Psalms* 117:16
[7] *Isaiah* 6:1   [8] *Isaiah* 3:13

ment, *Come ye to him and be enlightened;*[9] and again as a starting-point, *They that depart from thee shall be written in the earth.*[10] Therefore God is a body.

ON THE OTHER HAND, John writes: *God is spirit.*[11]

REPLY: In no sense is God a body, and this may be shown in three ways.

First, experience can offer no example of a body causing change without itself being changed. Now God has been shown above to be the unchanging first cause of change.[12] Clearly then God is not a body.

Secondly, in the first existent thing everything must be actual; there can be no potentiality whatsoever. For although, when we consider things coming to exist, potential existence precedes actual existence in those particular things; nevertheless, absolutely speaking, actual existence takes precedence of potential existence. For what is able to exist is brought into existence only by what already exists. Now we have seen that the first existent is God.[13] In God then there can be no potentiality. In bodies, however, there is always potentiality, for the extended as such is potential of division. God, therefore, cannot be a body.

Thirdly, it is evident from what has been said that God is the most excellent of beings.[14] A body, however, cannot be the most excellent of beings. For bodies are either living or non-living, and of these living bodies are clearly the most excellent. Now a living body is not alive simply in virtue of being a body (otherwise all bodies would be living); it is alive because of some other principle, in our case, the soul. Such a principle will be more excellent than body as such. God therefore cannot be a body.

Hence: 1. We remarked earlier that the Scriptures make use of bodily metaphors to convey truth about God and about

---

9 *Psalms* 33:6   10 *Jeremiah* 17:3   11 *John* 4:24
12 1a. 2, 3 above   13 ibid   14 ibid

spiritual things.[15] In ascribing, therefore, three dimensions
to God, they are using bodily extension to symbolize the extent of God's power: depth, for example, symbolizes his
power to know what is hidden; height, the loftiness of his
power above all other things; length, the lasting quality of his
existence; breadth, the universality of his love. Or there is
Dionysius' explanation of depth as the incomprehensibility
of God's nature: length as the penetration of all things by
God's power, and breadth the boundless reach of God's
guardianship enveloping all things.[16]

2. Man is said to be to God's image, not because he has a
body, but because of his superiority to other animals; and this
is why *Genesis*, after saying, *Let us make man in our image
and likeness*, adds, *that he may have dominion over the fishes
of the sea*, and so on.[16] This superiority man owes to reason
and intellect. So that man is to God's image because of his
intellect and reason, which are not bodily characteristics.

3. Parts of the body are ascribed to God in the Scriptures
by a metaphor drawn from their functions. Eyes, for example,
see, and so, we call God's power of sight his eye, though it is
not a sense-power, but intellect. And so with other parts of
the body.

4. The ascribing of posture to God is again simply metaphor. Sitting symbolizes his authority and his steadfastness;
standing his might triumphing in the face of all opposition.

5. One comes to God and one departs from him not by
bodily movement, since he is everywhere, but by movement
of the heart. Approaching and drawing away are metaphors
which picture being moved in spirit as being moved in space.

Article 2. Is God composed of 'form' and 'matter'?

THE SECOND POINT: 1. God seems to be composed of 'form'
and 'matter'.[a] For since soul is the form of the body, anything

---

[15] 1a. 1, 9 above   [16] *Divine names* IX, 5. PG 3, 913

[a] The vocabulary is technical, but easily mastered. The terms refer
to the two principles in bodily things, called 'body' and 'soul' in liv-

with a soul is composed of matter and form. Now the Scriptures ascribe soul to God; thus in *Hebrews* we find quoted as if from the mouth of God: *my righteous one shall live by faith, and if he shrinks back my soul will have no pleasure in him.*[1] God therefore is composed of matter and form.

2. Moreover, according to Aristotle, anger, joy and the like, affect body and soul together.[2] Now the Scriptures ascribe such dispositions to God: *the anger of the Lord was kindled against his people.*[3] God then is composed of matter and form.

3. Moreover, individualness derives from matter. Now God seems to be an individual, and not something common to many individuals. So God must be composed of matter and form.

ON THE OTHER HAND, since dimension is an immediate property of matter, anything composed of matter and form will be a body. Now we have seen that God is not a body.[4] God therefore is not composed of matter and form.

REPLY: God cannot contain matter.

First, because the very existence of matter is a being potential; whilst God, as we have seen, contains no potentiality, but is sheer actuality.[5] God cannot therefore be composed of matter and form.

Secondly, in complexes of form and matter it is the form which gives goodness and perfection. Such complexes therefore are but partakers of goodness, for matter merely partakes of form. Now whatever is good of itself is prior to anything merely partaking goodness; so that God, the first and most perfect good, is no mere partaker of goodness, and thus cannot be composed of matter and form.

Thirdly, an agent acts in virtue of its form, and so the way

---

ing bodily things. Matter is the underlying and persisting principle, the 'potential' with regard to the shaping or actual form.

[1] *Hebrews* 10:38   [2] *De Anima* I, 1. 403a3   [3] *Psalms* 105:40
[4] art. 1 above   [5] ibid

in which it is an agent will depend upon the way in which it has form. A primary and immediate source of activity must therefore be primarily and immediately form. Now God is the primary source of all activity, since, as we saw, he is the first cause.[6] God then is essentially form, and not composed of matter and form.

Hence: 1. Soul is ascribed to God by a metaphor drawn from its activity. For since soul is the seat of volition in men, we call what is pleasing to God's will, pleasing to his soul.

2. Anger and the like are ascribed to God by a metaphor drawn from their effects. For it is characteristic of anger that it stimulates men to requite wrong. Divine retribution is therefore metaphorically termed anger.

3. If form be considered in itself, free of extraneous factors, then any form assumed by one material thing can be assumed by more than one; individualness derives from matter, which, as the primary substrate of form, cannot be assumed by anything else. A form however of the sort that is not assumed by material things, but itself subsists as a thing, cannot be assumed by anything else, and is thus individual of itself. Now God is such a form, and therefore does not require matter.

Article 3. Is God to be identified with his own essence or nature, with that which makes him what he is?

THE THIRD POINT: 1. It seems that God is not to be identified with his essence or nature.[a] For the essence or nature of God is godhead, and godhead is said to reside in God. Now noth-

---

[6] 1a. 2, 3 above

[a] A note on three terms used by St Thomas will be useful for this and the following discussions, and indeed throughout. All derive from the Latin word *esse*, to be. *Esse* in its pointed sense signifies the act of 'be-ing', and, despite some disadvantages, is usually translated 'existence'. *Ens* is being as subject, and is translated being, thing, existent, existing thing. *Essentia* specifies what a thing is, and is generally translated 'nature', and sometimes 'essence' or 'whatness'.

ing resides in itself. It seems therefore that God must differ from his essence or nature.

2. Moreover, effects resemble their causes, for what a thing does reflects what it is. Now we do not identify created things with their natures: human nature is not a man. Neither then is godhead God.

ON THE OTHER HAND, God is not only called living, but life: *I am the way, the truth and the life.*[1] Now godhead bears the same relationship to God, as life does to the living. God then is godhead itself.

REPLY: God is to be identified with his own essence or nature.

We shall understand this when we see why things composed of matter and form must not be identified with their natures or essences. Essence or nature includes only what defines the species of a thing: thus human nature includes only what defines man, or what makes man man, for by 'human nature' we mean that which makes man man. Now the species of a thing is not defined by the matter and properties peculiar to it as an individual; thus we do not define man as that which has this flesh and these bones, or is white, or black, or the like. This flesh and these bones and the properties peculiar to them belong indeed to this man, but not to his nature. An individual man then possesses something which his human nature does not, so that a man and his nature are not altogether the same thing. 'Human nature' names, in fact, the formative element in man; for what gives a thing definition is formative with respect to the matter which gives it individuality.

The individuality of things not composed of matter and form cannot however derive from this or that individual matter, and the forms of such things must therefore be intrinsically individual and themselves subsist as things. Such things are thus identical with their own natures.

---

[1] John 14:6

In the same way, then, God, who, as we have seen, is not composed of matter and form,[2] is identical with his own godhead, with his own life and with whatever else is similarly said of him.

Hence: 1. In talking about simple things we have to use as models the composite things from which our knowledge derives. Thus when God is being referred to as a subsistent thing, we use concrete nouns (since the subsistent things with which we are familiar are composite); but to express God's simpleness we use abstract nouns. So that when we talk of godhead or life or something of that sort residing in God, the diversity this implies is not to be attributed to God himself, but to the way in which we conceive him.

2. God's effects resemble God as far as they can, but not perfectly. One of the defects in resemblance is that they can reproduce only manifoldly what in itself is one and simple. As a result they are composite, and so cannot be identified with their natures.

Article 4. Can one distinguish in God nature and existence?

THE FOURTH POINT: 1. It is not, it seems, the nature of God simply to exist.[a] If it were, there would be nothing to specify that existence; and since unspecified existence is existence in general and belongs to everything, the word 'God' would mean an existent in general, and would name anything. Now this is false according to Scripture: *they invested stocks and stones with the incommunicable name*.[1] So it is not God's nature simply to exist.

2. Moreover, as we remarked earlier, we can know clearly that there is a God, and yet cannot know clearly what he is.[2] So the existence of God is not to be identified with what God is, with God's 'whatness' or nature.

---

[2] art. 2 above   [a] See art. 3 above note *a*
[1] *Wisdom* 14:21   [2] 1a. 2, 2

ON THE OTHER HAND, Hilary writes, *Existence does not add anything to God; it is his very substance.*[3] The substance of God is therefore his existence.

REPLY: That God is his own essence, we have seen;[4] that he is also his own existence can be shown in a number of ways.

First, properties that belong to a thing over and above its own nature must derive from somewhere, either from that nature itself, as do properties peculiar to a particular species (for example, the sense of humour peculiar to man derives from his specific nature), or from an external cause (as heat in water derives from some fire). If therefore the existence of a thing is to be other than its nature, that existence must either derive from the nature or have an external cause. Now it cannot derive merely from the nature, for nothing with derived existence suffices to bring itself into being. It follows then that, if a thing's existence differs from its nature, that existence must be externally caused. But we cannot say this about God, whom we have seen to be the first cause.[5] Neither then can we say that God's existence is other than his nature.

Secondly, forms and natures are realized by existing: thus, we express actual realization of goodness or human nature by saying that goodness or human nature exists. When a nature is not itself existence, then, it must be potential of existence. Now, as we have seen, God does not contain potentialities,[6] so in him nature must not differ from existence. It is therefore God's very nature to exist.

Thirdly, anything on fire either is itself fire or has caught fire. Similarly, anything that exists either is itself existence or partakes of it. Now, God, as we have seen, exists.[7] If then he is not himself existence, and thus not by nature existent, he will only be a partaker of existence. And so he will not be the primary existent. God therefore is not only his own essence, but also his own existence.

---

[3] *On the Trinity* VII. PL 10, 208   [4] 1a. 3, 3
[5] 1a. 2, 3   [6] art. 1 above   [7] 1a. 2, 3

Hence: 1. 'Unspecified' is an ambiguous word. For it may imply on the one hand that further specification is excluded by definition, as reason is excluded by definition from irrational animals. Or it may imply that further specification is not included in the definition, as reason is not included in the definition of animals in general, though neither is it excluded. Understood in the first way, unspecified existence is divine existence; understood in the second way, unspecified existence is existence in general.

2. The verb 'to be' is used in two ways: to signify the act of existing, and to signify the mental uniting of predicate to subject which constitutes a proposition. Now we cannot clearly know the being of God in the first sense any more than we can clearly know his essence. But in the second sense we can, for when we say that God is we frame a proposition about God which we clearly know to be true. And this, as we have seen, we know from his effects.[8]

Article 5. Can one distinguish in God genus and difference?

THE FIFTH POINT: 1. God seems to belong to a genus. For the definition of a substance—something self-subsistent—is most fully applicable to God. God therefore belongs to the genus of substance.

2. Moreover, any measure must belong to the same genus as the things it measures: lengths are measured by length, and numbers by number. Now it appears from Averroes that God is the measure of all substances.[1] God must therefore belong to the genus of substance.

ON THE OTHER HAND, a generic idea is logically prior to the things which exemplify it. Now nothing is prior to God in either the real or logical order. Hence God does not belong to a genus.

---

[8] 1a. 2, 2   [1] *Commentary on Aristotle's Metaphysics* x, 7

REPLY: There are two ways of belonging to a genus: immediately and strictly, as do species and members of species; and mediately, as unity and the point belong to the genus of quantity because they generate number and extension, or as a defect like blindness belongs mediately to the genus of the corresponding perfection. In neither of these ways does God belong to a genus.

That he cannot be a species within a genus can be shown in three ways.

First, because species are defined by differentiating some generic notion. Such differentiation is always based on some actualization of the potentiality which gave rise to the generic notion. Thus sense-life, envisaged in the concrete, gives rise to the notion of animal (an animal being that which lives by sense-perception); whilst mental life gives rise to the notion of a reasoning creature (that is a creature which lives by its mind); the mind-life of man, however, realizes potentialities of his sense-life. And we see the like in other cases. So, since realization of potentialities does not occur in God, he cannot be a species within a genus.

Secondly, since the genus of a thing states what the thing is, a genus must express a thing's nature. Now God's nature, as we have seen,[2] is to exist; so that the only genus to which God could belong would be the genus of existent. Aristotle, however, has shown that there is no such genus:[3] for genera are differentiated by factors not already contained within those genera, and no differentiating factor could be found which was not already existent (it could not differentiate if it did not exist). So we are left with no genus to which God could belong.

Thirdly, all members of a genus share one essence or nature, that of the genus stating what they are. As existents, however, they differ, for a horse's existence is not a man's, and this man's existence is not that man's. So that when something belongs to a genus, its nature, or what it is, must

_____

[2] art. 4 above   [3] *Metaphysics* III, 3. 998b22

differ from its existence. In God, however, we saw that there is not this difference.[4] Clearly then God cannot be a species within a genus.

And this shows why one cannot assign either genus or difference to God, nor define him, nor demonstrate anything of him except by means of his effects; for definitions are composed of genus and difference, and demonstration depends upon definition.

That God does not belong mediately to a genus by initiating or generating it, is also clear. For anything which so initiates a genus that it mediately belongs to that genus, is ineffective outside the genus: the point generates only extension and unity only number. Now God initiates everything that is, as we shall see later.[5] He does not therefore so initiate any particular genus that he belongs to it.

Hence: 1. The word 'substance' does not mean baldly that which exists of itself, for existence, as we have seen, cannot determine a genus. Rather 'substance' means that which is possessed of a nature such that it will exist of itself. But this nature is not itself the thing's existence. So it is plain that God does not belong to the genus of substance.

2. This argument holds of measurement by commensuration in the strict sense, for then measure and measured must be of the same genus. Now nothing is commensurate with God; though he is called the measure of all things, inasmuch as the nearer things come to God, the more fully they exist.

Article 6. Is God composed of substance and accidents?

THE SIXTH POINT: 1. It seems that there must be accidents in God.[a] For Aristotle says that *substance is never accidental*

---

[4] art. 4 above   [5] 1a. 44, 1

[a] accident: a property which can be asserted of a thing without defining what that thing is. Real or 'predicamental' accident: a modification of a thing. Logical or 'predicable' accident: what is incidentally, not necessarily, attributed to a subject.

to anything;[1] so that one cannot have something that is accidental in one thing being the substance of another. The fact that heat, for example, is an accidental form of some things proves that it cannot be the substantial form of fire. Now wisdom, power and the like which are ascribed to God are accidental in us. They must therefore be accidental in God as well.

2. Moreover, each genus has its prototype. So, unless the prototypes of the many genera of accidents are to be found in God, there will be many other prototypes besides God; and this does not seem right.

ON THE OTHER HAND, every accident is an accident of some subject. Now God cannot be a subject, since, as Boethius says, *no simple form can be a subject.*[2] So there cannot be accidents in God.

REPLY. What we have already said makes it clear that accidents cannot exist in God.

First, because accidents realize some potentialities of their subject, an accident being a mode in which the subject achieves actuality. But we have seen already that potentiality is to be altogether ruled out from God.[3]

Secondly, because God is his own existence, and as Boethius says, *you may add to an existent, but you cannot add to existence itself*[4] (just as a hot thing can be other things than hot—white, for example—but heat itself is nothing else but heat).

Thirdly, because what exists by nature is prior to what exists by accident, so that if God is to be the absolutely prime existent, nothing can exist in him by accident. Nor can there be accidents existing in him by nature, as a sense of humour exists in man by nature; for such accidents are derivative from the essential nature of the subject. In God however there is

---

[1] *Physics* 1, 3. 186b1   [2] *On the Trinity* II. PL 64, 1250
[3] art. 1 above   [4] *De hebdomadibus.* PL 64, 1311

nothing derivative, but all derivation starts from him. We are left to conclude that God contains no accidents.

Hence: 1. Power and wisdom are not ascribed to God and to us in the same sense, as we shall see later.[5] For this reason it does not follow that, because they are accidental in us, they will be accidental in God also.

2. Substance is prior to accidents, so that prototypal accidents are themselves subordinate to prior substantial prototypes. Although God is not even a prototype within the genus of substance, but the prototype of all being, transcending all genera.

Article 7. Is there any way in which God is composite, or is he altogether simple?

THE SEVENTH POINT: 1. God, it seems, is not altogether simple. For the things which derive from God resemble him: thus everything deriving from the first being exists, and everything deriving from the first good is good. Now nothing deriving from him is altogether simple. Neither then is God altogether simple.

2. Moreover, whatever attributes display the more perfection must be ascribed to God. Now, in the world with which we are familiar, composite things are more perfect than simple ones: compounds than elements, for example, and elements than their constituent parts. So we ought not to assert that God is altogether simple.

ON THE OTHER HAND, Augustine says that God is the most truly simple thing there is.[1]

REPLY: There are many ways of showing that God is altogether simple.[a]

First, relying on what we have already said. For God, we said, is not composed of extended parts, since he is not a

---

[5] 1a. 13, 5   [1] *On the Trinity* VI, 4–8. PL 42, 927–9
[a] Yet embraces the variety of all perfections: see 1a. 4, 2 below.

body; nor of form and matter; nor does he differ from his own nature; nor his nature from his existence; nor can one distinguish in him genus and difference; nor substance and accidents. It is clear then that there is no way in which God is composite, and he must be altogether simple.

Secondly, everything composite is subsequent to its components and dependent upon them; whilst God, as we have seen, is the first of all beings.[2]

Thirdly, everything composite is caused; for essentially diverse elements will not combine unless made to do so by a cause. God however is not caused, as we have seen,[3] but is himself the first cause.

Fourthly, in any composite there is a realizing of potentialities, such as cannot occur in God: for either the potentialities of one component are realized by another, or at any rate all the components together are potentially the whole.

Fifthly, nothing composite can be predicated of its own component parts. In heterogeneous composites this is obvious, for no part of a man is a man, and no part of the foot a foot. And, although in homogeneous composites certain ways of describing the whole apply also to the parts (every bit of air, for example, is air, and every drop of water water), yet there are other ways which do not (thus if all the water occupies two cubic feet, no part of it will do so). So that in all composites there is some element not sharing a common predicate with the whole. Now even though one grants that a thing possessed of a form may contain such elements (thus, a white thing contains elements not covered by the predicate 'white'), nevertheless in the form itself there can be nothing foreign. Now God is form itself, indeed existence itself; so he can in no way be composite. And this was what Hilary was pointing out when he said: *God, being power, is not compounded of weakness; and, being light, is not pieced together from darkness.*[4]

Hence: 1. Things deriving from God resemble him as effects resemble a primary cause. Now it is in the nature of an

_____

[2] 1a. 2, 3   [3] ibid   [4] *On the Trinity* VII. PL 10, 223

effect to be composite in some way, because even at its simplest it is not its own existence. This we shall see later.[5]

2. In the world with which we are familiar composite things excel simple ones, because created perfection needs building up from many elements, and not just from one. Divine perfection is, however, simple and single, as we shall show shortly.[6]

Article 8. Does God enter into composition with other things?

THE EIGHTH POINT: 1. God seems to enter into composition with other things. For Dionysius declares that *the being of everything is the godhead beyond being.*[1] Now the being of everything enters into the composition of each. God therefore enters into composition with other things.

2. Moreover, God is a form, for Augustine says that *the Word of God* (which is God) *is unformed form.*[2] Now form is a component of things. God then must be a component in something.

3. Moreover, things which exist without differing are identical. Now God and the ultimate matter of things exist without differing. They are therefore completely identical. And since ultimate matter enters into the composition of things, God must do so too.—To prove the middle step in this argument: things that differ do so by certain differentiating factors, and must therefore be composite. God and ultimate matter are however altogether simple, and so cannot differ.

ON THE OTHER HAND, Dionysius says that *nothing can come into contact with God or partially intermingle with him in any way.*[3]

---

[5] 1a. 50, 2 ad 3   [6] cf 1a. 4, 2 ad 1
[1] *Heavenly hierarchy* IV, 1. PG 3, 177
[2] *Sermons* CXVII, 1. PL 38, 662
[3] *Divine names* II, 5. PG 3, 643

REPLY: On this point three mistakes have been made. Some people have held that God is the soul of the world, as we learn from Augustine;[4] and with these people we can include those who said that God was the soul of the outermost heaven. Others have said that God is the form of all things: the view, it is said, of Amaury of Bène and his followers. The third mistake was the really stupid thesis of David of Dinant that God was the ultimate unformed matter of things.[a] All these opinions are clearly wrong: God cannot enter into composition with anything in any way, be it as form or as matter.

First, because we have said above that God is the first cause of things.[5] Now the form of an effect, though similar in species to its cause (man begets man), is not to be identified with the cause. And matter is neither identifiable with the cause nor similar to it in species, since matter is only able to be what the cause is already.

Secondly, since God is a cause, he is a primary and immediate source of activity. A component, however, is not itself a primary and immediate source of activity; this belongs rather to the composite thing. Thus a hand does not act, but man by means of his hand; and it is the fire which warms by virtue of its heat. God then cannot be a component of anything.

Thirdly, no component, not even those primary components of composite things, matter and form, can be called, without qualification, a primary being. For matter is potential, and it is only in a qualified sense, as we have shown, that the potential precedes the actual.[6] Again, form, when a component, is something of which a composite partakes. Now, just as that which is essentially *x* takes precedence over that which partakes *x*, so also over *x* as partaken: that which

---

[4] *City of God* VII, 6. PL 41, 199. The reference is to Varro.

[a] Amaury of Bène and David of Dinant were two French professors of the late twelfth and early thirteenth century. Their views were condemned in 1210 by a provincial council at Paris. See E. Gilson, *Christian Philosophy in the Middle Ages* (London, New York, 1955), pp. 240–44.

[5] 1a. 2, 3   [6] art. 1 above

is by nature fire takes precedence over the being on fire of
other things. We have however already shown that God is the
primary being, without qualification.[7]

Hence: 1. Dionysius means that godhead is archetypally
and causatively the being of all things, but not substantially
their being.

2. The Word is not a component form, but a form upon
which things are patterned.

3. Simple things do not differ from one another by added
differentiating factors as composites do. Thus, although the
factors 'rational' and 'irrational' differentiate men and horses,
these factors themselves do not then require further factors
to differentiate them one from another. Indeed, if we may
point the words we are using, these factors are not *differentiated*, but *diverse*. According to Aristotle diversity is absolute,
but difference is difference in some respect.[8] So, emphasizing
our words, God and ultimate matter are not *differentiated*,
but are of themselves *diverse*. One cannot conclude therefore
to their identity.

---

[7] 1a. 2, 3   [8] *Metaphysics* x, 3. 1054b24

DISCUSSION OF God's simpleness must be followed by a study of his perfection. And since things perfect are called 'good', we shall discuss

first, God's perfection,
secondly, his goodness.

Question 4. God's perfection

About the first of these questions there are three points of inquiry:

1. is God perfect?
2. is his perfection all-embracing, containing, so to say, the perfection of everything else?
3. can creatures be said to resemble God?

Article 1. Is God perfect?

THE FIRST POINT: 1. 'Perfect' does not seem a suitable term to apply to God, for etymologically it means 'thoroughly made'. Now since we would not say that God is made, we should not say that he is perfect.

2. Moreover, God is the first origin of things. But things have imperfect origins: plants and animals, for example, begin from seed. God therefore is imperfect.

3. Moreover, as we have shown, the nature of God is simply to exist.[1] Now simply to exist is seemingly most imperfect: the lowest common denominator of all things. God then is not perfect.

ON THE OTHER HAND, we read in Matthew: *be ye perfect, as your heavenly Father is perfect.*[2]

---

[1] 1a. 3, 4   [2] Matthew 5:48

REPLY. Aristotle tells us that certain ancient philosophers—the Pythagoreans and Speusippus—did not regard the first origin of things as the acme of goodness and perfection;[3] the reason being that they only paid attention to the matter out of which things originated, and primordial matter is the most imperfect of all things. For matter as such is only potential, and primordial matter is therefore sheer potentiality and entirely imperfect.[a]

We however hold God to be not primordial matter but the primary operative cause of things, and thus the most perfect of things. For just as matter as such is potential, so an acting thing as such is actual. Thus the first origin of all activity will be the most actual, and therefore the most perfect, of all things. For things are called perfect when they have achieved actuality, the perfect thing being that in which nothing required by the thing's particular mode of perfection fails to exist.

Hence: 1. What is not made cannot properly be called perfect, but, as Gregory says, *stammering, we echo the heights of God as best we can.*[4] And so, because things that are made are called perfect when the potentiality of them has been actualized, we extend the word to refer to anything that is not lacking in actuality, whether made or not.

2. The imperfect matter from which the things around us originate, is not their ultimate origin, but is itself preceded by something perfect. For even when an animal is generated from seed, the original seed itself derives from some previous animal or plant. Anything potential must be preceded by something actual, since only the already actual can actualize a thing which exists potentially.

3. The most perfect thing of all is to exist, for everything else is potential compared to existence. Nothing achieves ac-

---

[3] *Metaphysics* XII, 7. 1072b30

[a] So imperfect in fact that it is a contradiction in term for primordial or 'bare' matter to exist. It exists only under some form as the potential principle within a material thing.

[4] *Morals* v, 36. PL 75, 715

tuality except it exist, and the act of existing is therefore the
ultimate actuality of everything, and even of every form. So
it is that things acquire existence, and not existence things.
For in the very phrases 'the existence of man' or 'of a horse'
or 'of some other thing', it is existence that is regarded as an
acquisition like a form, not the thing to which existence
belongs.

Article 2. Is God's perfection all-embracing, containing, so to say, the perfection of everything else?

THE SECOND POINT: 1. God, it seems, does not contain the
perfections of everything. For God, as we have seen, is
simple,[1] and the perfections of things are many and diverse.
So God does not contain every perfection of things.

2. Moreover, opposites cannot exist together. Now the perfections of things are opposed to one another; for each species is perfected by that which differentiates it from other
species in the same genus, and such constitutive differences
are opposed to one another. So it seems that, because opposites cannot exist together in the same thing, God does not
contain all the perfections of things.

3. Moreover, a living thing is more perfect than a merely
existent thing, and one that is wise more perfect than one
that is merely alive; so that to live is more perfect than to
be, and to be wise more perfect than to live. Now it is the
nature of God simply to be. Perfections like life and wisdom
therefore are not to be found in him.

ON THE OTHER HAND, we have Dionysius saying that *all existent things are contained in a primordial unity in God.*[2]

REPLY: The perfections of everything exist in God. For this
reason we call his perfection 'all-embracing', for, as Averroes

---

[1] 1a. 3, 7   [2] *Divine names* v, 9. PG 3, 825

says, he lacks no excellence of any sort.[3] There are two ways of showing this.

Firstly, because any perfection found in an effect must be found also in the cause of that effect; and this either without modification when cause and effect are of the same sort (thus man begets man), or in a more perfect manner when cause and effect are not of the same sort (thus the sun's power produces things having a certain likeness to the sun). This is because effects obviously pre-exist potentially in their causes. Now to pre-exist potentially in a cause is to pre-exist in a more perfect, not in a less perfect, manner, even if to pre-exist potentially in matter is to pre-exist less perfectly; for although matter as such is imperfect, agents as such are perfect. Since God then is the primary operative cause of all things, the perfections of everything must pre-exist in him in a higher manner. And Dionysius is touching upon this argument when he refuses any description of God as *this and not that*, saying God *is everything, inasmuch as he is everything's cause.*[4]

Secondly, because as we have seen God is self-subsistent being itself,[5] and therefore necessarily contains within himself the full perfection of being. For clearly a hot thing falls short of the full perfection of heat only because it does not fully partake of the nature of heat; to a self-subsistent heat nothing of the virtue of heat could be lacking. Nothing therefore of the perfection of existing can be lacking to God, who is subsistent existence itself. Now every perfection is a perfection of existing, for it is the manner in which a thing exists that determines the manner of its perfection. No perfection can therefore be lacking to God. And Dionysius is touching upon this argument when he says that God *does not exist in any qualified way, but possesses primordially in himself all being, without qualification and without circumscrip-*

---

[3] *Commentary on Aristotle's Metaphysics* v, 21
[4] op. cit. v, 8. PG 3, 824　　　[5] 1a. 3, 4

tion. And later he adds that *God is the being of all that subsists*.[6]

Hence: 1. If the sun, as Dionysius says, *possesses in itself, primordially and without diversity, the divers qualities and substances of the things we can sense, while yet maintaining the unity of its own being and the homogeneity of its light, how much more must everything pre-exist in unity of nature in the cause of all?*[7] Perfections therefore which are diverse and opposed in themselves, pre-exist as one in God, without detriment to his simpleness.

2. The above answer solves this argument also.

3. In the same chapter Dionysius[8] tells us that, when considered as notionally separate, existence as such is more perfect than life as such, and life as such more perfect than wisdom as such. Nevertheless, living things, which both live and exist, are more perfect than things which merely exist; and one who is wise also exists and also lives. So, although being an existent thing does not involve being living or wise (for nothing partaking of existence need partake every mode of existence), nevertheless, existence itself does involve life and wisdom (for subsistent existence itself cannot lack any perfection of existence).

Article 3. *Can creatures be said to resemble God?*

THE THIRD POINT: 1. No creature, it seems, can resemble God. For the psalm says *there is none like thee among the gods, O Lord*.[1] Now the creatures to which we extend the word 'god' are among the more excellent ones. So one has even less grounds for saying that other creatures resemble God.

2. Moreover, resemblance is a sort of comparison; so that things of diverse genera, which cannot be compared, cannot be alike. Thus no one talks of a resemblance between sweetness and whiteness. Now no creature can be of one genus

---

[6] op. cit. v, 4. PG 3, 817   [7] op. cit. v, 8. PG 3, 824
[8] op. cit. v, 3. PG 3, 817   [1] *Psalms* 85:8

with God, for God, as we say, does not belong to a genus.[2]
No creature then can resemble God.

3. Moreover, things are said to be alike when they agree in
form. Now nothing agrees with God in form, for nothing but
God alone has as its nature simply to exist. No creature then
can be like God.

4. Moreover, resemblance is mutual, for like is like to like.
If then some creature were like God, God would be like a
creature, which Isaiah denies: *to whom will you liken God?*[3]

ON THE OTHER HAND, we read in *Genesis, Let us make man
after our image and likeness*;[4] and in John's first epistle, *when
he appears we shall be like him.*[5]

REPLY: Resemblance results from sharing a common form,
and there are as many sorts of resemblance as there are ways
of sharing a form.

Some things are called alike because they share a form of
the same type to the same degree (and such we call not
merely alike, but exactly alike). Thus, two equally white
things are said to resemble one another in whiteness. And
this is the best likeness.

Other things are called alike because they share a form
of the same type, though to different degrees. Thus, something less white is said to resemble something more white.
And this is a less perfect likeness.

Thirdly, things are called alike because they share a form,
though not of one type. An example would be an agent and
its effect, when not in the same genus. For what a thing does
reflects what its active self is; and, since a thing is active in
virtue of its form, its effect must bear a likeness to that form.
If then agent and effect are of one species their like forms
will be of the same specific type, as when man begets man.
If, however, the agent is outside the species, the forms will
be alike, but not of the same specific type: thus a certain

---

[2] 1a. 3, 5   [3] *Isaiah* 40:18   [4] *Genesis* 1:26
[5] 1 *John* 3:2

likeness exists between the sun and the things the sun produces, even though such things do not receive a form of like
species to the sun's. If now there be an agent outside even
genus, its effects will bear an even remoter resemblance to
the agent. The likeness borne will not now be of the same
specific or generic type as the form of the agent, but will
present the sort of analogy that holds between all things because they have existence in common. And this is how things
receiving existence from God resemble him; for precisely as
things possessing existence they resemble the primary and
universal sources of all existence.

Hence: 1. As Dionysius says, when the Scriptures state that
nothing is like to God, *they are not denying all likeness to
him. For the same things are like and unlike God: like in so
far as they imitate as best they can him whom it is not possible to imitate perfectly; unlike in so far as they fall short
of their cause,*[6] not only in degree (as less white falls short
of more white), but also because they do not share a common species or genus.

2. Creatures are not related to God as to a thing of a different genus, but as to something outside of and prior to all
genera.

3. Creatures are said to resemble God, not by sharing a
form of the same specific or generic type, but only analogically, inasmuch as God exists by nature, and other things
partake existence.

4. Although we may admit in a way that creatures resemble
God, we may in no way admit that God resembles creatures;
for, as Dionysius points out, *mutual likeness obtains between
things of the same order, but not between cause and effect:*[7]
thus we would call a portrait a likeness of a man, but not
vice-versa. Similarly, we can say in a way that creatures resemble God, but not that God resembles creatures.

---

[6] *Divine names* IX, 7. PG 3, 916   [7] op. cit. IX, 6. PG 3, 913

WE ASK next about good.

first, the general notion of good,
secondly, the goodness of God.

Question 5. The general notion of good

The first question has six points of inquiry:

1. is being good really the same thing as existing?
2. if one assumes that being good and existing differ merely as ideas, which idea is the more fundamental?
3. if one assumes that existing is more fundamental, is everything that exists good?
4. what kind of causality is implicit in the notion of goodness?
5. is goodness a matter of being in condition, form and order?
6. the division of good into the worthy, the useful and the delightful.

Article 1. Is being good really the same thing as existing?

THE FIRST POINT: 1. There is a real difference, it seems, between being good and existing.[a] For Boethius says, *I observe*

---

[a] The reader will notice that articles 1 and 3 raise practically the same question and give it practically the same answer. But whereas article 3 is asking whether any particular things qualified as beings escape being qualified as goods, article 1 is rather asking whether these are different qualifications at all. One might say that article 3 treats the words *ens* and *bonum* as nouns, article 1 as adjectives. It is to mark this difference that *ens* has been translated as 'existing' and *bonum* as 'being good' quite often in the following pages.

that it is one thing for things to be good, another for them to exist.[1] So there is a real difference between being good and existing.

2. Moreover, nothing can be a mode of itself. The commentary on the *Book of Causes*[b] remarks, however, that being good is a mode of existing.[2] So existing and being good really differ.

3. Moreover, there are degrees of goodness but not of existence. So being good and existing must really differ.

ON THE OTHER HAND Augustine says that *inasmuch as we exist, we are good.*[3]

REPLY: To be good is really the same thing as to exist, but the words have different meanings. This is made clear as follows. The goodness of a thing consists in its being desirable; hence Aristotle's dictum that *good is what all things desire.*[4][c] Now clearly desirability is consequent upon perfection, for things always desire their perfection. And the perfection of a thing depends on how far it has achieved actuality. It is clear then that a thing is good inasmuch as it exists, for as we saw above it is by existing that everything achieves actuality.[5] Obviously then being good does not really differ from existing, though the word 'good' expresses a notion of desirability not expressed by the word 'existent'.

Hence: 1. Although being good is really the same thing as existing, one cannot use the words 'good' and 'existent' interchangeably without qualification, due to a difference in meaning. For 'existent' properly means actual, and actuality properly involves reference to potentiality, so that, used without qualification, 'existent' names a thing in its initial distinct-

---

[1] *De hebdomadibus.* PL 34, 1312

[b] a Latin translation of excerpts from Proclus

[2] *Proposition 19*   [3] *On Christian teaching* I, 32. PL 34, 32

[4] *Ethics* I, 1. 1094a3

[c] desire: all appetite is included, both conscious and unconscious.

[5] 1a. 3, 4; 4, 1 ad 3

ness from sheer potentiality. Now it is being a substance that thus distinguishes a thing, and things are therefore said to exist, without qualification, when they exist as substances. As possessed of some further actuality they are said to exist only in a certain respect; to be white, for example, is to exist only in a certain respect; it is not being white which removes a thing from sheer potentiality, for to be white a thing must already actually exist. 'Good', on the other hand, expresses the idea of desirable perfection and thus the notion of something complete. So things are called 'good', without qualification, when they are completely perfect; when their perfection is not so complete as it should be, then, even though having some perfection inasmuch as they actually exist, they will nonetheless not be called perfect or good without qualification but only in a certain respect.

It follows therefore that when we consider the initial existence of something as substance we talk of it existing without qualification and being good in a certain respect (namely, inasmuch as it exists); but when we consider the actualization which completes a thing we talk of that thing existing in a certain respect and being good without qualification. Hence Boethius' remark that *it is one thing for things to be good and another for them to exist*[d] refers to existing and being good understood without qualification; for to exist without qualification is to achieve an initial actuality, and to be good without qualification is to achieve complete actuality. However, a thing's initial actuality is a sort of goodness, and the actuality completing it a sort of existence.

2. 'Being good' describes a mode of existence when used without qualification to mean achieving complete actuality.

3. In the same way, degrees of goodness result from actuality over and above existence, such as knowledge or virtue.

Article 2. *Which idea is the more fundamental, being good or existing?*

THE SECOND POINT: 1. Being good seems to be a more fundamental idea than existing. For one lists epithets in the order

---

[d] quoted in 1st objection

of the ideas they express. Now in Dionysius' list of divine epithets 'good' precedes 'existent'.[1] The idea of the good is therefore prior to the idea of the existent.

2. Moreover, the more fundamental idea is the one with wider application. Now good is of wider application than existent, for as Dionysius says *good comprehends things that exist and things that do not exist, but existent only things that exist*.[2] Hence good is a more fundamental idea than existent.

3. Moreover, the more universal an idea the more fundamental it is. Now good seems more universal than existent, for it conveys the notion of desirability, and even non-existence is desirable—thus we read of Judas that *it would have been good for him never to have been born*.[3] The good is therefore a more fundamental idea than the existent.

4. Moreover, not only existence is desirable, but also life, wisdom and many similar things. Existence seems then to be only one of many desirable goods. So the good is without qualification a more fundamental idea than the existent.

ON THE OTHER HAND the *Book of Causes* says that *existence is the first thing created*.[4]

REPLY: Existing is a more fundamental idea than being good. For the idea expressed in a word is something the intellect conceives from things and expresses in speech. A more fundamental idea then is one met with earlier in this process of intellectual conception. Now the first idea met with in intellectual conception is that of an existent, for as Aristotle says in order to be known a thing must actually be.[5] This is why existent being is the primary and distinctive object of intellect, just as sound is the primary object of hearing. Existing therefore is a more fundamental idea than being good.

Hence: 1. Dionysius is concerned with divine epithets implying causality in God, for as he himself says, God's names

---

[1] *Divine names* III, 1. PG 3, 680   [2] op. cit. V, 1. PG 3, 816
[3] *Matthew* 26:24   [4] *Proposition* 4
[5] *Metaphysics* IX, 9. 1051a31

are drawn from creatures, like those of other causes from their effects.[6] Now being good, conveying as it does the notion of desirability, implies being an end or goal, and this is where causality starts, for no agent acts except for some end, and except some agent acts no matter acquires form (hence we call the end the cause of causes). In causation then the good precedes the existent as end precedes form; and for this reason in any list of epithets signifying divine causality 'good' will precede 'existent'.

A further reason is that the Platonists, not differentiating between potential being and lack of being, said that matter was non-existent, and consequently held that goodness is partaken of more widely than existence. For since unformed matter desires good, it partakes it (what a thing desires reflects what it is); it does not however partake existence since supposed to be non-existent. And this is why Dionysius says that *good comprehends things that do not exist.*[7]

2. Clearly this answers the second argument also. Or one could say instead that it is not to good as predicate but to good as cause that both existent and non-existent things are subject; understanding by non-existence not total and absolute non-existence but potential existence not yet actualized. For the good is a goal, in which not only things that have achieved actuality come to rest, but towards which things not actualized but only potential are in movement. Existing, on the other hand, involves no causal relation at all, unless it be that of form—either intrinsic form or extrinsic pattern, and only actually existent things are subject to the causality of form.

3. Non-existence is desirable not in itself, but for the incidental reason that it removes an evil which it is desirable to remove. Now removing evil is desirable only because evil is lack of some sort of existence. So that the desirable thing itself is existence, and non-existence is desirable only incidentally, inasmuch as a man can no longer abide the lack of

---

[6] op. cit. 1, 7. PG 3, 596   [7] op. cit. v, 1. PG 3, 816

an existence such as he desires. And it is for such incidental reasons that non-existence is called good.

4. Life, wisdom and so on are desired as modes of actual existence; so that what is desired from them is existence of a certain sort. Nothing therefore is desirable except it exist, and in consequence nothing is good except it exist.

Article 3. Is everything that exists good?

THE THIRD POINT: 1. Not everything that exists is good, it seems. For previous discussion has shown that being good adds something to existing.[1] Now adding something to the idea of existing will produce a narrower idea: being a substance, for example, or being of such a size or such a sort. Being good is therefore a narrower idea than existing. And so not everything that exists is good.

2. Moreover, nothing bad is good: witness Isaiah, crying *woe to those who call evil good*.[2] Now some things that exist are called bad. So not everything that exists is good.

3. Moreover, the good is, by definition, desirable. Now the ultimate matter of things is not desirable but only desires. Matter then is not good. And so not everything that exists is good.

4. Moreover, Aristotle says that mathematics does not concern itself with the good.[3] Nevertheless the objects of mathematics must somehow exist for there to be science of them. So not everything that exists is good.

ON THE OTHER HAND, anything that exists is either God or created by God. Now *every creature of God is good*, says St Paul.[4] And God himself is supremely good. So everything that exists is good.

REPLY: Inasmuch as they exist, all things are good. For everything, inasmuch as it exists, is actual and therefore in some

---

[1] art. 1 above   [2] *Isaiah* 5:20   [3] *Metaphysics* III, 2. 996a29
[4] 1 *Timothy* 4:4

way perfect, all actuality being a sort of perfection. Now we have shown above that anything perfect is desirable and good.[5] It follows then that, inasmuch as they exist, all things are good.

Hence: 1. Being a substance, or being of such a size or sort, as also any idea less general than these, narrows the idea of existing by mentioning what kind of thing is existing. Being good does not add to existing in this way, but adds merely the notion of a desirability and perfection associated with the very existence of things, whatever kind of things they be. Being good then is no narrower than existing.

2. Nothing that exists is called bad because it exists, but rather because it fails to exist in some way; thus a man is called bad when he fails to be virtuous, and an eye bad when its vision fails.

3. Just as matter only potentially exists, so it is only potentially good. Although one might say if one were a Platonist that matter is non-existent, being accompanied by lack of existence, and yet partakes something of goodness, being a predisposition towards good. This is why matter, though not desirable, nevertheless desires.

4. Mathematical objects have no separate existence; if they did, that existence itself would be good. We separate them only conceptually, by prescinding from matter and change, and thus from the idea of an end or goal motivating change. Now conceiving something to exist without conceiving it to be good is admissible, for as we have already seen existing is a more fundamental concept than being good.[6]

Article 4. What kind of causality is implicit in the notion of goodness?

THE FOURTH POINT: 1. Being good seems to imply not so much being an end or goal as being one of the other kinds of cause.[a]

---

[5] art. 1 above   [6] art. 2 above

[a] Aristotle, Metaphysics v, 2, enumerates four causes: material cause, that from which and in which a thing comes into being; for-

For Dionysius says that *the good is esteemed beautiful.*[1] Now beauty involves the notion of form. Goodness therefore conveys the idea of form.

2. Or another approach: good things pour forth their own being, as Dionysius gives us to understand, saying that *from the good comes all subsistence and existence.*[2] Now pouring out involves the idea of an operative cause. Being good therefore conveys the idea of being an operative cause.

3. Moreover, Augustine says that *we exist because God is good.*[3] Now existence comes from God as an operative cause. So being good implies being an operative cause.

ON THE OTHER HAND we have the words of Aristotle, *That for the sake of which things exist is their good and their goal.*[4] Being good therefore involves being an end or goal.

REPLY: Since good is what all things desire, and this involves the idea of a goal, clearly being good involves being a goal. Nevertheless, presupposed to the idea of good are the notions of operative cause and form.

For we observe that an act of causation begins from what will be caused last; thus fire begins by heating other things and then elicits the form of fire in them, and yet the heat of a fire is consequent upon its substantial form. Now in the act of causation we begin with the good end which influences the agent to act, then follows the action of the agent eliciting the form, and finally there arises the form. Necessarily then the opposite order is found within the caused thing: first, there occurs the form itself which gives the thing existence; second for consideration occurs the thing's operative power through which it achieves perfect existence (for a thing is perfect, Aristotle says, when it can reproduce itself[5]); and finally

---

mal cause, its own inner shaping principle; efficient cause, the active originator of its production; final cause, the end for the sake of which it is.

[1] *Divine names* IV, 7. PG 3, 701   [2] op. cit. IV, 4. PG 3, 700
[3] *On Christian teaching* I, 32. PL 34, 32
[4] *Physics* II, 3. 195a23   [5] *Meteorology* IV, 3. 380a12

the thing realizes the idea of good and so can pour forth perfection within being.

Hence: 1. A good thing is also in fact a beautiful thing, for both epithets have the same basis in reality, namely, the possession of form; and this is why *the good is esteemed beautiful.* Good and beautiful are not however synonymous. For good (being *what all things desire*) has to do properly with desire and so involves the idea of end (since desire is a kind of movement towards something). Beauty, on the other hand, has to do with knowledge, and we call a thing beautiful when it pleases the eye of the beholder. This is why beauty is a matter of right proportion, for the senses delight in rightly proportioned things as similar to themselves, the sense-faculty being a sort of proportion itself like all other knowing faculties. Now since knowing proceeds by imaging, and images have to do with form, beauty properly involves the notion of form.

2. Good things are said to pour forth their being in the same way that ends are said to move one.

3. Beings with wills are called good when those wills are good, since will determines the use to which everything else in us is put. A good man therefore is not one who has a good intellect, but one who has a good will. Now the special function of the will is the pursuit of ends. So saying that *we exist because God is good* does have reference to the causality of an end.

Article 5. Is goodness a matter of being in condition, form and order?

THE FIFTH POINT: 1. Goodness does not seem a matter of being in condition, form and order. For we have already seen that being good does not mean the same as existing.[1] Condition, form and order, however, seem part of what existence means. For the book of *Wisdom* declares, *Thou hast created all things by number and weight and measure,*[2] a threefold-

---

[1] art. 1 above   [2] *Wisdom* 11:21

ness Augustine shows to be the basis of form, condition and order, when he says, *Measure determines the condition of everything, number supplies everything with form, and weight attracts everything toward steadiness and rest.*[3] Goodness therefore does not consist in condition, form and order.

2. Moreover, condition, form and order are themselves goods of a certain sort. If then being good is to consist in being in condition, form and order, each of these must be in a condition, form and order of its own. And so on for ever.

3. Moreover, to be bad is to be out of condition, form and order. Now a bad thing never lacks goodness altogether. So that goodness does not consist in condition, form and order.

4. Moreover, that in which goodness consists cannot be called bad. But we talk of things being in bad condition, bad form and bad order. Goodness does not therefore consist in condition, form and order.

5. Moreover, condition, form and order are caused by weight, number and measure, as the above quotation from Augustine shows. But some good things do not possess weight, number and measure, for Ambrose declares that *it is the nature of light not to be created in number, weight and measure.*[4] Goodness therefore does not consist in condition, form and order.

ON THE OTHER HAND Augustine says that *these three—condition, form and order—are goods always found in everything God makes; where these three bulk large things are very good, where they are of small account things are of little good, where they do not exist at all things are no good.*[5] Now none of this would be so unless goodness consisted in these three things. Goodness therefore consists in condition, form and order.

REPLY: To be called 'good' things must be perfect, for only then as we have said are they desirable.[6] Being perfect means

---

[3] *On Genesis to the letter* IV, 3. PL 34, 299
[4] *On the Hexameron* I, 9. PL 14, 143
[5] *On the nature of good* 3. PL 42, 553   [6] art. 1 above

lacking nothing requisite to one's own mode of perfection. Now what a thing is its form determines, and form presupposes certain things and has certain necessary consequences. So, to be perfect and good, a thing must possess form and the prerequisites and consequences of form.

Now form presupposes that a thing's material elements and operative causes are somehow appropriate or commensurate to that form, and this is expressed in the word 'condition'. This is why *measure* is said to *determine condition*.[7] To express form itself Augustine used the word *species* since form determines the species of things. And this is why *number* is said to *supply form*; for according to Aristotle definitions of species are like numbers, and just as adding or subtracting one changes the species of numbers, so also does adding or subtracting a differentiating factor in definitions.[8] Finally, form issues in a proneness to some end or action or the like, for activity is consequent upon actuality, and things gravitate toward what is natural to them. And this is expressed by 'weight' and 'order'. So because being good consists in being perfect, it also consists in being in condition, form and order.

Hence: 1. An existent thing possesses these three qualities only when it is perfect, and then it is good.

2. We talk of condition, form and order as good in the same way that we talk of them existing, not as subjects of existence themselves, but as constituting other things in existence and goodness. Nevertheless they themselves are good without being so constituted in goodness. For they are not called good as being formally constituted good, but because other things are formally constituted good by them, in the same way that whiteness is said to exist inasmuch as it constitutes things in a mode of existence (namely, existing as white) and not because it is constituted in any mode of existence itself.

3. Every mode of existence is determined by some form, and so condition, form and order accompany every mode in which a thing exists. Thus man has one condition, form and

---

[7] *On Genesis* loc. cit.   [8] *Metaphysics* VIII, 3. 1043b34

order as a man, and another condition, form and order again as white, or as virtuous, or as knowledgeable, or as anything else he is. Now something gone bad, like a blind eye, lacks some particular mode of existence, in this case being able to see; and so loses, not all condition, form and order, but only that condition, form and order associated with being able to see.

4. Augustine says that *condition as such is always good* (and the same could be said of form and order) *but condition, form and order are called bad either because they fall short of what they should be, or because they are unfitted for the things for which they are meant, and thus bad in the sense of foreign and incongruous.*[9]

5. No one says it is the nature of light to lack number, weight and measure altogether, but only as compared to bodies; for light is all-pervasive in its influence on bodies, being the form of energy proper to the ultimate physical source of change, namely, the heavens.[a]

Article 6. *The division of good into the worthy, the useful and the delightful*

THE SIXTH POINT: 1. It seems wrong to divide good into the worthy, the useful and the delightful. For as Aristotle says goods are divided into ten categories,[1] in each of which we can find worthy, useful and delightful things. Such a division is therefore inappropriate.

2. Moreover, all division results from dissociation. Now these three classes of goods do not seem dissociate, for worthy things are also delightful, and nothing unworthy is useful, as Cicero remarks.[2] So the suggested division is inappropriate.

3. Moreover, things related as means to end must be treated

---

[9] *On the nature of good* 22 & 23. PL 42, 558

[a] According to the Aristotelean theory all changes on the earth below are eventually traceable to the influence of the changes in the heavens. This is evidently true to a very great extent where seasonal and biological changes are concerned.

[1] *Ethics* I, 6. 1096a23   [2] *De officiis* II, 3

as one. Now the useful is good only as a means to either the
delightful or the worthy. We should not then divide the useful from the delightful and the worthy.

ON THE OTHER HAND Ambrose divided the good in this way.[3]

REPLY: This division seems properly to apply to what is good
for man. Nevertheless, a deeper and more general consideration of the concept of good reveals that the division properly
applies to good as such. For a thing is good because desirable,
and because movements of desire terminate in it. Now the
termination of such movements can be discussed on analogy
with the movements of physical bodies. Physical movement
terminates, simply speaking, at its final point; but also, in a
certain sense, at points part of the way there, which since
they end some part of the movement can be called stops in
the movement. Moreover, one can consider that which finally
stops the movement to be either the actual thing aimed at
(a place, say, or a form), or rest in that thing. By analogy
then in movements of desire things desirable as putting a
partial stop to the movement, being partway toward some
other thing, we call 'useful'. That which is desirable as putting a full stop to the movement of desire because it is the
actually desired thing itself we call 'worthy', for worthy means
desirable in itself. That which puts a stop to the movement
of desire because it is rest in the desired thing is 'delight'.

Hence: 1. As existent things goods divide into ten categories; the suggested division however is proper to goods precisely as good.

2. The division is based not on dissociation of things, but
on dissociation of ideas. Although those things are properly
called delightful which are desirable solely because they give
delight and can at times be harmful and unworthy. And those
things are said to be useful which are desirable not in themselves but solely as means to other things (for example, the

---

[3] De officiis 1, 9. PL 16, 31

drinking of bitter medicine). Those things are called worthy which are desirable in themselves.

3. The word 'good' is not used in exactly the same sense within these three divisions, but in a graded sequence of analogical senses. The primary sense of 'good' is worthy, the second delightful, and the third useful.

Question 6. The goodness of God

This question is composed of four points of inquiry:

1. can one associate goodness with God?
2. is God supremely good?
3. is God alone good by nature?
4. does God's goodness make everything good?

Article 1. Can one associate goodness with God?

THE FIRST POINT: 1. One must not it seems associate goodness with God. For goodness consists in condition, form and order, which seem out of place in a God who is immeasurable and not subordinate to anything. So goodness must not be associated with God.

2. Moreover, *the good is what everything desires.*[1] But not everything desires God, because not everything knows him and one can only desire what one knows. Goodness therefore must not be associated with God.

ON THE OTHER HAND we read in *Lamentations, The Lord is good to those who wait for him, to the soul that seeks him.*[2]

REPLY: Goodness should be associated above all with God. For goodness is consequent upon desirability. Now things desire their perfection; and an effect's perfection and form consists in resembling its cause, since what a thing does reflects what it is. So the cause itself is desirable and can be called 'good', what is desired from it being a share in resem-

---

[1] *Ethics* I, 1. 1094a3   [2] *Lamentations* 3:25

bling it. Clearly then, since God is the primary operative cause of everything, goodness and desirability fittingly belong to him. And so Dionysius ascribes goodness to God as to the primary operative cause, saying that God is called good *as the source of all subsistence*.[3]

Hence: 1. Goodness consisting in condition, form and order is created goodness. Goodness belongs to God as to a cause, however, so he it is that imposes condition, form and order on others. The three qualities do belong to God, therefore, but as to a cause.

2. In desiring its own perfection everything is desiring God himself, for the perfections of all things, as we saw, somehow resemble divine existence.[4] And so, of the things that desire God, some know him in himself and this is the privilege of reasoning creatures, others know his goodness as participated somewhere or other and this is possible even to sense-knowledge, whilst yet other things, having no knowledge, desire by nature, directed to their goal by some higher being with knowledge.

Article 2. Is God supremely good?

THE SECOND POINT: 1. It seems that God is not supremely good. For supreme goodness is something over and above goodness, otherwise every good would be supremely good. Now adding one thing to another produces something composite. The supreme good is therefore composite. God, then, who has been shown to be simple,[1] is not the supreme good.

2. Moreover, Aristotle says that *good is what everything desires*.[2] Now the only thing which everything desires is the goal of all things, namely, God. So that nothing except God is good. This is also apparent from something *Matthew* says, *No one is good but God alone*.[3] Now calling a thing 'supreme' involves comparing it with other things: the su-

---

[3] *Divine names* IV, 4. PG 3, 700

[4] 1a. 4, 3   [1] 1a. 3, 7   [2] *Ethics* I, 1. 1094a3

[3] Quoted from *Luke* 18:19. Parallel place, *Matthew* 19:17

premely hot, for example, with all hot things. So one cannot
call God supremely good.

3. Moreover, 'supreme' involves a comparison. Now one
can only compare things of the same genus: it is odd to say
that sweetness is bigger or smaller than a line. Since then we
already know that God and other good things are not in the
same genus,[4] it seems that he cannot be called supremely
good by comparison with them.

ON THE OTHER HAND Augustine tells us that the three divine
Persons *are the supreme good seen by the supremely clean
of heart.*[5]

REPLY: God is not just supremely good within a particular
genus or order of reality; he is the absolutely supreme good.
For we saw that God was called good as being the first source
of every perfection things desire.[6] And these perfections, as
we have shown, flow out from God not as from an agent in
the same genus, but as from an agent agreeing neither in
species nor in genus with its effects.[7] Now an agent in the
same genus mirrors its effects with unchanged form, but an
agent not in the same genus mirrors them more perfectly,
the heat of the sun, for example, excelling that of fire. So,
since it is as first source of everything not himself in a genus
that God is good, he must be good in the most perfect manner possible. And for this reason we call him supremely good.

Hence: 1. What supreme goodness adds to goodness is
something not absolute but merely relative. Now the relations
that God is said to bear to creatures, though represented
mentally as existing in God, really exist not in God but in
the creatures, just as things are called objects of knowledge
not because they are related to knowledge, but because
knowledge is related to them. So the supreme good does not
have to be composite, but other good things must fall short
of him.

---

[4] 1a. 3, 5; 4, 3 ad 2　　[5] *On the Trinity* 1, 2. PL 42, 822
[6] art. 1 above　　[7] 1a. 4, 3

2. The assertion that *good is what everything desires* does not mean that every good is desired by everything, but that whatever is desired is good. And the assertion that *no one is good but God alone,* means 'good by nature' as we shall see.[8]

3. There is no way of comparing things not in the same genus, when they are actually in different genera. But we say God is not in the same genus as other goods, not because he belongs to another genus but because he exists outside all genera and initiates them all. And so he is related to other things by surpassing them; and this is the comparison implied by supreme goodness.

Article 3. Is God alone good by nature?

THE THIRD POINT: 1. Not only God it seems is good by nature. For as we saw above everything that exists is good, just as it is one.[1] Now Aristotle shows that every existing thing is one by nature.[2] Every existing thing therefore is good by nature.

2. Moreover, if *good is what everything desires* the very existence of a thing must be its good, for everything desires to exist. Now things exist by nature. Everything then is good by nature.

3. Moreover, there is a goodness in things which makes them good. If then there exists a thing not by nature good, the goodness of such a thing will not be its nature. Yet because it exists in some way, that goodness must itself be good, and if again by some goodness different from itself, we must go on and ask about this other goodness. The only way of stopping the process is by arriving at some goodness not good by another goodness. But then we might as well have begun with this. All things then are good by nature.

ON THE OTHER HAND Boethius says that everything else besides God participates goodness.[3] Nothing else therefore is by nature good.

---

[8] art. 3 below   [1] 1a. 5, 1–3   [2] *Metaphysics* IV, 2. 1003b32
[3] *De hebdomadibus.* PL 64, 1313

REPLY: God alone is good by nature.

For to be called 'good' a thing must be perfect. Now there is a threefold perfection in things: firstly, they are established in existence; secondly, they possess in addition certain accidents necessary to perfect their activity; and a third perfection comes when they attain some extrinsic goal. Thus the primary perfection of fire lies in existing according to its own substantial form, a secondary perfection consists in heat, lightness, dryness, and so on; and a third perfection is being at rest in its appropriate place.

Now this threefold perfection belongs by nature to no caused thing, but only to God; for he alone exists by nature, and in him there are no added accidents (power, wisdom and the like which are accidental to other things belonging to him by nature, as already noted). Moreover, he is not disposed towards some extrinsic goal, but is himself the ultimate goal of all other things. So it is clear that only God possesses every kind of perfection by nature. He alone therefore is by nature good.

Hence: 1. Being one does not denote being perfect, but only being undivided, and this belongs to everything by nature. For the natures of simple things are both undivided and indivisible, and the natures of composite things are at least undivided. So things whilst necessarily one by nature, are not, as we have shown, necessarily good by nature.

2. Although things are good inasmuch as they exist, nevertheless existence is not the nature of any created thing, and so it does not follow that created things are good by nature.

3. The goodness of a created thing is not its nature, but something additional: either its existence, or some added perfection, or some relatedness to a goal. This additional goodness however is said to be good in the same way that it is said to exist. Now it is said to exist as a mode in which something exists, not as something having its own mode of existence. And so it is said to be good because things that possess it are good, not because it itself possesses some other goodness making it good.

Article 4. Does God's goodness make everything good?

THE FOURTH POINT: 1. It seems that God's goodness makes all things good. For Augustine writes, *Consider this good and that good; abstract from the this and the that and gaze simply at good, if you can; so shall you see God, the good of all things, himself not good by any other good.*[1] So everything is good by the good we call God.

2. Moreover, Boethius says that everything is called good because it has God for its goal,[2] and this is because of the goodness of God. So it is the goodness of God that makes all things good.

ON THE OTHER HAND things are good inasmuch as they exist. Now things are said to exist, not by divine existence, but by their own. So things are good, not by God's goodness, but by their own.

REPLY: There is nothing to stop things being named by reference to others, if the name is a relative term, as when things are said to be 'in place' by reference to place, or 'measured' by reference to measure. But concerning non-relative terms opinions have differed. Plato believed that the forms of things exist separately, and that individual things are named after these separate forms which they participate in some way: Socrates, for example, is called a 'man' by reference to some separate Idea of man. And just as he believed in separate Ideas of man and horse, calling them Man Himself and Horse Itself, so also Plato believed in separate Ideas of being and unity, called Being Itself and Unity Itself, by participating which everything was said to be or to be one. The existent Good Itself and Unity Itself he believed to be the supreme God, by reference to whom all things were said to be good by

---

[1] *On the Trinity* VIII, 3. PL 42, 949
[2] *De hebdomadibus.* PL 64, 1312

participation. And although, as Aristotle repeatedly proves, the part of this opinion which postulates separate, self-subsistent Ideas of natural things appears to be absurd, nonetheless that there exists some first thing called God, good by nature, is absolutely true, as we have shown.[3] And with this opinion Aristotle also is in agreement.[a]

One may therefore call things good and existent by reference to this first thing, existent and good by nature, inasmuch as they somehow participate and resemble it, even if distantly and deficiently, as was pointed out earlier.[4] And in this sense all things are said to be good by divine goodness, which is the pattern, source and goal of all goodness. Nevertheless the resemblance to divine goodness which leads us to call the thing good is inherent in the thing itself, belonging to it as a form and therefore naming it. And so there is one goodness in all things, and yet many.

And this clears up the difficulties.

---

[3] art. 3 above

[a] This rendering of Plato derives partly from Aristotle (e.g. *Metaphysics* I, 9. 990a33) and partly from Neo-Platonists of about six centuries later. That Aristotle accepts some first good thing by nature St Thomas deduces from *Metaphysics* II, 1. 993b24.

[4] 1a. 4, 3

NEXT FOR CONSIDERATION after God's perfection we have his limitlessness and then his presence in things. For it is because he is boundless and unlimited that God is said to exist everywhere in everything.

Question 7. God's limitlessness

The first of these questions contains four points of inquiry:

1. is God unlimited?
2. is anything other than God unlimited in being?
3. can anything be unlimited in size?
4. can there exist an unlimited number of things?

Article 1. Is God unlimited?

THE FIRST POINT: 1. God, it seems, is not unlimited. For to be unlimited is to be incomplete and unrealized, as Aristotle says, and therefore imperfect.[1][a] Now God is the very summit of perfection. He is not therefore limitless.

2. Moreover, Aristotle says that to be limited or unlimited a thing must first be extended.[2] Now God is not extended, since he is not a body, as we have shown.[3] Unlimited is therefore not an apt description of God.

3. Moreover, so to be in one place that one is not in another is to be spatially limited; so to be one thing, then, that one is not another is to be limited in being. Now God is one thing

---

[1] *Physics* III, 6. 207a27

[a] Aristotle 'defines' the infinite as that which always has something further to offer, which you can therefore never 'define' or complete. It is in this sense that he says it resembles a part (lacking wholeness) or matter (lacking form). The translation adopts 'incomplete and unrealized'.

[2] op. cit. I, 2. 185b2   [3] 1a. 3, 1

and no other: not a stone, for example, nor a piece of wood. He is therefore not limitless in being.

ON THE OTHER HAND Damascene calls God *limitless, eternal and unbounded.*[4]

REPLY: Aristotle tells us that in ancient times all philosophers considered the first principle to be unlimited,[5] and reasonably so since they saw no limit to the things deriving from the first principle. But because they made a mistake about the nature of the first principle they made a corresponding mistake about its limitlessness. They thought of the first principle as matter, and hence assigned to it a material limitlessness, saying that the first principle of things was some limitless body.

We must therefore remember that anything not limited can be called limitless. Now there is both a sense in which matter is limited by form, and a sense in which form is limited by matter. Form limits matter because before assuming form matter is potential of many forms, but afterwards is determined by the one assumed. Matter limits form because a form as such may be shared by many things, but when acquired by matter becomes determinately the form of this thing. Now a form in limiting matter perfects it, so that material limitlessness is imperfect in character: a sort of matter without form. Matter however does not perfect a form but rather restricts its full scope, so that the limitlessness of a form undetermined by matter is perfect in character.

Now the notion of form is most fully realized in existence itself, as we showed above.[6] And in God existence is not acquired by anything, but, as we saw earlier, God is existence itself subsistent.[7] It is clear then that God himself is both limitless and perfect.

Hence: 1. The answer to the first difficulty is now plain.

2. The boundary of an extended thing is, so to speak, the

---

[4] *Orthodox faith* 1, 4. PG 24, 800   [5] *Physics* III, 4. 203b4
[6] 1a. 3, 4; 4, 3 ad 1   [7] ibid

form of its extension; the fact that setting bounds to extension produces shape, a sort of dimensional form, indicates this. So limitlessness of extension is the kind of limitlessness associated with matter, and such limitlessness, as we have said, is not to be ascribed to God.

3. The very fact that God's existence itself subsists without being acquired by anything, and as such is limitless, distinguishes it from everything else, and sets other things aside from it. Just so, if whiteness subsisted of itself, the very fact that it was not the whiteness of something would distinguish it from all whiteness ingredient in things.

Article 2. Is anything other than God unlimited in being?

THE SECOND POINT: 1. Other things, it seems, can be unlimited in being besides God. For a thing's power is commensurate with its being; so that if God is unlimited in being he must also be unlimited in power. This means that he can produce an unlimited effect, for power is measured by the effects it can produce.

2. Moreover, unlimited power is a mark of unlimited being. Now the powers of a created intellect are unlimited, for it perceives universal ideas capable of applying to an unlimited number of individuals. So every created being endowed with intellect is unlimited.

3. Moreover, the ultimate matter of things, though not God as we have shown,[1] is nonetheless unlimited. So something other than God can be unlimited.

ON THE OTHER HAND Aristotle says that what is unlimited cannot be derived from anything else.[2] Now everything other than God derives primarily from him. Nothing other than God then is unlimited.

REPLY: Things other than God can be unlimited in some, but not in all, respects. For if we talk of the limitlessness

---

[1] 1a. 3, 8   [2] Physics III, 4. 203b7

associated with matter, then clearly everything that actually exists possesses form, and its matter therefore is determined by that form. But because matter determined by a substantial form is still potential of many accidental forms, that which simply speaking is limited may yet in some respect be called unlimited. Wood, for example, limited by its form, is yet in a certain respect unlimited, inasmuch as it is capable of an unlimited number of shapes.

If however we talk of the limitlessness associated with form, then clearly things composed of form and matter are limited in all respects and unlimited in none. But if there exist created forms not assumed by matter but subsisting themselves, as some people say is the case with angels,[a] then such forms will be in a certain respect unlimited, inasmuch as they are not contained or restricted by matter. Since such subsistent created forms however acquire their existence, and are not identical with it, that existence itself is of necessity contained and restricted by some specifying nature. Such a form then cannot be in all respects unlimited.

Hence: 1. To make something the nature of which is simply to exist, is a contradiction in terms, for subsistent existence is noncreated existence; and so it is a contradiction in terms to make something in all respects unlimited. Hence, although God's power is unlimited, he still cannot make an absolutely unlimited thing, no more than he can make an unmade thing (for this involves contradictories being true together).

2. That the extent of an intellect's powers is in some sense unlimited follows from the fact that the intellect is a form not contained by matter. For either it is completely separate, as angelic beings are, or, in the case of an intellectual soul joined to a body, it is at least able to understand independently of bodily organs.

3. Nowhere in the world does ultimate matter exist by itself, for it is not an actually existent thing, but only po-

---

[a] cf 1a. 50, 2. The opinion referred to is that of some Neo-Platonists and Arabian Aristoteleans.

tential of existence; hence not so much a product as a by-product of creation. And again even the potentiality of ultimate matter is unlimited only in some, not in all, respects; for matter can only assume physical forms.

Article 3. Can anything be unlimited in size?

THE THIRD POINT: 1. It seems that things can be actually unlimited in size. For mathematical concepts are not without foundation: *abstraction*, as Aristotle says, *is not falsification*.[1] Now mathematics employs the concept of unlimited size; for a geometer proving something will say 'Let this line be infinite'. So something of unlimited size is not impossible.

2. Moreover, a thing may have any property which does not contradict its nature. Now limitlessness does not contradict the nature of extension; indeed to be limited or unlimited a thing must first it seems be extended.[a] So something unlimited in extent is quite possible.

3. Moreover, extension is divisible without limit, for Aristotle defines the continuum as *that which is capable of unlimited division*.[2] Now alternatives are substitutable one for the other; and the alternative to division and subtraction is addition and multiplication. So it seems that extension can

---

[1] *Physics* II, 2. 193b35

[a] St Thomas's words for extension are a little difficult to translate uniformly. His most generic word is *quantitas* which is literally 'muchness', and divides into *quantitas continua*—'unbroken muchness'—and *quantitas discreta*—'broken-up muchness'. Connected with the first kind of quantity are such words as *magnitudo* (magnitude), *continuum* and *quantitas dimensiva* (volume), and the word 'extension' has been generally used in this translation in this connection. Connected up with the second kind of quantity are such words as *multitudo* (manyness), *numerus* (number), and this last word 'number' has been generally used. Literally then the translation of the sentence to which this note is appended should read: 'limitlessness does not contradict the nature of extension; indeed to be limited or unlimited a thing must first it seems possess muchness'.

[2] op. cit. III, 1. 200b20

be multiplied without limit, and thus unlimited size is possible.

4. Moreover, the continuity and extent of both movement and time derive according to Aristotle from the spatial extension movement must traverse.[3] Now conceivably both time and movement could be endless, since any point you choose in time or in circular movement is a beginning as well as an end. Endless extension is therefore also conceivable.

ON THE OTHER HAND all bodies have surfaces, and any body having a surface is limited since surface is the boundary of bodies. All bodies then are limited. The same argument applies to surfaces and lines. So that nothing extended can be unlimited.

REPLY: To be unlimited in size is not the same thing as to be unlimited in being. For even if there existed bodily things, say fire or air, of unlimited size, these would still be limited in being: limited to a particular species by their form, and to a particular individual of the species by their matter. So although we have already proved that no creature is unlimited in being,[4] we have still to decide whether anything created can be unlimited in size.

We must realize then the two aspects under which bodies, which have all-round extension, can be considered: the mathematical aspect, which takes account only of the extension, and the physical aspect which includes matter and form. That physically a body cannot actually exist without limits is clear. For physical bodies have determinate forms. Now when a substantial form is determinate, the accidents which follow on that form must also be determinate, and extension is one of these accidents. Every physical body therefore has a determinate maximum and minimum size. And so it is impossible for any physical body to be unlimited. Considering movement will confirm this. To any physical body some movement comes naturally. But to an unlimited body no

---

[3] op. cit. IV, 11. 219a12   [4] art. 2 above

movement could be natural. Not rectilinear movement, because things only move naturally in straight lines when not
in their natural place; now this could not happen to an unlimited body, since it would fill all space, and one place
would not be more natural to it than another. Neither could
it revolve, since in such movement one part of the body
changes places with another part, and this would be impossible if the revolving body was unlimited in size. For the further from the centre of a body two lines are produced, the
further the distance between them becomes. In an unlimited
body they would become infinitely distant from one another,
and one line would never be able to reach the place of the
other.

For the mathematical body things are no different. For if
we imagine a mathematical body in actual existence we shall
have to imagine it with a form, for actuality requires form.
Now the form of anything extended as such is its shape, so
the body will have to have a shape. And it will therefore be
limited, because a shape must be contained within a boundary or boundaries.

Hence: 1. Geometers need not postulate lines which are
actually infinite, but lines from which they can cut off whatever length they require, and such are the lines they call
infinite.

2. Lack of limits may be compatible with the notion of
extension in general, but it contradicts the notion of any
specific extension: be it two feet, or a yard, or a circle, or a
triangle. Now things cannot exist in a genus without existing
in some species of the genus. So that because no species
of extension can be limitless, all limitless extension is impossible.

3. The limitlessness of extension is as we said the kind of
limitlessness associated with matter.[5] Now division breaks a
whole down into its matter, for parts have the nature of material elements; whilst addition is a movement towards com-

---

[5] art. 1 ad 2 above

pletion which has the nature of form. And so only unlimited division of extension can occur, not unlimited addition.

4. Movement and time do not exist all at once but bit by bit, and thus their actuality is shot through with potentiality. Spatial extension however exists all at once. So since potentiality characterizes matter, the extensive limitlessness associated with matter is incompatible with space in its entirety, but compatible with time and movement in their entirety.

Article 4. Can there exist an unlimited number of things?

THE FOURTH POINT: 1. It seems there can actually exist an unlimited number of things. For what potentially exists can be brought into actual existence. Now it is possible to multiply number indefinitely. An unlimited number of things can therefore actually exist.

2. Moreover, any type can be realized in some actual individual of the type. Now there are unlimited types of geometrical figure. So there can actually exist an unlimited number of such figures.

3. Moreover, only things which conflict with one another preclude one another. Now, given any set of things, one can find another set which does not conflict with the first, and can therefore co-exist with it; and so on without limit. So an unlimited number of things can actually exist.

ON THE OTHER HAND we read in the book of *Wisdom, By weight, number and measure thou didst order all things.*[1]

REPLY: On this point there have been two opinions. Certain people like Avicenna and Algazel,[a] held that a number of things cannot actually be inherently unlimited, though there can exist a number of things which just happen to be un-

---

[1] *Wisdom* 11:21

[a] Avicenna (Ibn Sina, d. 1087). Algazel (Al Gazali, d. about 1111) known to the Scholastics as the *abbreviator* of Avicenna; in fact his abridgement was intended as a preliminary to a refutation.

limited. A number of things is called inherently unlimited when its being unlimited is essential in some connection. Now this can never be, for something would then depend necessarily on an unlimited number of other things, and consequently would never finally achieve existence, for no one can traverse the infinite. We say however that a number of things happens to be unlimited, when nothing requires it to be unlimited, and yet in fact it is so. To make the distinction clear: a certain number of things is inherently necessary to carpentry, namely, a hammer, a hand to wield it, and a mind with practical knowledge. And if the number of such things is to be multiplied indefinitely the job of carpentry will never get finished, for it will depend on an unlimited number of causes. But if, in fact, a number of hammers is used, a second being picked up when the first one breaks, then there just happens to be a number of hammers; as it happens many hammers are used for the work, but it makes no difference whether one or two or more, or indeed an unlimited number, if unlimited time is available for the work.[b] In the same way then these people believed that a number of things that happens to be unlimited could actually exist.

This however is impossible. For any set of things one considers must be a specific set. And sets of things are specified by the number of things in them. Now no number is infinite, for number results from counting through a set in units. So no set of things can actually be inherently unlimited, nor can it happen to be unlimited. Again, every set of things existing in the world has been created, and anything created is subject to some definite purpose of its creator, for causes never act to no purpose. All created things must be subject

---

[b] Notice that St Thomas is perfectly prepared to allow infinite time for the work, though he complains earlier against an inherently unlimited number of causes that 'the job will never get finished'. 'Never' does not mean 'at no time finitely distant', but 'at no time even infinitely distant'. Understanding this point is vital to his numerous remarks about the impossibility of infinite regress. cf 1a. 46, 1 & 2.

therefore to definite enumeration. Thus even a number of things that happens to be unlimited cannot actually exist.

But an unlimited number of things can exist potentially. For increase in number results from division of a continuum; the more one divides a thing, the greater number of things one obtains. So that, just as there is potentially no limit to the division of a continuum, which we saw to be a breakdown into matter,[2] so, for the same reason, there is potentially no limit to numerical addition.

Hence: 1. Whatever potentially exists is brought into actual existence in accordance with its own way of existing: thus days do not come into existence all at once, but one after another. And in the same way, an unlimited number of things is not brought into existence all at once, but bit by bit, first a certain number, then an additional one, and so on without limit.

2. There are unlimited types of geometrical figure because number is unlimited, and the figures are typified as three-sided, four-sided and so on. So just as an unlimited number of things cannot be brought into actual existence all at once, neither can the multitude of geometrical figures.

3. Although positing one set of things will not conflict with the positing of another set, nonetheless positing an unlimited number will conflict with each specific number. So one cannot have an actually unlimited number of things.

---

[2] art. 3 ad 3 above

AN UNLIMITED THING ought it seems to exist everywhere in everything; we must therefore consider whether this is so of God.

Question 8. God's existence in things

This question has four points of inquiry:

1. does God exist in everything?
2. is God everywhere?
3. is God everywhere in substance, power and presence?
4. is being everywhere something that belongs to God alone?

Article 1. Does God exist in everything?

THE FIRST POINT: 1. God, it seems, does not exist in everything. For one cannot be both in everything and above everything. Yet according to the psalms God is above everything, *The Lord is high above all nations, etc.*[1] So he is not in everything.

2. Moreover, one is contained by what one is in. Now God is not contained by things but rather contains them. So things are in God rather than God in things. This is why Augustine says that *he is not in place, but is rather the place of everything else.*[2]

3. Moreover, the more powerful an agent, the more extended is its sphere of action. Now God is the most powerful of all agents. So his action can reach to things far distant from him, and he has no need to be present in them.

4. Moreover, there are certain things called devils. Now God does not exist in devils, for *light hath no communion*

---

[1] *Psalms* 112:4   [2] *83 Questions* 20. PL 40, 15

with darkness, as St Paul says.[3] So God does not exist in everything.

ON THE OTHER HAND a thing is present wherever it is active. But God is active in everything, according to Isaiah, *Thou hast wrought all our works in us, O Lord.*[4] So God exists in everything.

REPLY: God exists in everything; not indeed as part of their substance or as an accident, but as an agent is present to that in which its action is taking place. For unless it act through intermediaries every agent must be connected with that upon which it acts, and be in causal contact with it: compare Aristotle's proof that for one thing to move another the two must be in contact.[5] Now since it is God's nature to exist, he it must be who properly causes existence in creatures, just as it is fire itself sets other things on fire. And God is causing this effect in things not just when they begin to exist, but all the time they are maintained in existence, just as the sun is lighting up the atmosphere all the time the atmosphere remains lit. During the whole period of a thing's existence, therefore, God must be present to it, and present in a way in keeping with the way in which the thing possesses its existence. Now existence is more intimately and profoundly interior to things than anything else, for everything as we said is potential when compared to existence.[6] So God must exist and exist intimately in everything.

Hence: 1. The perfection of his nature places God above everything, and yet as causing their existence he also exists in everything, as we have been saying.

2. That in which bodily things exist contains them, but immaterial things contain that in which they exist, as the soul contains the body.[a] So God also contains things by exist-

---

[3] II *Corinthians* 6:14   [4] *Isaiah* 26:12
[5] *Physics* VII, 2. 243a4   [6] 1a. 3, 4
[a] The word 'contains' does not always refer to surrounding something spatially; thus, for instance, the phrase 'to contain oneself'. The reply, which is working with two opposed metaphors, is highly

ing in them. However, one does use the bodily metaphor and talk of everything being in God inasmuch as he contains them.

3. However powerful an agent be its action can only reach to distant things by using intermediaries. The omnipotence of God, though, is displayed by his acting in everything without intermediary, for nothing is distant from him in the sense of God not being in it. Nevertheless one does speak of the unlikeness of things to God in nature or grace being distance from him, just as the perfection of his nature places him above everything.

4. When referring to devils one may be thinking either of their nature, which comes from God, or of the disfigurement due to sin, which does not. And so one can only admit that God exists in devils if one adds the qualification: inasmuch as they, too, are things. But no qualification is needed when saying that God is present in things the nature of which is not disfigured.

Article 2. Is God everywhere?

THE SECOND POINT: 1. God, it seems, is not everywhere. For this would mean that God was in every place. Now it is not fitting for God to be in every place, because it is not fitting for God to be in place at all; as Boethius says, *Only bodies are in place*.[1] So God is not everywhere.

2. Moreover, place is related to the permanent in the same way as time to the transient. Now it is impossible for any indivisible instant of action or change to occur at more than one time. It is therefore equally impossible for any indivisible permanent thing to exist in more than one place. Now God's existence is not transient but permanent. He cannot, therefore, exist in more than one place, and thus cannot be everywhere.

---

compressed. God is in things as their efficient and final cause, not as their formal cause or soul. They are in him because he it is who holds them together.

[1] *De hebdomadibus*. PL 64, 1311

3. Moreover, if a thing exists wholly in one place it can in nowise exist outside it. Now wherever God exists he exists wholly, for he has no parts. So none of him exists anywhere else. God then does not exist everywhere.

ON THE OTHER HAND we read in *Jeremiah*, *I fill heaven and earth*.[2]

REPLY: Place is itself a sort of thing, and so there are two ways of understanding 'being in place': firstly, on an analogy with other things, that is to say, in whatever way we understand 'being in' when talking of other things, and the attributes of any place are in the place in this sense; or secondly, in the way peculiar to place alone, namely the way in which things occupying places are in those places. In both these ways there is a sense in which God is in every place, or in other words is everywhere.

First, he is in every place giving it existence and the power to be a place, just as he is in all things giving them existence, power and activity. Secondly, just as anything occupying a place fills that place, so God fills all places. But not as bodies do (for bodies fill places by not suffering other bodies to be there with them, whilst God's presence in a place does not exclude the presence there of other things); rather God fills all places by giving existence to everything occupying those places.

Hence: 1. Only bodies are in place through dimensional contact; other things are in place through causal contact.

2. Indivisibility is twofold. In one sense it characterizes any stopping-place within continuity, such as an instant in the transient, or a point in the permanent. In anything permanent such indivisible points have a set position, and so cannot be in more than one place or part of a place; and similarly in any action or change indivisible instants occur in a set order, and so cannot occur in more than one period of time. But in another sense indivisibility characterizes things

[2] *Jeremiah* 23:24

outside all kind of continuousness, and in this sense substances like God, the soul and angels, which are not bodies, are called indivisible. Such indivisible things are related to a continuum, not as being part of it, but as being in causal contact with it. And so, according as their sphere of action is small or large and comprehends one or more things, they are present in a small place or a large one, and in one place or more than one.

3. Whole is said relatively to parts. And part may mean either a part of a nature, as the form and matter composing certain things or the generic and differentiating notions composing definitions are called parts; or it may mean an extended part, into which some extended whole has been divided. So what is wholly in a place to its whole extent cannot extend outside that place; for the extent of anything occupying place is measured by the extent of the place, and unless the place were the thing's whole place the extent would not be the thing's whole extent. Wholeness of nature, however, is not measured by wholeness of place, so that what is wholly in something according to its whole nature can yet be in some wise outside it. This is clear even of accidents that happen to be extended; for if wholeness of nature is meant, whiteness is wholly present everywhere on a surface, its full specific nature being realized in every part; but if the wholeness of the extent it happens to possess is meant, then whiteness is not wholly present everywhere on the surface. Now the only wholeness that things which are not bodies either inherently possess, or happen to possess, is the wholeness of their essential nature. And so just as the soul exists wholly everywhere in the body, so God exists wholly in each and every thing.

Article 3. Is God everywhere in substance, power and presence?

THE THIRD POINT: 1. To say that God exists in things by substance, presence and power[a] hardly seems a satisfactory classi-

---

[a] The traditional phrase, ascribed to St Gregory the Great without

fication of the ways God exists in things. For to exist in something by substance is to reside substantially within it. Now God does not reside substantially in things, since he forms no part of their substance. So we ought not to say that God exists in things by substance, presence and power.

2. Moreover, being present is the same as not being absent. Now God, precisely as existing in all things by substance, is not absent from them. So to exist in everything by substance and by presence are the same. It was therefore redundant to say that God exists in things by substance, presence and power.

3. Moreover, just as the source of everything is God's power, so also is it his knowledge and will. Now God is not said to exist in things by knowledge and will; neither then should he be said to do so by power.

4. Moreover, there are many perfections, like grace, added to the substance of things.[b] If God then is said to exist in some people in a special way by grace, it seems we ought to acknowledge special ways in which he exists in things corresponding to each perfection.

ON THE OTHER HAND Gregory tells us that *in the ordinary way God exists in all things by presence, power and substance, but he is said to exist in certain things in a more intimate way by grace.*[1]

REPLY: God is said to exist in things in two ways. Firstly, as an operative cause, and in this way he exists in everything he creates. Secondly, as an object attained by some activity exists within the acting subject, and this applies only to mental activities where the known exists in the knower, and the de-

---

reference, appears in the *Glossa ordinaria*, or received running commentary, on *Canticles* 5:7.

[b] Catholic theologians apply the word 'grace' not only to the favour which is the act of God, but also to the goodness thereby produced in the creature: it is this to which the argument refers. cf 1a2æ. 110, 1

[1] cf note *a* above

sired in the one who desires. In this latter way, therefore, God exists in a special fashion in those reasoning creatures that are actually knowing and loving him, or are disposed to do so. And since we shall see this to be the result of a grace to the reasoning creature,[2] God is said to exist in this way in holy people by grace.

But to grasp the way in which he exists in other created things we must draw an analogy from human affairs. Thus in virtue of his power a king can be said to exist throughout his kingdom, though not everywhere present. Again, in virtue of its presence, a thing exists in everything within its field of view, so that everything in a house is said to be present even to a person not existing substantially in every part of that house. Finally, a thing exists in substance in the place where its substance is.

Now in the past certain people called Manichees declared that immaterial and imperishable things are subject to God's power, but visible and perishable things to some contrary power. As against this we must say that God exists by power in everything. Other people believed everything to be subject to God's power, but yet withdrew things here below from his providence; and a typical representative is he who *walks on the vault of heaven and does not see our doings*.[3] As against this we must say that God exists by presence in everything. Yet others said that God's providence oversees everything, but nevertheless asserted that God did not create everything without intermediaries, but only the first creatures, who then created others. As against this we must say that God exists in substance in everything.

Thus God exists in everything by power inasmuch as everything is subject to his power, by presence inasmuch as everything is naked and open to his gaze, and by substance inasmuch as he exists in everything causing their existence, as we said earlier.[4]

Hence: 1. God exists in all things by substance, not how-

---

[2] 1a. 43, 3. 1a2æ. 109, 1 & 3   [3] *Job* 22:14
[4] art. 1 above

ever by their substance as though he belonged to the substance of things, but by his own which, we have said, exists in everything as causing their existence.[5]

2. We can talk of something being present to someone whenever it lies within his field of vision, even if in substance it is far away from him, as we said. Hence the necessity of asserting the two ways, by substance and by presence.

3. It is of the nature of knowledge and volition that the known should exist in the knower and the thing willed in the one willing; and so, by his knowledge and will, things exist in God rather than God in things. But it is of the nature of power to initiate activity in some other thing, so that in virtue of its power an agent is brought into contact and relation with outside things. And this is why an agent can be described as existing in some other thing by power.

4. Grace is the only perfection added to the substance of things which makes God exist in them as a known and loved object; grace alone then makes God exist in things in a unique way. There is, however, another unique way in which God exists in a man, by being one with him, and we will deal with this in its proper place.[c]

Article 4. Is being everywhere something belonging to God alone?

THE FOURTH POINT: 1. It seems that being everywhere is not something belonging to God alone. For Aristotle says that universals exist everywhere and always,[1] and the ultimate matter in all bodies must also be everywhere. Now we have already made it clear that neither of these is God.[2] Being everywhere then is not something belonging to God alone.

2. Moreover, there is number in all numbered things. Now the book of *Wisdom* declares the whole world to have been

---

[5] ibid

[c] The reference is to unity of God and man in the person of Jesus Christ. cf 3a. 2 & 17

[1] *Posterior Analytics* I, 31. 87b33   [2] 1a. 3, 5 & 8

created numbered.[3] Some number then exists in the whole world, that is to say, everywhere.

3. Moreover, according to Aristotle the whole world is in its way a complete and perfect body.[4] Now the whole world is everywhere, for there can be no place outside it. So not only God is everywhere.

4. Moreover, there would be no place outside of an unlimited body, if such existed. And so it would be everywhere. Being everywhere then need not it seems belong to God alone.

5. Moreover, souls, says Augustine, are *wholly in the whole and wholly in every part of the whole*.[5] If then nothing existed in the world but one animal, its soul would be everywhere. Being everywhere then need not belong to God alone.

6. Again, Augustine says *wherever the soul sees it perceives, and wherever it perceives there it lives, and wherever it lives there it exists*.[6] Now the soul sees everywhere in a sense, for bit by bit it sees the whole heavens. The soul then exists everywhere.

ON THE OTHER HAND Ambrose asks *who would dare to name creature the Holy Ghost who exists always, everywhere, in everything; for this without doubt is something belonging to God alone*.[7]

REPLY: Being everywhere outright and essentially belongs to God alone. By being everywhere outright I mean being everywhere in one's completeness. For to exist everywhere, but with a different part in each different place, is not to be everywhere outright, since any property of a part is not the outright property of the whole: thus the whiteness of a man with white teeth belongs outright to the teeth, not to him. By being everywhere essentially I mean not just happening to be everywhere in certain circumstances, as the grain of wheat would be everywhere if no other bodies existed. When a

[3] *Wisdom* 11:21   [4] *De cælo et mundo* I, 1. 268b8
[5] *On the Trinity* VI, 6. PL 42, 929
[6] *Epistles* CXXXVII, 2. PL 33, 518
[7] *On the Holy Ghost* I, 7. PL 16, 723

thing is such that it would exist everywhere in any circumstances, it exists everywhere essentially. Now this belongs to God alone. For no matter how many places one may think up, even infinitely more than now exist, God would necessarily exist in them all, since nothing can exist except he cause it to do so.

And so to be everywhere outright and essentially belongs to God and to God alone, for no matter how many places one may think up God himself will necessarily exist in them, and not just parts of him.

1. Universals and the ultimate matter of things are indeed everywhere but not with one and the same existence.

2. Number, being an accident, is not essentially in place but only happens to be there. Nor is it complete in each numbered thing, but partly exists in each. So one cannot conclude that number is everywhere outright and essentially.

3. The whole body of the world is everywhere piece by piece, not whole in every place, and so not everywhere outright. Nor essentially everywhere, for if there were other places it would not be in them.

4. An unlimited body, if it existed, would exist everywhere piece by piece.

5. If only one animal existed, then its soul would indeed exist everywhere outright, but nevertheless only happen to do so.

6. One can interpret the phrase 'wherever the soul sees' in two ways. The first interpretation takes the adverb 'wherever' as determining the object of the seeing. And in this sense it is true that when the soul is seeing the heavens it is seeing in the heavens and thus perceiving in the heavens; but it does not follow that it lives or exists in the heavens because these two verbs do not name actions going out to external objects. The other interpretation takes the adverb 'wherever' as determining the position of the one seeing. And in this sense it is true that the soul lives and exists where it sees and perceives. But then it does not follow that it exists everywhere.

AS A NEXT STEP we must consider God's unchangeableness and consequent eternity.

Question 9. God's unchangeableness

For this question about unchangeableness there are two points of inquiry:

1. is God altogether unchangeable?
2. is only God unchangeable?

Article 1. Is God altogether unchangeable?

THE FIRST POINT: 1. It seems that God is not altogether unchangeable. For anything that moves itself is in some way changeable. Now Augustine says that *the creating spirit moves himself, though not in space and time.*[1] So in some way God is changeable.

2. Moreover, wisdom is described in Scripture as *more mobile than any moving thing.*[2] Now God is wisdom itself. God then is movable.

3. Moreover, drawing near and drawing away are descriptions of movements. Yet Scripture applies them to God: *Draw nigh to God and he will draw nigh to you.*[3] God then is changeable.

ON THE OTHER HAND we read in *Malachy, I am God, I change not.*[4]

REPLY: Our findings so far prove God to be altogether unchangeable.

---

[1] *On Genesis to the letter* VIII, 20. PL 34, 388
[2] *Wisdom* 7:24   [3] *James* 4:8   [4] *Malachy* 3:6

First, because we have proved that there must be some first existent, called God, sheerly actual and unalloyed with potentiality, since actuality, simply speaking, precedes potentiality.[5] Now any changing thing, whatsoever the change, is somehow potential. So it clearly follows that God cannot change in any way.

Secondly, because anything in change partly persists and partly passes, as a thing changing from white to black persists in substance. Things in change are therefore always composite. Now God we have shown to be not at all composite, but altogether simple.[6] Clearly then he cannot change.

Thirdly, because anything in change acquires something through its change, attaining something previously not attained. Now God, being limitless and embracing within himself the whole fullness of perfection of all existence, cannot acquire anything, nor can he move out towards something previously not attained. So one cannot in any way associate him with change.

And this is why some of the ancient philosophers, bowing to the truth, so to speak, held that the first source of things is unchangeable.

Hence: 1. Augustine is here using a Platonic way of speaking, according to which the first source of movement is said to move itself, meaning by 'movement' any operation at all, even understanding, willing and loving. So since God understands and loves himself, the Platonists said that God moves himself, not however meaning, as we are doing at the moment, the movement and change of something potential.

2. To call wisdom mobile is a metaphorical way of saying that wisdom spreads its own likeness throughout the length and breadth of things. For nothing can exist except it be a sort of reflection deriving from God's wisdom as from its primary operative and formal cause; just as works of art derive from craftsmanship. Inasmuch then as this likeness to divine wisdom is transmitted step by step from the highest things, which share the likeness most, to the lowest, which

_____
[5] 1a. 2, 3; 3, 1   [6] 1a. 3, 7

share it least, we talk of God's wisdom sallying forth as it were and moving into things. It is as though we talked of the sun sallying forth on earth when its light-rays touched earth. And this is the explanation Dionysius gives, when he says that *every emanation of the divine majesty comes to us set in motion by the Father of lights.*[7]

3. The scripture is here talking of God in metaphors. For just as the sun is said to enter or depart from a house by touching the house with its rays, so God is said to draw near to us when we receive an influx of his goodness, or draw away from us when we fail him.

Article 2. Is only God unchangeable?

THE SECOND POINT: 1. Not only God, it seems, is unchangeable. For Aristotle says that anything in change contains matter.[1] Now there are people who believe that certain created substances, such as souls and angels, exist without matter.[a] So not only God is unchangeable.

2. Moreover, all change has a goal in view, so that things which have already achieved their ultimate goal will not change. Now some creatures such as saints have already achieved their ultimate goal. Some creatures then are unchangeable.

3. Moreover, changeable things can vary. Forms, however, are invariable, as the *Book of the Six Principles* says, *Form is that which subsists with simple and invariable being.*[2] So not only God is unchangeable.

ON THE OTHER HAND Augustine says, *God alone is unchangeable; while the things God makes are made from nothing and therefore changeable.*[3]

---

[7] *Heavenly hierarchy* I, 1. PG 3, 120

[1] *Metaphysics* II, 2. 994b25. See critical apparatus, Ross.

[a] including St Thomas himself: 1a. 50, 2

[2] The reputed work of Gilbert de la Porrée. PL 188, 1257

[3] *On the nature of good* 1. PL 42, 551

REPLY: Only God is altogether unchangeable; creatures can all change in some way or other.

For one must realize that there are two possible grounds for calling a thing changeable, its own potentiality, and something else's power. Before creatures existed their existence was possible not because of any created potentiality, since nothing created exists eternally, but simply because God had the power to bring them into existence. Now just as bringing things into existence depends on God's will, so also preserving them in existence. For he preserves them in existence only by perpetually giving existence to them, and were he therefore to withdraw his activity from them all things, as Augustine makes clear, would fall back into nothingness.[4] So just as before things existed on their own it was in the creator's power for them to exist, so now that they do exist on their own it is in the creator's power for them not to exist. They are thus changeable because of power present in somebody else, namely, God, who was able to bring them into existence out of nothing, and is able to reduce them again from existence to nothingness.

Yet even if we talk of changeableness in things due to their own potentiality, every creature is still changeable in some way. For we must distinguish in creatures both active and passive potentialities. I call 'passive potentiality' the capacity of a thing to be perfected, either in being or by attaining the goal of its action. If we consider then the changeableness consequent upon a thing's potentiality to being, not everything is changeable, but only those things in which possibilities can exist without being realized. Thus bodies here on earth can change substantially in being (for the matter in them can exist without assuming the form of those particular substances), and can change also in such accidental modes of being as the subject can do without (as man can change from white to some other colour because man as subject can do without whiteness). If, however, the accidental mode of being is derivative from the subject's essential nature, the sub-

---

[4] *On Genesis to the letter* IV, 12. PL 34, 305

ject cannot do without it, and cannot therefore change with respect to it; thus, snow cannot become black. In heavenly bodies, on the other hand, the potentiality of the matter is wholly realized by the form, so that the matter cannot exist without that form; and such bodies therefore cannot change substantially in being, though they are able to change place, for the subject can exist without being in this or that particular place. Again, substances which are not bodies but are forms subsisting in themselves, cannot do without existence, even though related to that existence as potentialities to some actualization; for existence follows immediately upon form, and a thing can perish only by losing its form. In a form as such then there is no potentiality of non-existence, and so such substances are unable to change or vary in being. And this is what Dionysius means when he says that *created intellectual substances are free from generation and from all variation, being neither bodies nor material.*[5] In two ways, however, such substances can change: firstly, because of their potentiality to some goal, they can, as Damascene says, change their minds and choose evil rather than good;[6] secondly, they can change place, because, their power being limited, they can bring it to bear on places not previously touched by it— which cannot be said of God who in his limitlessness, as we saw, fills all places.[7]

In all creatures then there exists potentiality to change, either substantially as with perishable bodies, or in place as with the heavenly bodies, or in orderedness to a goal and application of power to different things as with the angels. And in addition there is a changeableness common to the whole universe of creatures, since whether they exist or not is subject to the creator's power. So, because God cannot change in any of these ways, he alone is altogether unchangeable.

Hence: 1. This argument holds for changeableness in being, either substantial or accidental, for that is the kind of change which interests philosophers.

---

[5] *Divine names* IV, 1. PG 3, 693
[6] *Orthodox faith* II, 3. PG 94, 868   [7] 1a. 8, 2

2. In addition to unchangeable being belonging to them by nature, the good angels are endowed by God's power with unchangeable choice; but they can still change as regards place.

3. Forms are called invariable because they themselves cannot be the subjects of variation; but they take part nonetheless in variation, inasmuch as a subject may have now this and now that form. Clearly then they vary in exactly the same way as they exist; for they are said to exist not as subjects of existence, but because things have existence through them.

WE ASK NEXT about eternity.

Question 10. The eternity of God

For this question there are six points of inquiry:

1. what is eternity?
2. is God eternal?
3. does eternity belong to God alone?
4. is eternity different from the æon and time?
5. the difference between the æon and time.
6. is there only one æon, as there is one time and one eternity?

Article 1. What is eternity?

THE FIRST POINT: 1. The definition of eternity given by Boethius seems unsuitable. He says that *eternity is the instantaneously whole and perfect possession of unending life.*[1] Now 'unending' is a negative term, such as belongs only in the definition of a defective thing. Eternity, however, is not defective. So the word 'unending' should not occur in a definition of eternity.

2. Moreover, 'eternity' names a sort of duration, and duration is connected with existence rather than with life. So we ought to use the word 'existence' rather than 'life' when defining eternity.

3. Moreover, one uses the word 'whole' of something having parts. Now eternity is simple, and therefore has no parts. So it should not be described as 'whole'.

4. Moreover, several days or several times cannot occur instantaneously. Yet in speaking of eternity these words 'day'

---

[1] *Consolation of philosophy* v, 6. PL 63, 858

and 'time' are used in the plural. The prophet Micah says *his goings forth are from the beginning, from the days of eternity*,[2] and in St Paul we read, *According to the revelation of the mystery kept secret through times eternal*.[3] Eternity therefore is not instantaneously whole.

5. Moreover, wholeness is the same as perfection. Given that eternity is whole, then, it is redundant to add that it is perfect.

6. Moreover, possession is unconnected with duration. Now eternity is a sort of duration. It is not therefore possession.

REPLY: Just as we can only come to know simple things by way of composite ones, so we can only come to know eternity by way of time, which is merely the *numbering of before and after in change*.[4] For in any change there is successiveness, one part coming after another, and by numbering the antecedent and consequent parts of change there arises the notion of time, which is simply this numberedness of before and after in change. Now something lacking change and never varying its mode of existence will not display a before and after. So just as numbering antecedent and consequent in change produces the notion of time, so awareness of invariability in something altogether free from change produces the notion of eternity. A further point: time is said to measure things which begin and end in time, as Aristotle points out,[5] and this is because one can assign a beginning and end to any changing thing. But things altogether unchangeable cannot have a beginning any more than they can display successiveness.

So two things characterize eternity. First, anything existing in eternity is *unending*, that is to say, lacks both beginning and end (for both may be regarded as ends). Secondly, eternity itself exists as an *instantaneous whole* lacking successiveness.

Hence: 1. We often use negations to define simple things,

_____

[2] *Micah* 5:2   [3] *Romans* 16:25
[4] *Physics* IV, 11. 220a25   [5] op. cit. IV, 12. 221b28

as when we say that a point has no parts. Now this is not because they are negative in their essential nature, but because our mind first of all grasps composite things, and cannot come to know simple things except by denying compositeness of them.

2. In point of fact, that which is eternal is not only existent but living. Now living includes in a way activity, which existence does not. And flow of duration is more apparent in activity than in existence; time, for example, is a numbering of change.

3. Eternity is called whole, not because it has parts, but because nothing is lacking to it.

4. Just as Scripture describes God metaphorically in bodily terms, although he is not a body, so it describes eternity in temporal and successive terms although eternity exists instantaneously.

5. There are two things to be noted about time, namely, that time itself is successive, and that an instant of time is imperfect.[a] To deny that eternity is time Boethius uses 'instantaneously whole'; to deny temporal instantaneity the word 'perfect'.

6. To possess something is to hold it firmly and immovably. To signify then the unchangeableness and constancy of eternity, we use the word 'possession'.

Article 2. Is God eternal?

THE SECOND POINT: 1. God, it seems, is not eternal. For one cannot ascribe to God something produced. Now eternity is produced, for Boethius says that *the flowing instant produces time and the abiding instant eternity*,[1] whilst Augustine says that *God is the source of eternity*.[2] So God is not eternal.

---

[a] That time is successive means that as a whole it is not actual; that an instant of time is imperfect means that any actualization of time is momentary and not whole.

[1] *On the Trinity* IV. PL 64, 1253
[2] *83 Questions* 23. PL 40, 16

2. Moreover, eternity cannot measure what exists before and after eternity. Now, according to the *Book of Causes*, God exists before eternity,[3] and according to *Exodus*, where we read that *the Lord will reign to eternity and beyond*,[4] he also exists after eternity. So eternity cannot be ascribed to God.

3. Moreover, eternity is a sort of measure. But one cannot measure God. One cannot therefore ascribe eternity to him.

4. Moreover, present, past and future do not exist in eternity, which, as we have said, is instantaneously whole.[5] But the Scriptures use verbs in the present, past and future tenses, when talking of God. So God is not eternal.

ON THE OTHER HAND the *Athanasian Creed* proclaims, *Eternal the Father, eternal the Son, eternal the Holy Ghost*.[6]

REPLY: We have shown already that the notion of eternity derives from unchangeableness in the same way that the notion of time derives from change.[7] Eternity therefore principally belongs to God, who is utterly unchangeable. Not only that, but God is his own eternity, whereas other things, not being their own existence, are not their own duration. God, however, is his own invariable existence, and so is identical with his own eternity just as he is identical with his own nature.

Hence: 1. The abiding instant is said to produce eternity according to our way of conceiving the situation. For just as we become aware of time by becoming aware of the flowing instant, so we grasp the idea of eternity by grasping the idea of an abiding instant. Augustine's statement that *God is the source of eternity* must be taken to mean eternity as shared, for just as God shares his unchangeableness with other things, so he does his eternity.

2. And this gives us the key to the second difficulty. For

---

[3] *Proposition* 2   [4] *Exodus* 15:18   [5] art. 1 above
[6] Denzinger 39   [7] art. 1 above

God exists before the eternity shared by immaterial substances. Hence in the same passage we read that *intelligence is co-extensive with eternity*.ᵃ As to the statement in *Exodus* that *the Lord will reign to eternity and beyond* one must realize that 'eternity' is here a synonym for 'ages', the word used by another translation. So that God is said to reign beyond eternity because he outlasts all ages, outlasts, that is to say, any given duration; for, as Aristotle says, an age is nothing more than the period of a thing's life.[8] Or one can also say that God reigns beyond eternity, because even if something else were to exist for ever, as certain philosophers believed the rotation of the heavens to do, the Lord would still reign beyond it, because his reign is instantaneously whole.

3. Eternity and God are the same thing. So calling him eternal does not imply his being measured by something extrinsic; the notion of measurement arises only in our way of conceiving the situation.

4. Verbs of different tenses are used of God, not as though he varied from present to past to future, but because his eternity comprehends all phases of time.

Article 3. Does eternity belong to God alone?

THE THIRD POINT: 1. Eternity does not seem to belong to God alone. For Daniel prophesies that *they who turn many to righteousness shall be as the stars in perpetual eternities*.[1] Now if God alone was eternal there could be only one eternity. So not only God is eternal.

ᵃ The background to this statement is to be found in the Neo-Platonist hierarchy of beings emanating from a supreme being, which was presupposed by the author of the *Book of Causes*. 'Intelligence' here stands for an immaterial substance lower in the order of emanations than God. If eternity is defined as the duration in which the intelligence exists, then God must be prior to eternity in this sense.

[8] *De cælo et mundo* 1, 9. 279a23   [1] *Daniel* 12:3

2. Moreover, we read in *Matthew*, *Depart, ye cursed, into eternal fire*.[2] Not only God then is eternal.

3. Moreover, what is necessarily so is eternally so. Now there are many necessary things: the first principles of demonstration, for example, and all propositions employed in demonstrations. So not only God is eternal.

ON THE OTHER HAND Jerome writes to Marcella that *God alone has no beginning*.[3] Now whatever has a beginning is not eternal. So God alone is eternal.

REPLY: Eternity, in the true and proper sense, belongs to God alone, for eternity, we said, follows upon unchangeableness,[4] and God alone, as we showed, is altogether unchangeable.[5] Certain things, however, receive from God a share in his unchangeableness, and to that extent they share in his eternity. The unchangeableness some things obtain from God is such that they never cease existing, and so the earth, as we read in *Ecclesiastes*, *abideth eternally*.[6] Other things though perishable are called in the Scriptures eternal because they endure for a long time, and so the psalm sings of *eternal mountains*,[7] and *Deuteronomy* speaks of *the fruits of the eternal hills*.[8] Yet others share eternity still more fully, possessing unchangeableness of existence and even of activity, and such are the angels and saints enjoying sight of the divine Word.[a] For, as Augustine says, *eddying thoughts* have no part in the saints' vision of the Word.[9] And this is why those who see God are said to have eternal life, as in *John*, *this is eternal life to know thee etc.*[10]

---

[2] *Matthew* 25:41   [3] *Epistles* 15. To Damasus. PL 22, 257

[4] art. 1 above   [5] 1a. 9, 2   [6] *Ecclesiastes* 1:4

[7] *Psalms* 75:5   [8] *Deuteronomy* 33:15

[a] The joy of the saints in heaven is the vision of God face to face. Since the Word, the second person of the divine Trinity, is the self-revelation of God, the vision is often referred to, especially by St Augustine, as the vision of the Word.

[9] *On the Trinity* xv, 16. PL 42, 1079   [10] *John* 17:3

Hence: 1. One talks of many eternities because many are the things sharing God's eternity by contemplating him.

2. The fire of hell is called eternal only because it is unending. But the pains of the lost do change, for we read in *Job* that *they shall pass from waters of snow to excessive heat.*[11] In hell then there is no true eternity, but rather time; hence the psalm saying *their time shall last for ever.*[12]

3. Necessity is a mode of truth. Now truth, according to Aristotle, resides in the mind.[13] So necessary truths are eternal only if they exist in the eternal mind, which is nothing other than God's mind. So it does not follow that anything outside God is eternal.

Article 4. Is eternity different from time?

THE FOURTH POINT: 1. Eternity seems no different from time. For two measures of duration can only be simultaneous, if one is part of the other; thus two days or hours cannot occur simultaneously, but an hour and a day can for an hour is part of a day. Now eternity and time, both signifying some sort of measure of duration, exist together. So since eternity is not part of time but exceeds and comprehends it, time must seemingly be a part of eternity and identical with it.

2. Moreover, according to Aristotle, the 'now' persists unchanged throughout time.[1] But the nature of eternity seems to consist precisely in remaining unbrokenly the same throughout the whole course of time. Eternity then is identical with the 'now' of time. And since the 'now' of time is in substance identical with time itself, so must eternity be.[a]

3. Moreover, Aristotle says that the measure of the most fundamental change measures all change;[2] in the same way it seems that the measure of the most fundamental existence

---

[11] *Job* 24:19   [12] *Psalms* 80:16

[13] *Metaphysics* VI, 4. 1027b27   [1] *Physics* IV, 11. 219b11

[a] The 'now' of time is the part of time that is actual—the present. As such it is identical with time, in so far as time is actual.

[2] op. cit. IV, 14. 223b18

should measure all existence. Now eternity measures divine existence which is the most fundamental existence, and so measures all existence. The existence of perishable things, however, is measured by time. So time is either eternity or a part of eternity.

ON THE OTHER HAND eternity is an instantaneous whole, whilst in time there is before and after. So time and eternity differ.

REPLY: Time and eternity clearly differ. But certain people make the difference consist in time having a beginning and an end whilst eternity has neither. Now this is an accidental and not an intrinsic difference. For even if time had always existed and will always exist, as those hold who think the heavens will rotate for ever, there will still remain the difference Boethius points out between time and eternity: that eternity is an instantaneous whole whilst time is not,[3] eternity measuring abiding existence and time measuring change.

If, however, the suggested difference applies to the things measured rather than to the measures themselves, there is some ground for it; for, as Aristotle says, time measures only things beginning and ending in time.[4] So, even though the heavens rotated for ever, time would measure, not the whole duration of the movement, since the infinite is immeasurable, but each revolution separately as it began and ended in time.

Or again the suggested difference could apply validly to the measures themselves, if we were to talk of potential beginnings and ends. For even though time lasted for ever, it would be possible to mark off beginnings and ends in it by dividing it into parts, and so in fact we talk of the beginning and end of a day or year; and this cannot happen in eternity.

However, these differences are all consequent upon the primary and intrinsic difference that eternity exists as an instantaneous whole, whereas time does not.

---

[3] *Consolation of philosophy* v. 6. PL 63, 859. Aristotle is cited by name as holding that the heavens rotate eternally.
[4] *Physics* IV, 12. 221b28

Hence: 1. This would be a valid argument if time and eternity were measures of the same type, which clearly they are not if one considers the different things they measure.

2. The 'now' remains unchanged in substance throughout time, but takes on different forms, because, just as time corresponds to movement, so the 'now' corresponds to the thing moving. Now the thing moving remains in substance the same throughout the course of time, but it differs in position, first here and then there, its movement consisting in the change of position. In the same way time consists in the flow of the 'now' changing its form. But eternity remains unchanged both in substance and in form. Eternity therefore differs from the 'now' of time.

3. Just as eternity is properly the measure of existence as such, so time is properly the measure of change. In so far then as any existence falls short of permanence in its existing and is subject to change, so will it fall short of eternity and be subjected to time. So the existence of perishable things, being changeable, is measured by time and not by eternity. For time measures not only the actually changing but also the potentially changeable. It measures, therefore, not only movement but also rest, the state of the movable when not moving.

Article 5. The difference between the æon and time

THE FIFTH POINT: 1. 'Æon' seems to be another name for time. For the æon is defined as the measure of immaterial substances. Now Augustine talks of *God moving immaterial creatures through time*.[1] Time and the æon are therefore the same.[a]

---

[1] *On Genesis to the letter* VIII, 20 & 22. PL 34, 388–89

[a] The 'æon' is a term derived by a different route from the same word as 'eternity'. In the early years of Greek philosophy it was in use as a measure of duration, which became distinct from eternity strictly so-called. Lucretius, the early Gnostics, and the Neo-Platonists all make use of the term. How St Thomas understands it is clear from the text.

2. Moreover, according to their definitions, as we saw, time possesses before and after, whilst eternity is instantaneously whole.[2] Now the æon is not eternity, for according to *Ecclesiasticus* the eternal *wisdom exists prior to the æon*.[3] The æon therefore is not instantaneously whole but possesses a before and after, which makes it the same as time.

3. Moreover, were the æon to lack before and after, then, for things measured by the æon, existing in the present or past would be the same as existing in the future. Such things, consequently, since they cannot not have existed in the past, would not be able not to exist in the future. And this is false, for they can be annihilated by God.

4. Moreover, things in the æon are going to last into an unlimited future. But if the whole æon exists at an instant, the limitlessness of such created things is already actual, which is impossible. So the æon is no different from time.

ON THE OTHER HAND Boethius writes of him who orders time to go from the æon.[4]

REPLY: The æon is neither time nor eternity, but lies somewhere between the two.

Certain people[b] express the difference by saying that eternity has neither beginning nor end, the æon has a beginning but no end, whilst time has both beginning and end. But this, as we have seen, is an accidental difference;[5] for even if things in the æon always had existed and always will exist, as some hold, or even if God were to bring them to an end sometime, as he is able to do, the æon would still be distinguishable from both eternity and time.

Others[c] express the difference between the three measures by saying that eternity does not have before and after, time has before and after and also newness and oldness, whilst the

---

[2] art. 1 above   [3] *Ecclesiasticus* 1:1
[4] *Consolation of philosophy* III, 9. PL 63, 758
[b] e.g. Alexander of Hales   [5] art. 4 above
[c] e.g. St Bonaventure

æon has before and after but not newness and oldness. But this is self-contradictory. If it is newness and oldness of the measure itself that is meant, the contradiction is obvious. For the before and after of duration cannot be instantaneous; if then the æon has a before and after, as each fore-part moves away an after-part must become newly present, and so there will be newness in the æon just as there is in time. If newness and oldness of the things measured is meant, an inconsistency still arises. For it is due to their changeable existence that temporal things age with time, and, as Aristotle shows, from this changeableness in the thing measured the before and after of time derives.[6] So that if things in the æon cannot be new or old, this will be because their existence is unchangeable. And in that case the measure itself will have no before and after.

We therefore say that as eternity is the measure of abiding existence, the further a thing falls short of abiding existence, the further it falls short of eternity. Now some things fall far enough short of abiding existence to have an existence consisting in or subject to change, and such things time measures; all movements, for example, and in perishable things, even their existence. Other things do not fall so far short of abiding existence that their existence consists in or is subject to change, but nonetheless it is accompanied by some actual or potential change. An example is the heavenly bodies which, whilst existing unchanged in substance, combine with this unchangeable existence a changeableness of place. And for another example, take angels who combine unchangeable existence with changeability of choice at the natural level, and with changeability of thoughts, affections and, in their own fashion, places.[d] These sorts of thing then are measured by

---

[6] *Physics* IV, 22. 221a31

[d] The heavenly bodies were thought to be free from generation and corruption and the sort of change of quality which occurs in the sublunar world. But they changed their place, of course, in the heavens. The angels, though not in place like bodies because possessing no dimensions, are nevertheless conceived of as in causal contact with bodies which are in place and which change place.

the æon, which lies somewhere between eternity and time. Eternity itself measures any existence which is both unchangeable and unaccompanied by changeableness. To sum up, then, time has a before and after, the æon has no before and after in itself but can be accompanied by it, whilst eternity neither possesses a before and after nor can co-exist with it.

Hence: 1. Inasmuch as their thoughts and affections display successiveness, immaterial creatures are measured by time. And so Augustine says in the same passage that to be moved through time is to be moved in affections. But as regards their natural existence they are measured by the æon; and inasmuch as they contemplate God's glory they share in eternity.

2. Although the æon is instantaneously whole, it differs from eternity in being able to co-exist with before and after.

3. There is no difference of past and future in an angel's existence as such, but only consequent upon accompanying changes. But we distinguish between angels existing or having existed or existing in the future, because we talk in the way we think, and we think of the existence of angels by relating it to different periods of time. Now in talking of angels existing or having existed, we incorporate a supposition such that the opposite of what we say is no longer within God's power; but in talking of them existing in the future, we as yet make no such supposition. Absolutely speaking, that angels should or should not exist is within God's power, so God can cause an angel not to exist in future, even if he cannot cause it not to exist while it exists, or not to have existed when it already has.

4. The duration of the æon is unlimited in the sense of not being limited by time. But there is no difficulty about something created being unlimited, if we mean that it is not limited by some particular other thing.

Article 6. Is there only one æon?

THE SIXTH POINT: 1. More than one æon exists, it would seem. For we read in the apocryphal books of *Ezra* that *the majesty and power of the æons is with thee, O Lord*.[1]

2. Moreover, each kind of thing has its own measure. Now some things measured by an æon are bodies, namely the heavenly bodies, and some, namely the angels, are immaterial substances. There is therefore more than one æon.

3. Moreover, if 'æon' names a kind of duration, everything in one æon will have the same duration. Now not all things measured by an æon have the same duration, for some come into existence later than others; the clearest case is that of human souls. So there is not only one æon.

4. Moreover, things unconnected causally do not seem to have the same measure of duration. Thus, one time measures everything temporal, it seems, because time measures first the most fundamental process in the world, and this process is in a way the cause of everything else. Now things measured by æons are not in causal connection. There is thus more than one æon.

ON THE OTHER HAND the æon is simpler than time, and nearer to eternity. But only one time exists. Still more then is there only one æon.

REPLY: There are two opinions on this point, some people saying that there is only one æon, some that there are many. And to decide which is nearer the truth we must ask ourselves why time is one, for we come to understand the immaterial through the material.

Some derive the unity of time in all temporal things from the unity of a number in numbered things, time being, as

---

[1] III (1) *Ezra* 4:40

Aristotle says, *a numbering*.[2] But this is not enough, for time is not a number abstracted from the things it numbers, but a numberedness existing in the things themselves; otherwise it would lack continuity, just as the continuity of ten yards of cloth derives not from the number but from the thing numbered. Now the numberedness in things differs in different things, and is not the same for all.

Others therefore derive the unity of time from the unity of eternity, the source of all duration. All duration, these people say, is one at source, although multiplied according to the differing things receiving duration from this primary source. Others again derive the unity of time from the unity of ultimate matter, the fundamental subject of the changes time measures. Neither derivation seems adequate, however, for things that are one in source or in subject, especially when these are the distant source and subject, are not one simply speaking, but only one in certain respects.

The true ground of time's unity is therefore the unity of the most fundamental process in the world, by which—since it is the simplest—all other processes are measured, as Aristotle says.[3] Time is not only the measure of this process, but also an accident of it, and so receives unity from it. But time is merely a measure of other processes, and so is not diversified by their diversity, for one measure, when independently existent, can measure many things.

Given this foundation, we must note two opinions concerning immaterial substances. Certain people have held with Origen that they all came out from God equal, or with other thinkers that many of them were equal. Other people have held that all immaterial substances came out from God in a certain order and hierarchy. And this seems to be Dionysius's opinion, who says that among such substances some are first, some intermediate and others last, and this even within one order of angels.[4] Holders of the first opinion then must con-

---

[2] *Physics* IV, 12. 220b8   [3] *Metaphysics* X, 1. 1053a8
[4] *Heavenly hierarchy* X, 2. PG 3, 273

fess more than one æon, corresponding to the many equally primary substances measured by æons. Holders of the second opinion, however, must confess only one æon, for Aristotle says that the simplest thing in a genus measures the other things,[5] so that the simpler existence of the primary thing in the æon—simpler because more primary—will measure the existence of everything in the æon. And because as we shall see later the second opinion is nearer the truth,[6] we shall here admit only one æon.

Hence: 1. 'Æon' sometimes means age, that is to say the period of a thing's duration; and in this sense we talk of many æons, as of many ages.

2. Although the heavenly bodies differ in nature from immaterial things, both kinds of thing agree in existing unchangeably. And as such they are both measured by the æon.

3. Not all temporal things come into existence together, but all nonetheless are measured by one and the same time as the primary temporal thing. In the same way everything in the æon is measured by the same æon as some primary thing, even if they do not come into existence together.

4. In order for one thing to measure others, it does not have to cause them all, but only to be simpler than them all.

---

[5] *Metaphysics* x, 1. 1052b33   [6] 1a. 47, 2; 50, 4

WE MUST FOLLOW what we have so far said with a treatment of the oneness of God.

Question 11. The oneness of God

This question has four points of inquiry:

1. does being one add anything to existing?
2. is being one the opposite of being many?
3. is there one God?
4. is God supremely one?

Article 1. Does being one add anything to existing?

THE FIRST POINT: 1. Being one seems to add something to existing. For being in some determinate genus adds to existing, in itself common to all genera. Now to be one a thing must be in a determinate genus, for unity initiates number which is a species of the genus quantity. Being one therefore adds something to existing.

2. Moreover, subdivisions of a general concept add something to the general concept itself. Now being is subdivided into being one and being many. Being one adds something therefore to being.

3. Moreover, if being one added nothing to existing, the words 'one' and 'existent' would be synonymous. Now it is tautological to say that what exists is existent. It should therefore be tautological to say that what exists is one, which is not so. Being one must therefore add something to existing.

ON THE OTHER HAND Dionysius says that *nothing exists without being somehow one*.[1] But if being one added something to

---

[1] *Divine names* XIII, 2. PG 3, 977

existing, it would narrow its application, and Dionysius would be wrong. Being one therefore adds nothing to existing.

REPLY: Oneness adds nothing real to any existent thing, but simply denies division of it, for to be one means no more than to exist undivided. And from this it is clear that everything existing is one. For everything existing is either simple or composite. Now simple things are neither actually nor potentially divided, whilst composite things do not exist as long as their constituent parts are divided but only after these parts have come together to compose the thing. Clearly then everything's existence is grounded in indivision. And this is why things guard their unity as they do their existence.

Hence: 1. Two opposing positions have been adopted by those who identify the unity equivalent with existing and the unity initiating number. Pythagoras and Plato, seeing that the unity equivalent with existing adds nothing to existing but simply signifies the existent substance undivided, thought this also true of the unity initiating number. And since number is composed of unities, they believed number to be the substance of all things. Avicenna, on the other hand, seeing that the unity initiating number adds something to substance (for otherwise number composed of unities would not be a species of quantity), believed that the unity equivalent with existing added something to the substance of an existent thing, as whiteness adds something to man. Now this is clearly false, for everything is one of its very substance. If it were one by something else, that something else, being itself one, would be one by something else again, and so on and so on. Better not to embark on such a course, and say, therefore, that the unity equivalent with existing adds nothing to existing, whilst the unity initiating number adds something belonging to the genus of quantity.

2. There is nothing to stop things being divided from one point of view and undivided from another (numerically divided, for example, yet undivided in kind), and they will then be from one point of view one, and from another many. If a thing is simply speaking divided (either because undivided in essentials although divided in non-essentials, as

one substance having many accidents; or because actually undivided although potentially divisible, as one whole having
many parts), then such a thing will be simply speaking one,
and many only in a certain respect. On the other hand, if
things are simply speaking divided though in a certain respect
undivided (as things divided in substance although undivided in species or in causal origin), then they will be simply
speaking many, and one only in a certain respect, as things
many in number can be of one species or origin. Now being is
subdivided into being one and being many in the sense of
one simply speaking and many in a certain respect. For the
many as such cannot be said to exist, except in so far as they
have a certain unity. Thus, Dionysius says that *no manifold
exists without being somehow one: for many parts are one
whole, many accidents one in subject, many things one in
species, many species one in genus, and many processes one
in origin.*[2]

3. There is no tautology in saying that what exists is one,
because unity adds to existence conceptually.

Article 2. Is being one the opposite of being many?

THE SECOND POINT: 1. It seems that being one is not the opposite of being many. For one cannot assert one opposite of
the other. Yet the many are always in a certain respect one,
as has been said.[1] So being one is not opposed to being many.

2. Moreover, nothing is composed of its opposite. But the
many is composed of unities. Unity, therefore, is not opposed
to the many.

3. Moreover, one thing has one opposite. Now few is the
opposite of many. One, therefore, is not the opposite of
many.

4. Moreover, if the one and the many are opposed it must
be like indivision and division are, namely, as lack to possession. Now this does not seem right, for unity would then be
subsequent as an idea to the many, and defined in terms of it;

[2] loc. cit.   [1] 1a. 11, 1 ad 2

but in fact the many is defined in terms of unity. We would thus be defining in circles, which will not do. So one and many are not opposed.

ON THE OTHER HAND, things are opposed if their definitions are opposed. Now indivision defines unity, whilst division enters into the definition of the many. So one and many are opposed.

REPLY: One is the opposite of many in differing ways. Thus the unity initiating number is opposed to the manyness of number as a measure opposes what it measures, for unity is by definition the fundamental measure, and number is many measured in ones, as Aristotle says.[2] The unity convertible with existing, however, is opposed to the many as indivision is opposed to division, by lacking it.

Hence: 1. To lack something is not to cease existing entirely, for Aristotle defines lack as the non-existence of some attribute in some subject;[3] but it is to cease existing in some respect. And so it happens that lack of existence is grounded in an existent, existence being a universal attribute, a thing that does not happen when the lack is of some special attribute like sight or whiteness or the like. And what is true of existence is true of the unity and goodness convertible with existence: for lack of goodness is grounded in a good, and absence of unity in something one. So the many turn out to be somehow one, the bad thing a sort of good, and the non-existent a kind of existent. Nonetheless there is no contradiction involved for one term is understood simply speaking, the other only in a certain respect. For what is existent in a certain respect is non-existent simply speaking, for example, the potentially existent does not actually exist; and what is existent simply speaking does not exist in a certain respect, for example, a substance will lack certain accidents. Similarly, therefore, what is good in a certain respect is bad simply

---

[2] *Metaphysics* x, 1. 1052b18; 6. 1057a3
[3] op. cit. IV, 2. 1004a15

speaking, or vice versa. And what is one simply speaking is many in a certain respect, or vice versa.

2. A whole can be homogeneous, if composed of similar parts, or heterogeneous, if composed of dissimilar parts. In homogeneous wholes the component parts share the form of the whole, thus every bit of water is water. And this is the way a continuum is made up from its parts. In heterogeneous wholes the parts lack the form of the whole; thus no part of a house is itself a house, and no part of man a man. The many is this kind of whole. And so because no part of the many has the form of the many, the many is composed of unities, like the house from things not houses; but these unities compose the many inasmuch as they exist, not inasmuch as they are undivided and opposed to the many, just as the parts of a house make up the house inasmuch as they are bodies of a certain sort, not inasmuch as they are not houses.

3. 'Many' can be given two meanings: the straightforward one opposed to unity, and that connoting a certain excess and opposed to few. In the first sense two is many, but not in the second.

4. The one is opposed to the many because it lacks the division possessed by the many. So division must precede unity as an idea in our minds, though not in simple fact. For we grasp the simple things by way of the composite, defining a point as something without parts or as the beginning of a line. Even in our minds, however, the many is subsequent to unity, for we only conceive divided things as many by ascribing unity to each of them. So unity enters the definition of the many, but the many does not enter the definition of unity. Now division arises in the mind simply by negating existence. So that the first idea to arise in the mind is the existent, then that this existent is not that existent and so we grasp division, thirdly unity, and fourthly the many.

Article 3. Is there one God?

THE THIRD POINT: 1. God is not one, it seems. For St Paul says that *there are indeed many gods and many lords.*[1]

2. Moreover, the unity with which number begins cannot be attributed to a God to whom quantity cannot be attributed. Nor can the unity convertible with existence because it implies lack and lack imperfection, which cannot exist in God. So we cannot talk of one God.

ON THE OTHER HAND there is *Deuteronomy, Hear, O Israel, the Lord our God is one God.*[2]

REPLY: That there is one God can be shown in three ways.

First, because God is simple. For clearly no individual can share with others its very singularity. Socrates can share what makes him man with many others, but what makes him this man can belong to one alone. So if Socrates were this man just by being a man, there could no more be many men than there can be many Socrates. Now in God this is the case, for as we showed God is himself his own nature.[3] So to be God is to be this God. And it is thus impossible for there to be many Gods.

Secondly, because God's perfection is unlimited. For God, as we have seen, embraces in himself the whole perfection of existence.[4] Now many Gods, if they existed, would have to differ. Something belonging to one would not belong to the other. And if this were a lack the one God would not be altogether perfect, whilst if it were a perfection the other God would lack it. So there cannot be more than one God. And this is why philosophers in ancient times, bowing, so to speak, to the truth, held that if the source of things was unlimited it could not be many.[a]

---

[1] 1 *Corinthians* 8:5   [2] *Deuteronomy* 6:4   [3] 1a. 3, 3
[4] 1a. 4, 7
[a] cf *Physics* III, 4. 203b4

Thirdly, because the world is one. For we find all existent things in mutual order, certain of them subserving others. Now divers things only combine in a single order where there is a single cause of order. For unity and order is introduced into a plurality of things more perfectly by a single cause than by many, unity producing unity essentially whilst the many produce unity only incidentally in so far as they too are somehow one. So the primary source of unity and order in the universe, namely, God, must be one himself, for the primary is always most perfect and not incidental but essential.

Hence: 1. The words *many gods* allude to the mistaken beliefs of those who worshipped many gods, thinking the planets and the other stars and even each separate part of the world to be divine. And so the passage continues, *yet there is for us one God and Father,* etc.

2. The unity with which number begins is not attributed to God but only to material things. For it is studied in mathematics which treats of entities existing in matter but defined without reference to matter. The unity convertible with existence, on the other hand, is a sort of metaphysical entity which can exist outside of matter. And although God cannot lack anything, yet because of our ways of understanding things, he cannot be known by us except we conceive him as lacking or excluding certain attributes. And so there is nothing wrong with describing God as lacking things: being without a body, for example, or without limits. And in the same way we call God one.

Article 4. Is God supremely one?

THE FOURTH POINT: 1. God, it seems, is not supremely one. For unity is absence of division. Now for something to be more or less absent is impossible. So we cannot say God is more one than other things.

2. Moreover, nothing seems more indivisible than things like points and units which are indivisible both actually and potentially. Now the degree of unity we ascribe to a thing depends on its degree of indivisibility. So God is not more one than points and units.

3. Moreover, just as the supremely good is good of itself, so the supremely one must be one of itself. Now Aristotle tells us that everything that exists is one of itself.[1] So everything is supremely one. God is therefore no more one than anything else.

ON THE OTHER HAND Bernard says that *among all the things we say are one the unity of the divine Trinity takes pride of place.*[2]

REPLY: Since to be one is to exist undivided, anything supremely one must be both supremely existent and supremely undivided. Both characteristics belong to God. He exists supremely, because he has not acquired an existence which his nature has then determined, but is subsistent existence itself, in no way determined. He is also supremely undivided, because as we have seen he is altogether simple, not divided in any way, and this neither actually nor potentially.[3] Clearly then God is supremely one.

Hence: 1. Although there cannot be more or less absence as such, a thing can be said to have more or less of a lack inasmuch as it has less or more of the opposite attribute. So a thing is called more or less or supremely one, inasmuch as it is less or more or not at all divided or divisible.

2. The point and numerical unity are not supremely existent, since they only exist as accidents in a subject. Neither of them then is supremely one. For just as no subject is supremely one because of the heterogeneity of subject and accident, so also no accident.

3. Although everything that exists is one in substance, not every substance has the same relation to unity, for certain substances have many component parts and some not.

---

[1] *Metaphysics* IV, 2. 1003b32
[2] *De Consideratione* V, 8. PL 182, 799   [3] 1a. 3, 7

Question 12. How God is known by his creatures

Having considered what God is in himself we turn now to consider what our minds can make of him; how in fact is he known by his creatures? Here there are thirteen points of inquiry:

1. can any created mind see the essence of God?
2. does the mind see the essence of God by means of any created likeness?
3. can we see the essence of God with our bodily eyes?
4. can any created intellect see the essence of God by its own natural powers?
5. does the created mind need a created light in order to see the essence of God?
6. is the essence of God seen more perfectly by one than by another?
7. can a created mind comprehend the essence of God?
8. does it in seeing the essence of God see all things?
9. is it by means of any likeness that it knows what it sees there?
10. is all that is seen in God seen together?
11. can any man in this life see the essence of God?
12. can we know God through our natural reason in this life?
13. besides the knowledge we have of God by natural reason, is there in this life a deeper knowledge that we have through grace?

Article 1. Can any created mind see the essence of God?

THE FIRST POINT: It seems that no created mind can see God in his essence. For commenting on St John's words, *God no man has ever seen*,[1] Chrysostom says, *It is not only the*

---

[1] John 1:18

prophets who have never seen what God is; neither have the angels or the archangels seen him, for how could created nature see the uncreated?[2] Dionysius, too, says, *Sense cannot attain to him, nor imagination, nor opinion, nor reasoning, nor knowledge.*[3]

2. The unlimited is, as such, unknowable. But we have already shown that God is unlimited,[4] so he must be in himself unknown.

3. The created mind only knows what is already there to be known, for the first thing the mind grasps of anything is that it *is* something or other. God, however, is not there: he is beyond what is there, as Dionysius says,[5] hence he is not intelligible, he is beyond understanding.

4. Since in knowledge the thing known is some sort of perfection of the knower, it cannot be altogether out of proportion to the knower. But there is no proportion whatever between the created mind and God, they are infinitely distant from each other, hence such a mind cannot see the essence of God.

ON THE OTHER HAND we read in 1 *John, We shall see him just as he is.*[6]

REPLY: In so far as a thing is realized it is knowable; but God is wholly realized—there is nothing about him which might be but is not—and so in himself he is supremely knowable. What is in itself supremely knowable may, however, so far exceed the power of a particular mind as to be beyond its understanding, rather as the sun is invisible to the bat because it is too bright for it. With this in mind some have said that no created mind can see the essence of God.

This view, however, is not admissible in the first place on theological grounds as being inconsistent with faith. The ultimate happiness of man consists in his highest activity, which is the exercise of his mind. If therefore the created mind

---

[2] *Homilies on John* 15. PG 59, 98
[3] *Divine names* 1, 3. PG 3, 593   [4] 1a. 7, 1
[5] op. cit. IV, 2. PG 3, 697   [6] 1 *John* 3:2

were never able to see the essence of God, either it would
never attain happiness or its happiness would consist in something other than God. This is contrary to faith, for the ultimate perfection of the rational creature lies in that which is
the source of its being—each thing achieves its perfection by
rising as high as its source.

The view is also philosophically untenable, for it belongs
to human nature to look for the causes of things—that is how
intellectual problems arise. If therefore the mind of the rational creature were incapable of arriving at the first cause of
things, this natural tendency could not be fulfilled. So we
must grant that the blessed do see the essence of God.

Hence: 1. Both these authorities are speaking not simply
of seeing God's essence but of comprehending it. Thus Dionysius introduces the words quoted by saying, *All find it completely impossible to comprehend him, for sense cannot attain to him*, etc. and Chrysostom, soon after the passage
quoted says, *By vision is meant contemplation of the Father
and perfect comprehension of him such as the Father has of
the Son*.

2. The unlimited in the sense of indeterminate matter not
perfected by form is, as such, unknowable because it is
through the form that anything is known. But the unlimited
in the sense of a form not confined by matter is in itself supremely knowable. It is in this latter sense that God is unlimited or infinite, and not in the first sense, as is clear from
what has been said.[7]

3. God is not said to be 'not there' in the sense that he
does not exist at all, but because being his own existence he
transcends all that is there. It follows from this not that he
cannot be known but that he is beyond all that can be known
of him—this is what is meant by saying that he cannot be
comprehended.

4. When we say one thing is in proportion to another we
can either mean that they are quantitatively related—in this
sense double, thrice and equal are kinds of proportion—or

---

[7] 1a. 7, 1

else we can mean just any kind of relation that one thing may have to another. It is in this latter sense that we speak of a proportion between creatures and God, in that they are related to him as effects to cause and as the partially realized to the absolutely real; in this sense it is not altogether disproportionate to the created mind to know God.

Article 2. Does the mind see God's essence by means of any created likeness?

THE SECOND POINT: 1. It seems that the created mind sees the essence of God by means of a likeness. We read in 1 *John*, *We know that when he appears we shall be like him and we shall know him just as he is.*[1]

2. Augustine says, *When we know God a likeness of him comes to be in us.*[2]

3. Actual thought is the realized intelligibility of what is known, just as actual sensation is the realized sensibleness of what is known. But this only occurs when the sense is formed by a likeness of the sensible thing or the mind by a likeness of the intelligible thing. Hence if God is actually seen by the created mind he must be seen through some likeness.

ON THE OTHER HAND St Paul's words, *we see now in a mirror by dull reflection,*[3] Augustine says, *refer to any likeness that may help us to understand God.*[4] But to see God in his essence is not to see him 'in a dull mirror' but is contrasted with this; hence the divine essence is not seen through any likeness.

REPLY: In order to see, whether with the senses or the mind, two things are needed; there must be a power of sight and the thing to be seen must come into sight: for we do not see unless the thing is somehow in our sight. Obviously the visible corporeal thing is not by its essence in the one who sees, but

---

[1] 1 *John* 3:2   [2] *On the Trinity* IX, 11. PL 42, 969
[3] 1 *Corinthians* 13:12   [4] op. cit. XV, 9. PL 42, 1069

only by its image: we see a stone not because the stone itself is in the eye but because its image is.

If, however, one and the same thing were both the thing seen and the source of the power of sight, then the seer would receive from that thing both the power of sight and the image by which it sees. Now it is clear that God is the author of the power of understanding and also can be an object of the understanding. The power of understanding in the creature (since it is not itself the essence of God), must be a sharing by likeness in the nature of him who is the primordial intelligence. Thus we could call it a sort of intelligible light derived from the primordial light, and we could say this both of the natural power of understanding and of any additional power that comes from grace or glory. It is the power of sight itself, therefore, that needs, in order to be capable of seeing God at all, a certain likeness to him.

When, however, we consider the essence of God as an object of sight, it is impossible that it should be united with the power of sight by any created image. Firstly, because as Dionysius says, things of a higher order cannot be known through likenesses of an inferior order[5]—we cannot even know the essences of incorporeal things through bodily likenesses, much less could we see the essence of God through any kind of created likeness. Secondly, because, as we have said,[6] the essence of God is to exist, and since this could not be the case with any created form no such form could represent the essence of God to the understanding. Thirdly, the divine essence is beyond description, containing to a transcendent degree every perfection that can be described or understood by the created mind. This could not be represented by any created likeness since every created form is determinately this rather than that, whether it be wisdom, power, existence itself, or anything else. Hence to say that God is seen by means of a likeness is to say that his essence is not seen, which is erroneous.

Accordingly we should say that for the seeing of God's es-

---

[5] *Divine names* IV, 1. PG 3, 588   [6] 1a. 3, 4

sence some likeness is required on the part of the power of sight, namely the light of divine glory strengthening the mind, of which the *Psalm* speaks, *In thy light shall we see light.*[7] It is not that God's essence can be seen by means of any created likeness representing him as he is.

Hence: 1. This authoritative text is speaking of the likeness which comes through sharing in the light of glory.

2. Augustine is here speaking of the knowledge we can have of God in this life.

3. The divine essence is existence itself. Hence as other intelligible forms, which are not identical with their existence, are united to the mind according to a sort of mental existence by which they inform and actualize the mind, so the divine essence is united to a created mind so as to be what is actually understood and through its very self making the mind actually understanding.

Article 3. *Can we see God's essence with our bodily eyes?*

THE THIRD POINT: 1. It seems that we could see the essence of God with our bodily eyes. For Job says *In my flesh I shall see God,*[1] and, *With the hearing of the ear I have heard thee, but now my eye sees thee.*[2]

2. Augustine says, *The eyes* (of the blessed) *are made clearer, not in the sense that they become more piercing than those of eagles or serpents—for however acutely these beasts see, they see nothing but material things—but in the sense that they can see incorporeal things.*[3] But whatever can see incorporeal things could be raised up to see God, hence the eyes of the glorified body could see God.

3. A man can see God in the imagination, for we read in *Isaiah, I saw the Lord seated on his throne.*[4] But what we imagine has its origin in the senses, for the imagination, ac-

---

cording to Aristotle, is *a change brought about by the activity of the senses*,[5] hence God can be seen by bodily vision.

ON THE OTHER HAND Augustine says, *No man has ever seen God whether in this present life or in the angelic life in the way that our bodily eyes see visible things.*[6]

REPLY: It is impossible to see God by the power of sight or by any other sense or sensitive power. Any power of this kind is, as we shall be seeing later, the proper activity of some corporeal organ.[7] Such activity must belong to the same order as that of which it is the activity, hence no such power could extend beyond corporeal things. God, however, is not corporeal, as has been shown,[8] hence he cannot be seen by sense or imagination but only by the mind.

Hence: 1. *In my flesh I shall see God* does not mean that I shall see God by means of the bodily eye, but that I shall see him when I am in the flesh, i.e., after the resurrection. *Now my eye sees thee* refers to the eye of the mind, as when St Paul says, *May he grant you a spirit of wisdom in knowing him, may he enlighten the eyes of your mind.*[9]

2. Augustine here is merely making a suggestion and not committing himself to a definite position. This is clear from what he says immediately afterwards; *They (the eyes of the glorified body) would have to have an altogether different power if they were to see incorporeal things.* Later he finds his own solution; *It is extremely likely that we shall then see the bodies that make up the new heaven and the new earth in such a way as to see God present everywhere in them, governing everything, even material things. We shall not merely see him as we now do when 'the invisible things of God are made known to us by the things he has made' but rather as we now see the life of the living breathing people we meet. The fact that they are alive is not something we*

---

[5] *De Anima* III, 3. 429a1
[6] *Epistles* CXLVII, 11. PL 33, 609   [7] art. 4 below
[8] 1a. 3, 1   [9] *Ephesians* 1:17

come to believe in but something we see.[10] Hence it is evident that our glorified eyes will see God as now they see the life of another. For life is not seen by bodily eyesight as though it were visible in itself as a proper object of sight; it is an indirect sense-object, not itself perceived by sense, yet straightway known in sensation by some other cognitive power. That divine presence is instantly perceived by the mind on the sight of and through bodily things comes from two causes, from its own penetrating clearness and from the gleaming of divine brightness in our renewed bodies.

3. The essence of God is not seen in the imagination. What appears there is an image representing God according to some likeness, as is the way with the divine Scriptures which describe God metaphorically by means of material things.

Article 4. Can any created intellect see God's essence by its own natural powers?

THE FOURTH POINT: 1. It seems that a created mind might see the essence of God by its own natural powers. Dionysius says that an angel is *a pure and most clear mirror, reflecting, if one may dare to say it, the whole beauty of God.*[1] But to see something in a mirror is really to see it; since therefore, the angel by its own natural powers understands itself, it would seem that by these powers it must understand the divine essence.

2. What is supremely visible only becomes less visible to us through some defect in our vision, whether bodily or intellectual. An angel's mind does not suffer from any defect and therefore since God is in himself supremely intelligible he must be supremely intelligible to the angel. Since, therefore, the angel can understand less intelligible things by its own powers, much more will it be able to understand God.

3. The reason why the bodily senses cannot be raised up

---

[10] loc. cit., end of chapter. PL 41, 800
[1] *Divine names* IV, 18. PG 3, 724

to understand incorporeal being is that it is beyond their natural scope. If therefore seeing the essence of God were beyond the natural scope of a created mind it would seem that no such mind could attain to the essence of God; but this, as we have seen,[2] is erroneous. It would seem therefore that it must be natural to the created mind to see God.

ON THE OTHER HAND we read in Romans, *The grace of God is eternal life*.[3] Now eternal life, as we know from *John*, consists in seeing the divine essence, *This is eternal life, their knowing thee, the only true God*.[4] Hence to know the essence of God belongs to the created mind by grace and not by nature.

REPLY: It is impossible that any created mind should see the essence of God by its own natural powers. A thing is known by being present in the knower; how it is present is determined by the way of being of the knower. Thus the way something knows depends on the way it exists. So if the way of being of the thing to be known were beyond that of the knower, knowledge of that thing would be beyond the natural power of the knower.

But what is meant by the 'way of being' of a thing? Some things are of a nature that cannot exist except as instantiated in individual matter—all bodies are of this kind. This is one way of being. There are other things whose natures are instantiated by themselves and not by being in matter. These have existence simply by being the natures that they are: yet existence is still something they *have*, it is not what they are— the incorporeal beings we call angels are of this kind. Finally there is the way of being that belongs to God alone, for his existence is what he is.

Knowledge of things that exist in the first way is connatural to us, for the human soul, through which we know, is itself the form of some matter. There are two ways in which we

---

[2] art. 2 above　　[3] *Romans* 6:23　　[4] *John* 17:3

know such things, by sensing them and by understanding them. Sensing consists in the proper activity of certain bodily organs, and it is connatural to this power to know things precisely in so far as they are in individual matter; thus by sense we know only individual things. The power of understanding does not consist in the activity of corporeal organs and so, although the natures that it connaturally knows cannot exist except in individual matter, it knows them not merely as they are in such matter, but as made abstract by the operation of the mind. Thus by understanding we can know things universally, something that is beyond the scope of the senses.

Knowledge of things that exist in the second way is connatural to an angel's mind, which can know natures that are not in matter: this is beyond the natural scope of human understanding in this life while the soul is united to the body.

Finally, only to the divine intellect is it connatural to know subsistent existence itself. This is beyond the scope of any created understanding, for no creature *is* its existence, it has a share in existence. Hence no created mind can see the essence of God unless he by his grace joins himself to that mind as something intelligible to it.

Hence: 1. It is indeed connatural to the angel to know God by his likeness shining forth in the angel itself, but to know God by any kind of created likeness is not to know his essence, as we have seen.[5] Hence it does not follow that the angel knows the essence of God by its natural powers.

2. The angel's mind has no defect, if by 'defect' is meant a deprivation, a lack of what should be present. But if it means simply the absence of some perfection, then any creature is defective by comparison with God since it does not have all the excellence that is to be found in God.

3. Since eyesight is altogether corporeal it cannot be raised to what is immaterial. The human or angelic mind, however,

---

[5] art. 2 above

already by its nature to some extent transcends the material and so can be raised by grace beyond its nature to something higher than the material. An indication of this is that bodily sight is confined to knowing a nature as in *this* concrete thing, it cannot in any way come to know it in abstraction. The mind on the other hand can consider in abstraction what it knows in the concrete, for although we know things that have their forms in matter it can nevertheless untie the two and consider the form as such. Similarly, although it is connatural to the angelic mind to know existence as concrete in a particular nature, nevertheless it can so far distinguish the two as to know that the thing and its existence are not identical. Hence since the created mind has the capacity by nature to see the concrete form or concrete act of existence in abstraction by analysis, it can by grace be raised so that it may know unmixed subsistent being and unmixed subsistent existence.

Article 5. Does the created mind need a created light in order to see God's essence?

THE FIFTH POINT: 1. It seems that the created mind does not need a created light in order to see God. For amongst sensible things what is luminous of itself does not need any extra light in order to be visible. Neither therefore should this be the case with intelligible things. But God is intelligible light. Hence he is not to be seen by any created light.

2. When God is seen through some medium he is not seen in his essence. Yet if he were seen by some created light he would be seen through a medium, hence his essence would not be seen.

3. Whatever is itself a creature could belong to some creature by nature. If therefore there is a created light through which God's essence is seen, this light could belong by nature to some creature and such a creature at least would not need any additional light in order to see God: this however is a contradiction. Hence it is not necessary that every creature should require additional light in order to see God.

ON THE OTHER HAND we read in the *Psalm*, *In thy light we shall see light*.[1]

REPLY: Whatever is raised beyond its own nature must be made apt to this by a disposition beyond its own nature[a]— as air, if it is to receive the form of fire, needs to be predisposed to it. When however a created intellect sees the essence of God, that very divine essence becomes the form through which the intellect understands. Hence there must be some disposition given to the understanding beyond its own nature so that it can be raised to such sublimity. Since as we have shown,[2] the natural power of the intellect is not sufficient to see the essence of God, this power of understanding must come to it by divine grace. This increase in the power of understanding we call 'illumination' of the mind, as also we speak of the intelligible form as 'light'. This is the light that is spoken of in the *Apocalypse*, *The brightness of God will illuminate her*,[3] i.e., the community of the blessed enjoying the vision of God. By this light we are made 'deiform', that is, like to God, as is said by John, *When he shall appear we shall be like to him, and we shall see him just as he is*.[4]

Hence: 1. The function of the created light is not to make the essence of God intelligible, for it is intelligible of itself; its purpose is to strengthen our minds in understanding, rather as a skill increases the effectiveness of any of our pow-

---

[1] *Psalms* 35:10

[a] When a thing develops in accordance with its nature (for example, when a child grows up) it fulfils capacities or potentialities that it has by nature. It is because of this that the adult characteristics belong to the same person as did those of childhood. If a thing is to rise to a state beyond its nature, this too must be a fulfilment of capacities that it has, otherwise the higher condition would not really belong to the thing but would merely be, so to speak, stuck on to it. These capacities which it cannot of course have by nature are the predispositions of which St Thomas is speaking.

[2] art. 4 above   [3] *Revelation* 21:23   [4] 1 *John* 3:2

ers. As also light in bodily vision makes the medium actually transparent so that it can be altered by colour.

2. The light is not needed as a likeness in which the essence of God may be seen, but to perfect the mind and strengthen it so that it may see God. It is not the medium *in* which God is seen, but the means *by* which he is seen; so it makes the vision of God no less immediate.

3. A disposition to the form of fire could only belong by nature to something that has the form of fire. Hence the light of glory could be natural to a creature only if that creature were by nature divine, which is self-contradictory. It is by this light that the creature becomes godlike or deiform as we have already said.[5]

Article 6. Is God's essence seen more perfectly by one than by another?

THE SIXTH POINT: 1. It seems that, of those who see the essence of God, one does not see it more perfectly than another. We read in 1 John, *We shall see him just as he is*,[1] but he *is* in only one way. Hence he will only be seen in one way; not therefore more by some and less by others.

2. Augustine says that the *same thing cannot be better understood by one than by another*.[2] Now all who see God's essence understand it, for it is by the mind that we see him, not by the senses, as already noted.[3] Hence in seeing the divine essence one sees no better than another.

3. When a thing is seen more perfectly it is because of something either to do with the thing seen or with the power of sight. In the former case it might be that the object is more perfectly present to the one who sees—present in a more perfect likeness: this has no relevance to the present discussion, for God is present to the mind not by any likeness but by his own essence. So if someone sees God more perfectly than another it can only be because of a difference in the power

---

[5] in the explanation   [1] 1 *John* 3:2
[2] 83 *Questions* 32. PL 40, 22   [3] art. 3 above

of understanding; from this it would follow that he who is more intelligent would see God more clearly: this however is theologically awkward, for in beatitude man is promised equality with the angels.

ON THE OTHER HAND eternal life consists in the vision of God, as we know from *John, This is eternal life, that they might know thee, the only true God.*[4] If therefore all saw the essence of God equally, all would be equal in eternal life; but this is contrary to what St Paul says, *Star differs from star in brightness.*[5]

REPLY: Of those who see the essence of God one will see him more perfectly than another. This is not because of a likeness of God which is more perfect in one than in the other, for the vision of God is not through any likeness, as we have seen.[6] It is because one mind has a greater power or ability to see God than has the other. This ability to see God does not belong to the mind by its own nature but by the light of glory which renders the mind in some sense like to God, as we have said.[7]

Hence the mind that has a greater share in the light of glory will see God more perfectly. Those share more in the light of glory who have more charity; because a greater charity implies a greater desire, and this itself in some way predisposes a man and fits him to receive what he desires. So that he who has greater charity will see God more perfectly, and will be more blessed.[a]

Hence: 1. The adverbial 'just as' in *We shall see him just as he is* refers not to the manner in which we shall see him but to what we shall see. The sentence means that we shall see his existence which is his essence; it does not mean that the manner we shall see him is as perfect as the manner in which God is.

---

[4] John 17:3 [5] 1 Corinthians 15:41 [6] art. 2 above
[7] art. 5 above
[a] Most of all the mind of Christ united in person with the Word of God; see 3a. 10, 4.

2. The same solution applies to the second objection, for if you say, 'A thing cannot be thought better by one than by another without error,' this is true if 'better' refers to the thing thought, for to think of a thing as being better or worse than it actually is is to be mistaken, but not if it refers to the mode of knowing, for without error the thinking of one can be better than the thinking of the other.

3. The diversity between those who see God has nothing to do with the thing seen, for this, God's essence, is the same for all. Nor is it a diversity in likenesses through which the object is seen; it is due to a diversity of intellectual capability, not inborn, but, as stated above,[8] given by the light of glory.

Article 7. Can a created mind comprehend God's essence?

THE SEVENTH POINT: 1. It seems that those who see the essence of God comprehend him. For St Paul says, *I press on, seeking to comprehend.*[1] He does not do this in vain, for he says elsewhere, *I do not run as one uncertain of my goal.*[2] Moreover in the same place he bids others do the same, . . . *so run that you may comprehend.*

2. Augustine says, *We say that something is comprehended when the whole of it is so visible that nothing of it is hidden.*[3] But when God is seen in his essence, the whole of him is seen and nothing is hidden since God is altogether simple. Hence whoever sees his essence comprehends him.

3. It might be argued 'Yes, we see the totality of God but we do not see him totally.' But this will not do, for 'totally' here is meant to apply either to him or to the seeing. But certainly it is *him* in his totality that we see for *we shall see him just as he is,* as has been said.[4] Moreover we *see* him totally for the mind sees God with its whole power. Who-

---

[8] in the explanation   [1] *Philippians* 3:12
[2] 1 *Corinthians* 9:26
[3] *Epistles* CXLIV, 9. On seeing God. PL 33, 606
[4] art. 6 ad 1 above

ever, therefore, sees God in his essence sees him totally, and
this is to comprehend him.

ON THE OTHER HAND we read in *Jeremiah*, *O God most powerful, great and strong, Lord of armies is thy name, mighty
in thy designs, incomprehensible in thy thoughts.*[5]

REPLY: Augustine says that for the mind to attain God in
any way is a great happiness,[6] but it is impossible for any
created mind to comprehend him. To comprehend is to understand perfectly: a thing is perfectly understood when it is
understood as well as it can be. Thus we do not comprehend
a proposition that could be proved scientifically if all we
have is a probable opinion about it: a man who can prove
that the angles of a triangle equal two right angles may be
said to comprehend this fact; but one who is merely of the
opinion that it is so on the grounds that learned men say so
or that it is commonly accepted, does not comprehend it
because he has not attained the most perfect sort of understanding available in this case.

Now no created mind can attain the perfect sort of understanding that is intrinsically possible of God's essence. This
is made evident as follows: each thing can be understood to
the extent that it is actually realized. God, therefore, whose
actual being is infinite, as noted above,[7] can be infinitely
understood. The created mind, however, understands God
more or less perfectly according to the degree of the light of
glory that floods it. Since no matter what mind it is received
in the created light of glory cannot be infinite, it is impossible
for any created mind to understand God infinitely; impossible, therefore, to comprehend him.

Hence: 1. 'To comprehend' can mean two things. Strictly
and properly it means to contain something, and in this sense
God cannot be comprehended either by the mind or by anything else. The infinite cannot be contained in the finite;

[5] *Jeremiah* 32:18
[6] *Sermons to the people* CXVII, 9. PL 38, 663   [7] 1a. 7, 1

God exists infinitely and nothing finite could grasp him infinitely. It is of comprehension in this sense that we are now speaking.

In a broader sense, however, comprehending is the opposite of letting something slip: anyone who attains anything, when he lays hold on it could be said to comprehend it. It is in this sense that God is comprehended by the blessed; *I held him and will not let him go.*[8] It is in this sense that St Paul's authoritative texts use the word. And thus comprehension is one of the three endowments of the blessed, corresponding to hope as does vision to faith and fruition or enjoyment to charity. For in this life not everything in our vision is in our grasp—for we see some things in the distance and we see things that are not in our power, nor have we enjoyment of all we grasp—either because it does not please us or because it is not what ultimately we are seeking, the satisfaction and quiescence of all our desires. But the blessed have this triple gift in God, for they see him and seeing him they possess him, holding him for ever in their sight, and holding him they enjoy him as their ultimate goal fulfilling all their desires.

2. When we say that God is not comprehended we do not mean there is something about him that is not seen, but that he cannot be seen as perfectly as intrinsically he is visible. When a man has only a probable opinion about a proposition that could be proved, there is no part of the proposition hidden from him, he understands both subject and predicate and the fact that they are conjoined, nevertheless he does not understand the proposition as well as it could be understood. Thus Augustine, defining comprehension, says something *is totally comprehended when it is so seen that no part of it is hidden, or so that all its limits can be seen,*[9] for all the limits of a thing are reached when we reach to the limit in our way of knowing it.

3. The word 'totally' applies to the object, but it is not that we do not know of the whole way of being of the thing,

---

[8] *Song of Songs* 3:4   [9] loc. cit. in objection

but that our way of knowing does not measure up to this. Whoever sees God in his essence sees something that exists infinitely and sees it to be infinitely intelligible, but he does not understand it infinitely. It is as though a man might be of the opinion that a certain proposition could be proved without himself being able to prove it.

Article 8. Does a created mind in seeing God's essence see all things?

THE EIGHTH POINT: 1. It seems that those who see God in his essence see all things in him. Gregory says, *What is it that he does not see who sees the seer of all things?*[1] But God sees all things. Hence he who sees God sees all things.

2. Whoever sees a mirror sees what is reflected in it. But everything that is or could be is reflected in God as in a mirror, for he himself knows all things in himself. Hence whoever sees God sees all that is or could be.

3. He who understands the greater thing can understand the lesser, as Aristotle says,[2] but everything that God has done or can do is a lesser thing than his essence, therefore whoever understands God can understand all that God has done or can do.

4. The rational creature naturally wishes to know everything. If therefore in knowing God he were not to know all things his desires would not be satisfied and hence in seeing God he would not be happy, but this is not in accordance with the faith. In seeing God, therefore, he sees all things.

ON THE OTHER HAND the angels see the essence of God and yet do not know everything. According to Dionysius the lesser angels are purified of their unknowing by the greater.[3] Moreover angels do not know future contingents or the secrets of the heart, for knowledge of these things belongs to God alone. Hence it cannot be true that whoever knows the essence of God knows all things.

---

[1] *Dialogues* IV, 33. PL 77, 376   [2] *De Anima* III, 4. 429b3
[3] *Heavenly hierarchy* 7. PG 3, 208

REPLY: The created mind seeing the divine essence does not see in it all that God does or can do. It is obvious that how things are to be seen in God depends on how they are in him. Everything other than God, however, is in him as an effect is in its cause, so that all things are seen in God as effects in their cause. Now the more perfectly a cause is seen the more of its effects can be seen in it. A man of sharp intelligence who grasps a principle can see at once what is implied in it, whereas a duller man has to have each conclusion explained to him. Only a man who wholly comprehends a cause will see in it all its effects and everything about its effects. But no created mind can wholly comprehend God, as we have shown.[4] Thus no created mind seeing God sees all that God does or can do, for this would be to comprehend his power. But the more perfectly God is seen the more of what he does or can do is seen in him.

Hence: 1. Gregory is thinking of sufficiency from the point of view of what is seen; in himself God is sufficient to contain and show forth all things: it does not follow from this that anyone who sees God sees all things, for he would not perfectly comprehend him.

2. A man who sees a mirror does not necessarily see everything that is in it unless he sees it perfectly.

3. Although it is a greater thing to see God than to see all other things, nevertheless it is also a greater thing to see God in such a way that all other things are seen in him, than to see him in such a way that only a certain amount is seen in him. We have already shown[5] that the amount we see in God depends on how perfectly we see him.

4. As to the fourth: the natural desire of the rational creature is to know all things that belong to the perfection of the mind. He seeks to know the natures of things and the laws that govern their behaviour; this much is seen by anyone who sees the divine essence. But to know particular individuals and their thoughts and deeds, does not of itself belong to the perfection of the created mind, nor does the mind

---

[4] art. 7 above   [5] in the explanation

naturally seek after this; nor again, does it need to know the things that have not yet happened but can be brought about by God. Simply to see God who is the fount and source of all being and truth would so satisfy the creature's desire for knowledge that he would seek no further for his happiness. As Augustine says, *Unhappy the man who knows all* (creatures) *and knows not thee: blessed is he who knows thee, even though he knows them not. And he who knows both thee and them is not the happier because of them but is simply happy because of thee.*[6]

Article 9. Is it by means of any likeness that a created mind knows what it sees in God's essence?

THE NINTH POINT: 1. It seems that what is seen in God is seen through a likeness. For knowledge comes about through the assimilation of the knower to the known; the mind in its realization becomes the realized intelligibility of the thing to be known, and the sight in its realization becomes the realized visibility of the thing to be seen: this happens because the knowing power is formed by a likeness of the thing known, as the pupil of the eye is formed by the likeness of colour. If therefore the minds of those who see God in his essence are to understand other creatures they must be formed by the likenesses of these creatures.

2. We remember what we have previously seen, but St Paul who, according to Augustine,[1] saw the essence of God when he was rapt in his ecstasy, still remembered many things after he had ceased to see it; for he said, *I have heard secret words which it is not given to man to speak.*[2] Some likeness, therefore, of the things he remembered must have remained in his mind and so these likenesses must have been there when he was actually seeing God.

---

[6] *Confessions* v, 4. PL 32, 708
[1] *On Genesis to the letter* XII, 28. PL 34, 478
[2] II *Corinthians* 12:4

ON THE OTHER HAND it is with one view that we see the mirror and what is in it; but everything we see in God is seen as in a sort of intelligible mirror. Hence since God himself is not seen through any likeness but by his essence, neither are the things seen in him seen by any likeness.

REPLY: The things seen in the essence of God by those who see it are not seen through any likeness but through the essence of God itself in their minds. Each thing is known in so far as its likeness is in the knower. This can happen in two ways: since things which are like to the same thing are like to each other the power of knowing can be conformed to the thing known either by being formed directly by the likeness of the known thing, and then the thing is known in itself, or else by being formed by the likeness of something which is itself like to the known thing, and then the thing is known in a likeness. It is one thing to know a man himself and another to know him from his picture. Thus to know things through their own likenesses in the mind is to know them in themselves, or in their own natures; but to know them through their likenesses pre-existing in God is to see them in God. These two knowledges are different. Hence when things are known in God by those who see his essence, they are not seen through any likeness but in the same way that God himself is known, just by the essence of God present in the mind.

Hence: 1. The mind is assimilated to what it sees in God by being united to the divine essence in which the likenesses of all things pre-exist.

2. There are some powers of knowing which from likenesses first conceived can form others—as in the imagination we can form the image of a golden mountain from those of gold and a mountain, and as in the mind from genus and difference we can form the notion of a species; likewise, from the likeness of a picture we can form a likeness of him whose picture it is. This is how St Paul or anyone else who sees the essence of God could form, from his vision of the divine essence, the likenesses of the things that he sees there—and in St Paul's case these would remain after the vision itself had ceased.

But to see things through likenesses formed in this way is not to see them as they are seen in God.

Article 10. Is all that is seen in God seen together?

THE TENTH POINT: 1. It seems that what is seen in God is not seen all at once. For Aristotle says that we may know many things but we understand only one thing at a time.[1] It is however by our understanding that we see God and hence the things we see there are understood, they cannot therefore be seen all at once.

2. Augustine says, *God moves spiritual creatures in time*[2] —i.e. he moves them to know and love. But the angel who sees God is a spiritual creature, hence since time implies succession, some who see God know and love things successively.

ON THE OTHER HAND Augustine says, *Our thoughts will not fly back and forth, first to one thing then to another, but we shall see all our knowledge in a single view.*[3]

REPLY: The things that are seen in the Word are not seen successively but together. The reason why we cannot think of many things at once is that to think of them we need many likenesses in the mind, and one mind cannot be formed by many likenesses at once, any more than a body can be many shapes at once. When many things can be thought of through one likeness—as with the parts of a whole—they can be thought of together, but when each thing requires a different likeness they can only be thought of successively. Now if all things were to be thought of through one likeness of them all, they could all be thought of together. Now it has been shown[4] that all the things seen in God are seen not each by its own likeness but by the one essence of God, hence they are seen together and not successively.

---

[1] *Topics* II, 10. 114b34
[2] *On Genesis to the letter* VIII, 20. PL 34, 388
[3] *On the Trinity* XV, 16. PL 42, 1079   [4] art. 9 above

Hence: 1. We understand one thing at a time in the sense that we understand through one concept at a time, but many things may be understood at once if they are understood through the same concept—as in understanding the concept of man we understand both animality and rationality, and in the concept of a house both walls and roof.

2. Angels in their natural knowledge (in which they know things through different concepts that are innate in them) do not know everything at once. In this sense their minds are moved through time. But in so far as they see things in God they see them all at once.

Article 11. Can any man in this life see God's essence?

THE ELEVENTH POINT: 1. It seems that a man in this life could see God in his essence. For Jacob says, *I saw God face to face.*[1] But we know from 1 Corinthians that to see God face to face means to see his essence, *Now we see in a mirror by dull reflections but then we shall see face to face.*[2] Hence it is possible in this life to see the essence of God.

2. The Lord said of Moses, *I spoke to him mouth to mouth, he saw God clearly and not through images and signs.*[3] But this is to see God in his essence. Therefore someone in this life can see God in his essence.

3. That in which all other things are known and by which all other things are judged, must be known to us through itself. But even now we know all things in God, for Augustine says, *If we both see that what you say is true, and we both see that what I say is true; where do we see this? neither I in you nor you in me, but both of us in the immutable truth itself above our minds.*[4] Again he says that *we judge things according to divine truth.*[5] Also that *the business of reason is to judge these corporeal things by incorporeal and eternal*

---

[1] *Genesis* 32:30   [2] 1 *Corinthians* 13:12   [3] *Numbers* 4:8
[4] *Confessions* XII, 25. PL 32, 840
[5] *On true religion* XXX, 31. PL 34, 146

standards, and these must be beyond the mind if they are to be immutable.[6] Hence we see God in this life.

4. Augustine says that by our intellectual vision we see what is in the soul by its essence.[7] But intellectual vision does not see intelligible things by any likeness but by their essences, as he also says in the same place. Since therefore God is in our souls by his essence, he must be seen by us in his essence.

ON THE OTHER HAND on *Exodus, No man shall see me and live,*[8] the Gloss says, *So long as we live in this mortal life we can see God by certain images, but we cannot see him by that likeness which is his very nature.*[9]

REPLY: A mere man[a] cannot see the essence of God unless he be uplifted out of this mortal life. The reason for this is that, as we have said,[10] the way in which a thing knows depends on the way it has its being. Our souls, so long as we are in this life, have their being in corporeal matter, hence they cannot by nature know anything except what has its form in matter or what can be known through such things. It is obvious, however, that the divine essence cannot be known through the natures of material things, for we have shown[11] that any knowledge of God that we have through a created likeness is not a knowledge of his essence. Hence it is impossible for the human soul, as it is in this life, to see the essence of God. An indication of this is that the more the soul is abstracted from material things the greater capacity it has for understanding abstract intelligible things. Thus divine revelations and foresights of the future come

---

[6] *On the Trinity* XII, 2. PL 42, 999

[7] *On Genesis to the letter* XII, 24. PL 34, 474

[8] *Exodus* 33:20   [9] From Gregory. PL 76, 91

[a] 'Mere man'—this phrase is used to distinguish other men from Christ who is God and man, and who had the beatific vision during his earthly life.

[10] art. 4 above   [11] art. 2 above

more often during dreams and ecstasies. It is impossible,
therefore, that the soul while it lives normally on earth should
be raised to an understanding of that which is most intelligible of all, the divine essence.

Hence: 1. As Dionysius says, in the Scriptures God is said
to be seen when certain images of the divine are formed,
whether these be sensible or imaginary.[12] When he says, *I
saw God face to face*, Jacob refers not to the essence of God
but to an image representing it. It belongs to an especially
high form of prophecy to see God represented as one speaking, even though it be only in a vision of the imagination—as
we will explain later when we speak of the degrees of prophecy.[13] An alternative explanation would be that Jacob refers
to a high and extraordinary degree of contemplation.

2. God can work miracles with minds as well as bodies,
in either case raising them beyond the normal order of things
to a supernatural level. Thus he may raise up certain minds
to see his essence in this life but not by making use of their
bodily senses. Augustine says[14] that this is what happened
to Moses, the teacher of the Jews and to St Paul, the teacher
of the Gentiles. We will deal with this more fully when we
come to speak of ecstasy.[15]

3. We see everything in God and judge everything by him
in the sense that it is by sharing in his light that we are able
to see and judge, for the natural light of reason is a sort of
sharing in the divine light. We might say in the same sense
that we see and judge all sensible things in the sun—i.e. by
the light of the sun. Hence Augustine says, *The lessons of
instruction can only be seen as it were by their own sun*,[16]
namely God. Just as we can see sensible things without seeing
the essence of the sun, so we can see things intellectually
without seeing the essence of God.

4. By intellectual vision we see what is in the soul as a
thought in the mind. God is in the souls of the blessed in

---

[12] *Heavenly hierarchy* 4. PG 3, 180   [13] 2a2æ. 174, 3
[14] *On Genesis to the letter* XII, 26. PL 34, 476
[15] 2a2æ. 175, 3   [16] *Soliloquies* I, 8. PL 32, 877

this way but not in ours. He is in us by essence, presence and power.[a]

Article 12. Can we know God by our natural reason in this life?

THE TWELFTH POINT: 1. It seems that we cannot in this life know God by natural reason. For Boethius says, *The reason cannot grasp simple forms.*[1] Now God, as has been shown,[2] is supremely a simple form. Therefore natural reason cannot attain to knowledge of him.

2. According to Aristotle the soul understands nothing by natural reason without images.[3] But since God is incorporeal there can be no image of him in our imagination. So then he cannot be known to us by natural reason.

3. Natural reason is common to the good and the bad, for human nature is common to both. Knowledge of God, however, belongs only to the good, for Augustine says, *The weak eye of the human mind is not fixed on that excellent light unless purified by the justice of faith.*[4] Therefore God cannot be known by natural reason.

ON THE OTHER HAND we read in *Romans*, *What may be known about God is manifest to them,*[5] i.e. what can be known about him by natural reason.

REPLY: The knowledge that is natural to us has its source in the senses and extends just so far as it can be led by sensible things; from these, however, our understanding cannot reach to the divine essence. Sensible creatures are effects of God which are less than typical of the power of their cause, so knowing them does not lead us to understand the whole power of God and thus we do not see his essence. They are

---

[a] cf 1a. 8, 3 above
[1] *Consolation of philosophy* v, 4. PL 63, 84   [2] 1a. 3, 7
[3] *De Anima* III, 7. 431a16
[4] *On the Trinity* I, 2. PL 42, 822   [5] *Romans* 1:19

nevertheless effects depending from a cause, and so we can at least be led from them to know of God that he exists and that he has whatever must belong to the first cause of all things which is beyond all that is caused.

Thus we know about his relation to creatures—that he is the cause of them all; about the difference between him and them—that nothing created is in him; and that his lack of such things is not a deficiency in him but due to his transcendence.

Hence: 1. The reason can know *that* a simple form is, even though it cannot attain to understanding *what* it is.

2. God is known to the natural reason through the images of his effects.

3. Knowledge of God in his essence is a gift of grace and belongs only to the good, yet the knowledge we have by natural reason belongs to both good and bad. Augustine says, *I do not now approve what I said in a certain prayer, 'O God who hast wished only the clean of heart to know truth . . .' for it could be answered that many who are unclean know many truths,*[6] i.e., by natural reason.

Article 13. *Besides the knowledge we have of God by natural reason is there in this life a deeper knowledge that we have through grace?*

THE THIRTEENTH POINT: 1. It seems that by grace we do not have a deeper knowledge of God than we have by natural reason. For Dionysius says that he who is best united to God in this life sees him as utterly unknown,[1] and he refers to Moses who received such great graces of knowledge. But by natural reason we come to know God without knowing what he is. Hence grace gives us no greater knowledge of God than does natural reason.

2. With natural reason we only come to know God through

---

[6] *Retractations* 1, 4. PL 32, 589
[1] *Mystical theology* 1. PG 3, 1001

images in the imagination. Yet the same is true of the knowledge we have through grace, for Dionysius says, *It is impossible for the divine ray to shine upon us except as screened round about by the many-coloured sacred veils*.[2] So by grace we have no fuller knowledge of God than we have by natural reason.

3. By grace our minds are united to God in faith; but faith is not knowledge, for Gregory says we have *faith and not knowledge of the unseen*.[3] Therefore grace adds nothing to our knowledge of God.

ON THE OTHER HAND St Paul says, *God has revealed to us through his Spirit*, a wisdom which *none of this world's rulers knew*[4] and a gloss says that this refers to philosophers.[5]

REPLY: By grace we have a more perfect knowledge of God than we have by natural reason. The latter depends on two things: images derived from the sensible world and the natural intellectual light by which we make abstract intelligible concepts from these images.

In both these respects human knowledge is helped by the revelation of grace. The light of grace strengthens the intellectual light and at the same time prophetic visions provide us with God-given images which are better suited to express divine things than those we receive naturally from the sensible world. Moreover God has given us sensible signs and spoken words to show us something of the divine, as at the baptism of Christ when the Holy Spirit appeared in the form of a dove and the voice of the Father was heard saying, *This is my beloved Son*.[6]

Hence: 1. Although in this life revelation does not tell us what God is, and thus joins us to him as to an unknown, nevertheless it helps us to know him better in that we are shown more and greater works of his and are taught certain

---

[2] *Heavenly hierarchy* 1. PG 3, 121
[3] *Homilies* XXVI. PL 76, 1202   [4] 1 *Corinthians* 2:8 & 10
[5] interlinear from Jerome. PL 30, 752
[6] *Matthew* 3:17

things about him that we could never have known through natural reason, as for instance that he is both three and one.

2. The stronger our intellectual light the deeper the understanding we derive from images, whether these be received in a natural way from the senses or formed in the imagination by divine power. Revelation provides us with a divine light which enables us to attain a more profound understanding from these images.

3. Faith is a sort of knowledge in that it makes the mind assent to something. The assent is not due to what is seen by the believer but to what is seen by him who is believed. In that it lacks the element of seeing, faith fails to be genuine knowledge, for such knowledge causes the mind to assent through what is seen and through an understanding of first principles.[a]

---

[a] Cajetan notes that in this life the knowledge of God through grace is not a higher *manner* of knowledge than that through reason, which offers evidence; it is higher by its *object*, see 2a2æ. 4, 8. For God's own knowledge given to the blessed in heaven as the principle of faith and *sacra doctrina* see 1a. 1, 2 & 2a2æ. 2, 3.

Question 13. Theological language

Having considered how we know God we now turn to consider how we speak of him, for we speak of things as we know them. Here there are twelve points of inquiry:

1. can we use any words to refer to God?
2. do any of the words we use express something that he is?
3. can we say anything literally about God or must we always speak metaphorically?
4. are all the words predicated of God synonymous?
5. are words used both of God and of creatures used univocally or equivocally?
6. given that they are in fact used analogically, are they predicated primarily of God or of creatures?
7. in speaking of God can we use words that imply temporal succession?
8. does 'God' mean a thing of a certain kind or a thing having a certain operation?
9. is the name 'God' peculiar to God or not?
10. when it is used of God, of what shares in divinity and of what is merely supposed to do so, is it used univocally or equivocally?
11. is 'He who is' the most appropriate name for God?
12. can affirmative statements correctly be made about God?

Article 1. Can we use any words to refer to God?

THE FIRST POINT: 1. It seems that we can use no words at all to refer to God. For Dionysius says, *Of him there is no naming nor any opinion,*[1] and we read in Proverbs, *What is his name or the name of his son if thou knowest?*[2]

2. Nouns are either abstract or concrete. The concrete

---

[1] *Divine names* 1. PG 3, 593   [2] *Proverbs* 30:4

noun is inappropriate to God because he is altogether simple; and the abstract noun is also ruled out because it does not signify a complete subsistent thing. Hence no noun can be used to refer to God.

3. A noun signifies a thing as coming under some description, verbs and participles signify it as enduring in time, pronouns signify it as being pointed out or as in some relationship. None of these is appropriate to God: we have no definition of him nor has he any accidental attributes by which he might be described; he is non-temporal and cannot be pointed to because he is not available to the senses; moreover he cannot be referred to by relative pronouns since the use of these depends on the previous use of some other referring term such as a noun, participle or demonstrative pronoun. Hence there is no way of referring to God.

ON THE OTHER HAND we read in *Exodus, The Lord is a great warrior; Almighty is his name.*[3]

REPLY: Aristotle says that words are signs for thoughts and thoughts are likenesses of things,[4] so words refer to things indirectly through thoughts. How we refer to a thing depends on how we understand it. We have seen already[5] that in this life we do not see the essence of God, we only know him from creatures; we think of him as their source, and then as surpassing them all and as lacking anything that is merely creaturely. It is the knowledge we have of creatures that enables us to use words to refer to God, and so these words do not express the divine essence as it is in itself. In this they differ from a word like 'man' which is intended to express by its meaning the essence of man as he is—for the meaning of 'man' is given by the definition of a man which expresses his essence; what a word means is the definition.[6] [a]

---

[3] *Exodus* 15:3   [4] *De Interpretatione* I, 1. 16a3
[5] 1a. 12, 11   [6] *Metaphysics* IV, 7. 1012a22
[a] *Definition* for St Thomas is not primarily the explanation of the meaning of a word, but shows forth the essence of a thing by giving its genus and difference. He thought that things were of real kinds,

Hence: 1. God is said to have no name, or to be beyond naming because his essence is beyond what we understand of him and the meaning of the names we use.

2. Since we come to know God from creatures and since this is how we come to refer to him, the expressions we use to name him signify in a way appropriate to the material creatures we ordinarily know.[7] Amongst such creatures the complete subsistent thing is always a concrete union of form and matter; for the form itself is not a subsistent thing, but that by which something subsists. Because of this the words we use to signify complete subsistent things are concrete nouns which are appropriate to composite subjects. When, on the other hand, we want to speak of the form itself we use abstract nouns which do not signify something as subsistent, but as that by which something is: 'whiteness', for example, signifies the form as that by which something is white.[b]

Now God is both simple, like the form, and subsistent, like the concrete thing, and so we sometimes refer to him by abstract nouns to indicate his simplicity and sometimes by concrete nouns to indicate his subsistence and completeness; though neither way of speaking measures up to his way of being, for in this life we do not know him as he is in himself.

3. To signify a thing as coming under some description is to signify it as subsisting in a certain nature or definite form.

---

and that one aim of science should be to construct an 'ideal language' in which the meanings of nouns would correspond to the definitions of species. Such a technical scientific language would make the order of nature more perspicuous. Sometimes he talks as though this scientific ideal had been already achieved and the meanings of the words in actual use always expressed the definition of essences.

[7] 1a. 12, 4

[b] In St Thomas's view, 'man' and 'humanity' have the same meaning and differ only in their manner of signifying, *modus significandi*. 'Humanity' does not stand for a form (or 'an abstraction') in the way that 'man' may stand for a man. Both signify the nature of man, but one signifies it concretely as instantiated, the other as that by which an instance of man occurs. cf 1a. 32, 2.

We have already said that the reason we use concrete nouns
for God is to indicate his subsistence and completeness;[8] it
is for the same reason that we use nouns signifying a thing
under some description. Verbs and participles can be used
of him although they imply temporal succession because his
eternity includes all time. Just as we can understand what is
both simple and subsistent only as though it were composite,
so we can understand and speak of the simplicity of eternity
only after the manner of temporal things: it is composite
and temporal things that we ordinarily and naturally understand. Demonstrative pronouns can be used of God in so far
as they point, not to something seen, but to something understood, for so long as we know something, in whatever way,
we can point it out. And thus according as nouns and participles and demonstrative pronouns can signify God, so in
the same way relative pronouns can be used.

*Article 2. Do any of the words we use of God ex-
press something of what he is?*

THE SECOND POINT: 1. It seems that no word is used of God
to express what he is.[a] For John Damascene says, *The words*

---

[8] reply to preceding objection

[a] The inquiry literally translated is whether words can be used of
God 'substantially'. It concerns the logical form of our statements
about God. St Thomas is not asking whether we can give an account
of the substance or nature of God, for he has already insisted that
we do not know what God is. He is asking whether we can use the
logical form of giving-an-account-of-a-nature when speaking of God.
If not, our statements about God would all have to be either negative or relational.

His main theme here is that our ignorance of God's nature is not
such that some forms of statement are admissible and others not, but
that all language is quite inadequate. Substantial predication, which
looks as if it were saying what God is, is neither more nor less appropriate than any other kind. It is the same notion that underlies
his contention that we can speak of God literally as well as metaphorically. To penetrate the mystery of God is not, for St Thomas,

used of God signify not what he is but what he is not, or his relationship to something else, or something that follows from his nature or operations.[1]

2. Dionysius says, *You will find a chorus of holy teachers seeking to distinguish clearly and laudably the divine processions in the naming of God.*[2] This means that the names which the holy teachers use in praising God differ according to his different causal acts. However, to speak of the causal activity of a thing is not to speak of its essence, hence such words are not used to express what he is.

3. We speak of things as we understand them. But in this life we do not understand what God is, and so we can use no words to say what he is.

ON THE OTHER HAND Augustine says, *The being of God is to be strong, to be wise or whatever else we say of his simplicity in order to signify his essence.*[3] All such names then signify what God is.

REPLY: It is clear that the problem does not arise for negative terms or for words which express the relationship of God to creatures; these obviously do not express what he is but rather what he is not or how he is related to something else—or, better, how something else is related to him. The question is concerned with words like 'good' and 'wise' which are neither negative nor relational terms, and about these there are several opinions.

Some have said that sentences like 'God is good', although they sound like affirmations are in fact used to deny something of God rather than to assert anything. Thus for ex-

---

like passing from metaphor to literal statement, or from negative to substantial predication, it is to pass beyond language altogether. The possibility of speaking about God rests on the possibility of using words to 'try to mean' more than we can understand by them.

[1] *Orthodox faith* I, 9. PG 94, 835
[2] *Divine names* I, 2. PG 3, 589
[3] *On the Trinity* VI, 4. PL 42, 927

ample when we say that God is living we mean that God is not like an inanimate thing, and likewise for all such propositions. This was the view of the Rabbi Moses.[4]

Others[b] said that such sentences were used to signify the relation of God to creatures, so that when we say 'God is good' we mean that God is the cause of goodness in things, and likewise in other such propositions.

Neither of these views seem plausible, and for three reasons. Firstly, on neither view can there be any reason why we should use some words about God rather than others. God is just as much the cause of bodies as he is of goodness in things; so if 'God is good' means no more than that God is the cause of goodness in things, why not say 'God is a body' on the grounds that he is the cause of bodies? So also we could say 'God is a body' because we want to deny that he is merely potential being like primary matter.

Secondly it would follow that everything we said of God would be true only in a secondary sense, as when we say that a diet is 'healthy', meaning merely that it causes health in the one who takes it, while it is the living body which is said to be healthy in a primary sense.

Thirdly, this is not what people want to say when they talk about God. When a man speaks of the 'living God' he does not simply want to say that God is the cause of our life, or that he differs from a lifeless body.

So we must find some other solution to the problem. We shall suggest that such words do say what God is; they are predicated of him in the category of substance, but fail to represent adequately what he is. The reason for this is that we speak of God as we know him, and since we know him from creatures we can only speak of him as they represent him. Any creature, in so far as it possesses any perfection, represents God and is like to him, for he, being simply and universally perfect, has pre-existing in himself the perfections of

---

[4] Moses Maimonides. *The Guide for the Perplexed* 1, 58
[b] e.g. Alan of Lille. cf PL 210, 631

all his creatures, as noted above.[5] But a creature is not like
to God as it is like to another member of its species or genus,
but resembles him as an effect may in some way resemble a
transcendent cause although failing to reproduce perfectly the
form of the cause—as in a certain way the forms of inferior
bodies imitate the power of the sun. This was explained
earlier when we were dealing with the perfection of God.[6]
Thus words like 'good' and 'wise' when used of God do
signify something that God really is, but they signify it imperfectly because creatures represent God imperfectly.

'God is good' therefore does not mean the same as 'God is
the cause of goodness' or 'God is not evil'; it means that what
we call 'goodness' in creatures pre-exists in God in a higher
way. Thus God is not good because he causes goodness, but
rather goodness flows from him because he is good. As Augustine says, *Because he is good, we exist*.[7]

Hence: 1. John Damascene says that these words do not
signify what God is, because none of them express completely
what he is; but each signifies imperfectly something that he
is, just as creatures represent him imperfectly.

2. Sometimes the reason why a word comes to be used is
quite different from the meaning of the word. Thus the word
'hydrogen' derives from what produces water, but it does not
mean something that produces water, it means a particular
chemical element, otherwise everything that produced water
would be hydrogen.[c] In the case of words used of God we
may say that the reason they came to be used derives from his
causal activity, for our understanding of him and our language about him depends on the different perfections in
creatures which represent him, however imperfectly, in his
various causal acts. Nevertheless these words are not used to
mean his causal acts. 'Living' in 'God is living' does not mean

[5] 1a. 4, 2   [6] ibid, 3
[7] *On Christian teaching* 1, 32. PL 34, 32
[c] 'Hydrogen'—a substitute for *lapis*, stone, in the Latin text, with
its unfounded and therefore distracting etymology from *lædens
pedem*, foot-injuring.

the same as 'causes life'; the sentence is used to say that life does pre-exist in the source of all things, although in a higher way than we can understand or signify.

3. In this life we cannot understand the essence of God as he is in himself, we can however understand it as it is represented by the perfections of his creatures; and this is how the words we use can signify it.

Article 3. Can we say anything literally about God?

THE THIRD POINT: 1. It seems that no word can be used literally of God. For we have already said that every word used of God is taken from our speech about creatures, as already noted,[1] but such words are used metaphorically of God, as when we call him a 'rock' or a 'lion'. Thus words are used of God metaphorically.

2. A word is not used literally of something if it would be more accurate not to use it than to use it. Now according to Dionysius it would be truer to say that God is not good or wise or any such thing than to say that he is.[2] Hence no such thing is said literally of God.

3. Words for bodily things can only be used metaphorically of God because he is incorporeal. All our words, however, belong to a bodily context, for all imply such conditions as temporal succession and composition of matter and form which belong to the material world. Therefore such words can only be used metaphorically.

ON THE OTHER HAND Ambrose says, *There are some ways of referring to God which show forth clearly what is proper to divinity, and some which express the luminous truth of the divine majesty, but there are others which are used of God metaphorically and through a certain likeness.*[3] Hence not all words are used of God metaphorically; some are used literally.

---

[1] art. 1 above   [2] *Heavenly hierarchy* 2. PG 3, 41
[3] *On faith* II, prol. PL 16, 583

REPLY: As we have said,[4] God is known from the perfections that flow from him and are to be found in creatures yet which exist in him in a transcendent way. We understand such perfections, however, as we find them in creatures, and as we understand them so we use words to speak of them. We have to consider two things, therefore, in the words we use to attribute perfections to God, firstly the perfections themselves that are signified—goodness, life and the like—and secondly the way in which they are signified. So far as the perfections signified are concerned the words are used literally of God, and in fact more appropriately than they are used of creatures, for these perfections belong primarily to God and only secondarily to others. But so far as the way of signifying these perfections is concerned the words are used inappropriately, for they have a way of signifying that is appropriate to creatures.

Hence: 1. Some words that signify what has come forth from God to creatures do so in such a way that part of the meaning of the word is the imperfect way in which the creature shares in the divine perfection. Thus it is part of the meaning of 'rock' that it has its being in a merely material way. Such words can be used of God only metaphorically. There are other words, however, that simply mean certain perfections without any indication of how these perfections are possessed—words, for example, like 'being', 'good', 'living' and so on. These words can be used literally of God.

2. The reason why Dionysius says that such words are better denied of God is that what they signify does not belong to God in the way that they signify it, but in a higher way; thus in the same passage he says that God *is beyond all substance and life.*[5]

3. These words have a bodily context not in what they mean but in the way in which they signify it; the ones that are used metaphorically have bodily conditions as part of what they mean.

---

[4] art. 2 above   [5] loc. cit.

Article 4. Are all the words predicated of God synonymous?

THE FOURTH POINT: 1. It seems, for three reasons, that all words applied to God are synonymous. For synonyms are words that mean exactly the same thing. Now whatever we say about God we mean the same thing, for his goodness and his wisdom and such-like are identical with his essence. Hence all these expressions are synonyms.

2. It might be argued that although they signify the same thing they do so from different points of view; but this will not do, for it is useless to have different points of view which do not correspond to any difference in the thing viewed.

3. One thing that can only be described in one way is more perfectly one than one thing that can be described in many ways. God is supremely one. Hence he cannot be describable in many ways, and so the many things said about him all have the same meaning: they are synonymous.

ON THE OTHER HAND piling up synonyms adds nothing to the meaning; 'clothing garments' are just the same as 'garments'. If therefore all the things said about God were synonymous it would be inappropriate to speak of 'the good God' or anything of the kind. Yet Jeremiah says, *Most strong, mighty and powerful, the Lord of Armies is thy name.*[1]

REPLY: The words we use to speak of God are not synonymous. This is clear enough in the case of words we use to deny something of him or to speak of his causal relation to creatures. Such words differ in meaning according to the different things we wish to deny of him or the different effects to which we are referring. But it should be clear from what has been said[2] that even the words that signify what God is (although they do it imperfectly) also have distinct meanings.[3]

What we mean by a word is the concept we form of what

---

[1] *Jeremiah* 32:18   [2] art. 2 above   [3] art. 1 & 2 above

the word signifies. Since we know God from creatures we understand him through concepts appropriate to the perfections creatures receive from him. What pre-exists in God in a simple and unified way is divided amongst creatures as many and varied perfections. The many perfections of creatures correspond to one single source which they represent in varied and complex ways. Thus the different and complex concepts that we have in mind correspond to something altogether simple which they enable us imperfectly to understand. Thus the words we use for the perfections we attribute to God, although they signify what is one, are not synonymous, for they signify it from many different points of view.

Hence: 1. The solution of the first objection is then clear. Synonyms signify the same thing from the same point of view. Words that signify the same thing thought of in different ways do not, properly speaking, signify the same, for words only signify things by way of thoughts, as noted above.[4]

2. The many different points of view are not baseless and pointless, for they all correspond to a single reality which each represents imperfectly in a different way.

3. It belongs to the perfection of God's unity that what is many and diverse in others should in him be unified and simple. That is why he is one thing described in many ways, for our minds learn of him in the many ways in which he is represented by creatures.

Article 5. Are words used univocally or equivocally of God and creatures?

THE FIFTH POINT: 1. It seems that words used both of God and of creatures are used univocally:[a] the equivocal is based

---

[4] loc. cit.

[a] A word is said to be used univocally when it has exactly the same meaning in different applications; it is used equivocally when it has different meanings in different applications, as with all puns. Thus 'tap' is used equivocally of a knock on the door and the thing on the barrel. Some terms, however, are designedly equivocal, because of the likeness or proportion between the quite distinct objects

on the univocal as the many is based on the one. A word such as 'dog' may be used equivocally of a hound and a fish, but only because it is first used univocally—of hounds—otherwise there would be nowhere to start from and we should go back for ever. Now there are some causes that are called univocal because their effects have the same name and description as themselves—what is generated by a man, for example, is also a man. Some causes, however, are called equivocal, as is the sun when it causes heat, for the sun itself is only equivocally said to be hot. Since, therefore, the equivocal is based on the univocal it seems that the first cause upon which all others are based must be an univocal cause, hence what is said of God and of his creatures must be said univocally.

2. There is no resemblance between things that are only equivocally the same, but according to *Genesis* there is a resemblance between creatures and God; *Let us make man in our own image and likeness*.[1] So it seems that something can be said univocally of God and creatures.

3. Aristotle says that the measure must be of the same order as the thing measured,[2] and he also describes God as the first measure of all beings. God, therefore, is of the same order as creatures; and so something can be said univocally of both.

ON THE OTHER HAND for two reasons it seems that such words must be used equivocally. First, the same word when used with different meanings is used equivocally, but no word when used of God means the same as when it is used of a creature. 'Wisdom', for example, means a quality when it is used of creatures, but not when it is applied to God. So then it must have a different meaning, for we have here a difference in the genus which is part of the definition. The same applies to other words; so all must be used equivocally.

And second, God is more distant from any creature than

---

they represent: they are called 'analogical'. Such are the proper terms about God and creatures employed by theology. cf art. 10 below

[1] *Genesis* 1:26   [2] *Metaphysics* X, 1. 1053a24

any two creatures are from each other. Now there are some creatures so different that nothing can be said univocally of them—for example when they differ in genus. Much less, therefore, could there be anything said univocally of creatures and God.

REPLY: It is impossible to predicate anything univocally of God and creatures. Every effect that falls short of what is typical of the power of its cause represents it inadequately, for it is not the same kind of thing as the cause. Thus what exists simply and in a unified way in the cause will be divided up and take various different forms in such effects—as the simple power of the sun produces many different kinds of lesser things. In the same way, as we said earlier,[3] the perfections which in creatures are many and various pre-exist in God as one.

The perfection words that we use in speaking of creatures all differ in meaning and each one signifies a perfection as something distinct from all others. Thus when we say that a man is wise, we signify his wisdom as something distinct from the other things about him—his essence, for example, his powers or his existence. But when we use this word about God we do not intend to signify something distinct from his essence, power or existence. When 'wise' is used of a man, it so to speak contains and delimits the aspect of man that it signifies, but this is not so when it is used of God; what it signifies in God is not confined by the meaning of our word but goes beyond it. Hence it is clear that the word 'wise' is not used in the same sense of God and man, and the same is true of all other words, so they cannot be used univocally of God and creatures.

Yet although we never use words in exactly the same sense of creatures and God we are not merely equivocating when we use the same word, as some have said,[b] for if this were so we could never argue from statements about creatures to

---

[3] art. 4 above
[b] The reference is to Averroes and Maimonides.

statements about God—any such argument would be invalidated by the Fallacy of Equivocation. That this does not happen we know not merely from the teachings of the philosophers who prove many things about God but also from the teaching of St Paul, for he says, *The invisible things of God are made known by those things that are made.*[4]

We must say, therefore, that words are used of God and creatures in an analogical way, that is in accordance with a certain order between them. We can distinguish two kinds of analogical or 'proportional' uses of language. Firstly there is the case of one word being used of two things because each of them has some order or relation to a third thing. Thus we use the word 'healthy' of both diet and passing water, because each of these has some relation to health in a man, the former as a cause, the latter as a symptom of it. Secondly there is the case of the same word used of two things because of some relation that one has to the other—as 'healthy' is used of the diet and the man because the diet is the cause of the health in the man.

In this way some words are used neither univocally nor purely equivocally of God and creatures, but analogically, for we cannot speak of God at all except in the language we use of creatures,[5] and so whatever is said both of God and creatures is said in virtue of the order that creatures have to God as to their source and cause in which all the perfections of things pre-exist transcendently.

This way of using words lies somewhere between pure equivocation and simple univocity, for the word is neither used in the same sense, as with univocal usage, nor in totally different senses, as with equivocation. The several senses of a word used analogically signify different relations to some one thing, as 'health' for urine means a symptom of physiological health, and for a diet means a cause of that health.

Hence: 1. Even if it were the case that in speech the equivocal were based on the univocal, the same is not true of causality. A non-univocal cause is causal by reference to an

---

4 *Romans* 1:20   5 art. 1 above

entire species—as the sun is the cause that there are men. An univocal cause, on the other hand, cannot be the universal cause of the whole species (otherwise it would be the cause of itself, since it is a member of that same species), but is the particular cause that this or that individual should be a member of the species. Thus the universal cause which must be prior to the individual cause, is non-univocal. Such a cause, however, is not wholly equivocal, for then there would be no resemblance in any sense between it and its effects. We could call it an analogical cause, and this would be parallel to the case of speech, for all univocal predications are based on one non-univocal, analogical predicate, that of being.[c]

2. The resemblance of creatures to God is an imperfect one, for as we have said,[6] they do not even share a common genus.

3. God is not a measure that is proportionate to what is measured; so it does not follow that he and his creatures belong to the same order.

The two arguments in the contrary sense do show that words are not used univocally of God and creatures but they do not show that they are used equivocally.

Article 6. Are words predicated primarily of God or of creatures?

THE SIXTH POINT: 1. It seems that the words we use of God apply primarily to creatures. For we speak of things as we know them since, as Aristotle says, words are signs for things as understood.[1] But we know creatures before we know God, hence our words apply to creatures before they apply to God.

2. Dionysius says that *the language we use about God is*

---

[c] St Thomas means that whatever we say (affirmatively) of a thing, we say that it *is* such and such. In this sense every predication, in whatever category, is a predication of being. But 'being' itself is used non-univocally, for *being* a man and *being* upside down and *being* happy are not all being in the same sense.

[6] 1a. 4, 3   [1] *De Interpretatione* 1, 1. 16a3

derived from what we say about creatures.[2] But when a word
such as 'lion' or 'rock' is transferred from a creature to God it
is used first of the creature. Hence such words apply primarily to the creature.

3. Words used of both God and creatures are used of him
in that he is the cause of all things, as Dionysius says.[3] But
what is said of something in a causal sense applies to it only
secondarily—as 'healthy' applies primarily to a living body
and only secondarily to the diet that causes its health. Hence
such words are applied primarily to creatures.

ON THE OTHER HAND we read in *Ephesians, I bow my knees to
the Father of our Lord Jesus, from whom all fatherhood in
heaven and on earth is named;*[4] and the same seems to apply
to other words used of God and creatures. These words, then,
are used primarily of God.

REPLY: Whenever a word is used analogically of many things,
it is used of them because of some order or relation they have
to some central thing. In order to explain an extended or
analogical use of a word it is necessary to mention this central
thing.[5] Thus you cannot explain what you mean by a
'healthy' diet without mentioning the health of the man of
which it is the cause; similarly you must understand 'healthy'
as applied to a man before you can understand what is meant
by a 'healthy complexion'[a] which is the symptom of that
health. The primary application of the word is to the central
thing that has to be understood first; other applications will
be more or less secondary in so far as they approximate to
this use.

Thus all words used metaphorically of God apply primarily
to creatures and secondarily to God. When used of God they
signify merely a certain parallelism between God and the

---

[2] *Divine names* 1, 3. PG 3, 596
[3] *Mystical theology* 1. PG 3, 1000   [4] *Ephesians* 3:14-15
[5] cf *Metaphysics* IV, 7. 1012a23
[a] Literally, 'the meaning of health as applied to urine'.

creature. When we speak metaphorically of a meadow as 'smiling' we only mean that it shows at its best when it flowers, just as a man shows at his best when he smiles: there is a parallel between them. In the same way, if we speak of God as a 'lion' we only mean that, like a lion, he is mighty in his deeds. It is obvious that the meaning of such a word as applied to God depends on and is secondary to the meaning it has when used of creatures.

This would be the case for non-metaphorical words too if they were simply used, as some have supposed,[b] to express God's causality. If, for example, 'God is good' meant the same as 'God is the cause of goodness in creatures' the word 'good' as applied to God would have contained within its meaning the goodness of the creature; and hence 'good' would apply primarily to creatures and secondarily to God.[c]

But we have already shown[6] that words of this sort do not only say how God is a cause, they also say what he is. When we say he is good or wise we do not simply mean that he causes wisdom or goodness, but that he possesses these perfections transcendently. We conclude, therefore, that from the point of view of what the word means it is used primarily of God and derivatively of creatures, for what the word means —the perfection it signifies—flows from God to the creature. But from the point of view of our use of the word we apply it first to creatures because we know them first. That, as we have mentioned already,[7] is why it has a way of signifying that is appropriate to creatures.

Hence: 1. This is valid so far as our first application of the words is concerned.

---

[b] e.g. Alan of Lille

[c] 'God is good' means according to St Thomas, 1a. 13, 2, that what we call goodness in creatures pre-exists in him in a higher way. Our understanding of how to use 'God is good' is a function of our understanding of goodness in creatures, but the goodness of God is not therefore a function of the goodness of creatures. In this sense 'good' as applied to God does not have contained within its meaning the goodness of the creature.

[6] art. 2 above   [7] art. 3 above

2. Words used of God metaphorically are not in the same case as the others, as we have said.[8]

3. This objection would be valid if all words were used to express the causality of God and not to say what he is, as 'healthy' expresses the causality of a diet and not what it consists in.

Article 7. In speaking of God can we use words that imply temporal succession?

THE SEVENTH POINT: 1. It seems that we cannot apply to God words that imply temporal succession, even when we are speaking of his relation to creatures.[a] It is generally agreed that such words signify what God is in himself. Thus Ambrose says[1] that 'Lord' indicates his power, but this is the divine substance, and 'creation' indicates his action—but this is his essence. But God in himself is not temporal but eternal. Hence these words are not said of him in a temporal sense but as applicable from eternity.

2. Whatever is true of a thing in a temporal sense can be said to have been brought about—what is white in a temporal sense is made white. But nothing in God could be brought about. Therefore nothing is said of him in a temporal sense.

3. If the reason why we could use words of God in a temporal sense were that such words implied a relation to creatures then the same would be true of every word that implied such a relation. Now some of these are applied as from eternity; we say, for example, that from eternity he knew creatures and loved them—*With an everlasting love have I loved thee*.[2] Hence all other words, such as 'Lord' or 'Creator', are applicable from eternity.

4. These words signify a relation, and this must be a reality in God or in the creature alone. It cannot, however, be only

---

[8] in the explanation

[a] The question is whether you can say that God began or ceased to have certain relationships to creatures.

[1] *On faith* 1, 1. PL 16, 533   [2] *Jeremiah* 31:3

in the creature, for if this were so God would be called 'Lord' in virtue of the opposite relation existing in the creature; nothing, however, is named from its opposite. The relation, therefore, must be something real in God. Yet, since he is beyond time, it cannot be temporal. Such words, then, are not used of God in a temporal sense.

5. Something is said to be relative in virtue of some relationship it has. A man is called a lord because of the lordship he has, just as a thing is called white because of the whiteness it has. If, therefore, the relation of lordship were something that God did not really have, but were merely a way of thinking of him, it would follow that God is not truly Lord, which is clearly false.

6. When the two terms of a relationship are not of the same order, one may exist without the other—for example, the knowable can exist without knowledge, as is pointed out in the *Categories*.[3] But in the case of relations between God and creatures, the two terms are not of the same order, and so something could be said relatively of God even though the creature did not exist. In this way words like 'Lord' and 'Creator' can apply to God from eternity and are not used in a temporal sense.

ON THE OTHER HAND Augustine says that the relative term 'Lord' is applicable to God in a temporal sense.[4]

REPLY: Some words that imply a relation to creatures are said of God in a temporal sense and not as applicable from eternity.

In order to explain this we must first say something about relations.[b]

---

[3] Aristotle, 7. 7b30   [4] *On the Trinity* v, 16. PL 42, 922

[b] Ordinarily St Thomas does not see a relationship as something that subsists between two terms, but as a 'towardship' in each. The translation of this article is somewhat freer than that of others. For a fuller discussion see 1a. 28, 1–3; also the disputations *On the power of God* VIII, 2.

Some[c] have said that being related to something is never a reality in nature, it is something created by our way of thinking about things. But this is false for some things do have a natural order or relation to others. Since whenever we can say of x that it is related to y, we can also say of y that it is related to x, there are three possibilities here.

Sometimes both what we say of x and what we say of y is true of them not because of any reality in them, but because they are being thought of in a particular way. Thus when we say a thing is identical with itself, the two terms of the relation only exist because the mind takes one thing and thinks of it twice, thus treating it as though it had a relation to itself. Similarly any relation between a thing and nothing is set up by the mind treating *nothing* as though it were a term. The same is generally true of all relations that are set up as part of our thinking, for instance the relation of *being a species of a certain genus*.

In the second case both what we say of x and what we say of y is true of them because of some reality in x and y. They are related because of something that belongs to both—quantity, for example, as with the relations of *being bigger than* and *being smaller than*, *being double* and *being half*, and so forth. It is the same with the relations that result from causal activity as *being what is changed by* and *being what changes*, *being father of* and *being son of* and so forth.

In the third case the truth about x that it is related to y is due to something real in x, but the truth about y that it is related to x is not due to anything real in y. This happens when x and y are not of the same order. Take, for example, the relation of *being knowable by* and *knowing* (whether we mean knowledge by the senses or by the mind). When x is knowable by y, x is not in and by itself something knowable. In so far as it exists in its own right it lies outside the order of knowledge; hence while the relation of *knowing x* is a reality in the senses or mind of y—for knowing is what makes a real difference to these—*being knowable by y* is not a reality

---

[c] Disciples of Gilbert de la Porrée.

in x. Thus Aristotle says that some things are said to be relative not because they are related to others but because others are related to them.[5] One side of the pillar is said to be the right side because it is at somebody's right hand; the relation of *being on the right of* is real in the man but not in the pillar.

Now since God is altogether outside the order of creatures, since they are ordered to him but not he to them, it is clear that being related to God is a reality in creatures, but being related to creatures is not a reality in God, we say it about him because of the real relation in creatures. So it is that when we speak of his relation to creatures we can apply words implying temporal sequence and change, not because of any change in him but because of a change in the creatures; just as we can say that the pillar has changed from being on my left to being on my right, not through any alteration in the pillar but simply because I have turned round.

Hence: 1. Some relative words signify simply a relationship, others signify that on account of which there is a relationship. Thus 'lord' says nothing more about a lord except that he stands in some relationship. To be a lord precisely is to be related to a servant—the same is true of words like 'father' and 'son' and so forth. Other relative words, however, such as 'motor' and 'moved', 'head' and 'being headed', signify something on account of which there is a relationship. Some of the words we use of God are of the first kind and some of the second. 'Lord' for instance signifies nothing but a relation to creatures, though it presupposes something about what he is, for he could not be lord without his power which is his essence. Others such as 'Saviour' or 'Creator' which refer directly to an action of God which is his essence are of the second kind and signify something on account of which he has a relationship. Both sorts of word, however, are used of God in a temporal sense in so far as they convey expressly or by implication a relation to creatures; they are not said tem-

---

[5] *Metaphysics* v, 15. 1021a29

porally in so far as they signify directly or indirectly the divine essence.

2. The relations attributed to God in a temporal sense are not real in him but belong to him as a way of speaking of him. The same is true of any becoming that we attribute to him—as when we say, Lord, thou hast become a refuge to us.[6]

3. Thinking is not something we do to other things, but remains within us, and the same is true of willing. Hence expressions signifying relations that ensue from God's thinking and willing are applied to him from eternity. When, however, they signify relations that ensue from acts which, according to our way of thinking of God, proceed from him to external effects they can be used of him in a temporal sense. This is the case with such words as 'Creator' and 'Saviour'.

4. God's temporal relations to creatures are in him only because of our way of thinking of him, but the opposite relations of creatures to him are realities in the creatures. It is quite admissible to attribute a relation to God because of something that takes place in the creature, for we cannot express the reality in creatures without talking as though there were matching relations also in God, so that God is said to be related to a creature because the creature is related to him, just as, according to Aristotle, the knowable is said to be related to knowledge because knowledge is related to it.[7]

5. God is related to creatures in so far as creatures are related to him. Since the relation of subjection to God is really in the creature, God is really Lord. It is the relationship of lordship in him that is supplied by our minds, not the fact of his being the Lord.

6. When we ask whether the terms of a relation are of the same order or not, we are not asking about the things that are said to be related but about the meaning of the relative words used. If one entails the other and vice versa then they are of the same order—as with being double and being half of or with being father of and being son of. If, however, one entails the other but not vice versa then they are not of the

---

6 Psalms 89:1   7 Metaphysics v, 15. 1021a30

same order. This is the case with *knowing* and *being knowable by*. For x to be knowable by y it is not necessary that y should be knowing x; it is sufficient that it should have the power to know x. Thus 'being knowable' signifies intelligibility as something prior to actual knowledge. If, however, we take 'being knowable' to mean being actually here and now intelligible, then it is coincident with the actual exercise of knowledge, for a thing cannot so be known unless someone is knowing it. In a parallel way although God is prior to creatures (as being knowable is prior to knowing) since 'x is lord of y' and 'y is subject to x' entail each other, *being lord of* and *being subject to* are of the same order. Hence God was not lord until he had a creature subject to him.

Article 8. Does 'God' mean a thing of a certain kind?

THE EIGHTH POINT: 1. It seems that 'God' does not mean a being of a certain kind. For John Damascene says that *God (theos) is derived from theō, which means to take care of or foster all things; or else from aithō, which means to burn— for our God is a fire burning up all wickedness; or from Theaomai, which means to consider all things.*[1] All these refer to activity. Hence 'God' means an activity, not a thing.

2. We name things as we know them. We do not know what kind of thing God is. Therefore the name 'God' cannot signify what he is.

ON THE OTHER HAND Ambrose says that 'God' is a name signifying the divine nature.[2]

REPLY: What makes us use a word is not always what the word is used to mean. We come to understand what a thing is from its properties and its behaviour, and often it is from

---

[1] *Orthodox faith* I, 9. PG 94, 835. The reference is to *Deuteronomy* 4:24.

[2] *On faith* I, 1. PL 16, 553

some piece of its behaviour that we take our name for the
sort of thing it is. Thus the word 'hydrogen' is derived from
the fact that this gas when burnt produces water, but the
word does not mean something that produces water but a
particular sort of gas.[a] Things that we recognize immediately
like heat or cold or whiteness are not named from anything
else, and so in their case what makes us use the word is the
same as what it is used to mean.

Now God is not known to us in his own nature, but through
his works or effects, and so, as we have seen,[3] it is from these
that we derive the language we use in speaking of him. Hence
'God' is an operational word in that it is an operation of God
that makes us use it—for the word is derived from his universal providence: everyone who uses the word 'God' has in
mind one who cares for all things. Thus Dionysius says, *The
Deity is what watches over all things in perfect providence
and goodness.*[4] But although derived from this operation the
word 'God' is used to mean what has the divine nature.

Hence: 1. Everything John Damascene says here refers to
divine Providence, which is what makes us use this word in
the first place.

2. The meaning of the name we give to something depends on how much of its nature we understand from its
properties and effects. Since from its properties we can understand what a stone is in itself, the word 'stone' signifies the
nature of the stone as it is in itself. Its meaning is the definition of a stone, in knowing which we know what a stone is;
for *what a word means is the definition.*[5] But from divine
effects we do not come to understand what the divine nature
is in itself, so we do not know of God what he is. We know
of him only as transcending all creatures, as the cause of their
perfections and as lacking in anything that is merely creaturely, as already noted.[6] It is in this way that the word 'God'
signifies the divine nature: it is used to mean something that

---

[a] see note *c* art. 2 above   [3] art. 1 above

[4] *Divine names* XII, 1. PG 3, 969

[5] *Metaphysics* IV, 7. 1012a23   [6] 1a. 12, 12

is above all that is, and that is the source of all things and is distinct from them all. This is how those that use it mean it to be used.

Article 9. Is the name 'God' peculiar to God alone?

THE NINTH POINT: 1. It seems that 'God' is not peculiar to God, but can be used of other things. For whatever shares in what a name signifies can share in the name, but we have just said[1] that 'God' signifies the divine nature and this is something that can be communicated to others, according to Peter, *He has bestowed upon us precious and very great promises . . . that by this we may become partakers of the divine nature.*[2] Hence 'God' may be applied to others besides God.

2. Only proper names are altogether incommunicable. But 'God' is not a proper name as is clear from the fact that it can be used in the plural, as in the *Psalm, I say you shall be gods.*[3] Hence the word 'God' is applicable to many things.

3. The name 'God' is applied to God, as we have just seen,[4] because of his operations. But other words that are used of God because of his operations such as 'good', 'wise' and such-like, are all applicable to many things. So 'God' is as well.

ON THE OTHER HAND we read in *Wisdom, They gave the incommunicable name to sticks and stones,*[5] and the reference is to the name of the Godhead. Hence the name 'God' is incommunicable.

REPLY: A noun may be used of many things in two ways, either properly or by metaphor. It is properly used of many when the whole of what it means belongs to each of them; it is used metaphorically when some part of what it means belongs to each. The word 'lion', for example, properly speaking applies only to the things that have the nature it signifies,

---

[1] art. 8 above   [2] II *Peter* 1:4   [3] *Psalms* 81:6
[4] art. 8 above   [5] *Wisdom* 14:21

but it is also applied metaphorically to other things that have
something of the lion about them. The courageous or the
strong can be spoken of in this way as 'lions'.

To understand which nouns properly speaking apply to
many things we must first recognize that every form that is
instantiated by an individual either is or at least can be
thought of as being common to many; human nature can be
thought of, and in fact is, common to many in this way; the
nature of the sun, on the other hand, can be thought of as
being, but in fact is not, common to many. The reason for
this is that the mind understands such natures in abstraction
from the individual instances, hence whether it be in one
individual or in many is irrelevant to our understanding of
the nature itself; given that we understand the nature we can
always think of it as being in many instances.

The individual, however, from the very fact of being individual, is divided from all others. Hence a word that is used
precisely to signify an individual cannot be applicable to
many in fact, nor can it be thought of as applicable to many.
It is impossible to think that there could be many of this
individual. Hence no proper name is properly speaking communicable to many, though it may be communicable through
some resemblance—as a man may metaphorically be called
'an Achilles' because he has the bravery of Achilles.

But consider the case of forms which are not instantiated
by being the form of an individual, but by themselves (inasmuch as they are subsistent forms). If we understood these
as they are in themselves it would be clear that they are not
common to many in fact and also cannot be thought of as
being common to many—except perhaps by some sort of resemblance as with individuals. In fact, however, we do not
understand such simple self-subsistent forms as they are in
themselves, but have to think of them on the model of the
composite things that have their forms in matter. For this
reason, as we said earlier,[6] we apply to them concrete nouns
that signify a nature as instantiated in an individual. Thus

---

[6] art. 1 ad 2 above

the nouns we use to signify simple subsistent natures are grammatically the same as those we use to signify the natures of composite things.

Now 'God' is used, as we saw,[7] to signify the divine nature, and since this nature cannot have more than one instance,[8] it follows that from the point of view of what is in fact signified, the word cannot be used of many, although it can mistakenly be thought of as applying to many—rather as a man who mistakenly thought there were many suns would think of 'sun' as applying to many things. Thus we read in *Galatians*, *You were slaves to gods who by nature were not gods*, and a gloss says, *not gods by nature but according to the opinion of men*.[9]

Nevertheless the word 'God' does have several applications, though not in its full meaning. It is applied metaphorically to things that share something of what it means. Thus 'gods' can mean those who by resembling God share in some way in the divine, as in the *Psalm*, *I say you shall be gods*.[10]

If, however, a name were given to God, not as signifying his nature but referring to him as this thing, regarding him as an individual, such a proper name would be altogether incommunicable and in no way applicable to others—perhaps the Hebrew name of God, the Tetragrammaton[a] was used in this way: it would be as though someone were to use the word 'Sun' as a proper name designating this individual.

Hence: 1. The divine nature can be communicated to others only in the sense that they can share in the likeness of God.

2. 'God' is a common noun and not a proper name because it signifies in the concrete the divine nature, although God himself is neither universal nor particular. We do not,

---

[7] art. 8 above   [8] 1a. 11, 3

[9] *Galatians* 4:8. Interlinear gloss. PL 192, 139

[10] *Psalms* 81:6

[a] The word of four consonants, especially the Hebrew word YHWH, vocalized as *Yahweh*, the ineffable name of God, for which, in reading, the Jews used as a substitute, *Adonai*, Lord. cf below art. 11 ad 1

however, name things as they are in themselves but as they are to our minds. In actual fact the name 'God' is incommunicable rather as we said of the word 'Sun'.[11]

3. Words like 'good' and 'wise' are applied to God because of the perfections that flow from God to creatures. They do not mean the divine nature, they mean these perfections; and so not only can they be thought of as applicable to many things but they actually are in fact. But the word 'God' is applied to him because of the operation peculiar to him which we constantly experience, and it is used to signify the divine nature.

Article 10. Is the name used in the same sense of God, of what shares in divinity, and of what is merely supposed to do so?

THE TENTH POINT: 1. It seems for three reasons that 'God' is used univocally of what has the divine nature, what shares in this nature and what is supposed to have it. For when men have not the same meaning for the same word they cannot contradict each other, equivocation eliminates contradiction. But when the Catholic says, 'The idol is not God', he contradicts the pagan who says, 'The idol is God', hence 'God' is being used univocally by both.

2. An idol is supposed to be God but is not so in fact, just as the enjoyment of the delights of the flesh is supposed to be felicity but is not so in fact. But the word 'happiness' is used univocally of this supposed happiness and of true happiness. So also the word 'God' must be used univocally of the supposed and the real God.

3. A word is used univocally when its meaning is the same. But when the Catholic says there is one God he understands by 'God' something almighty, to be revered above all things, but the pagan means the same when he says that his idol is God. Hence the word is used univocally in the two cases.

---

[11] in the explanation

ON THE OTHER HAND for two reasons it seems that the word is used equivocally. What is in the mind is a sort of picture of what is in reality, as is said in *De Interpretatione*,[1] but when we say 'That is an animal', both of the real animal and of the one in a picture, we are using the word equivocally. Hence the word 'God' used of the real God and of what is thought to be God is used equivocally.

5. A man cannot mean what he does not understand, but the pagan does not understand the divine nature, so when he says, 'The idol is God', he does not mean true divinity. But when the Catholic says that there is one God he does mean this. Hence 'God' is used equivocally of the true God and of what is supposed to be God.

REPLY: The word 'God' in these three cases is used neither univocally nor equivocally but analogically. When a word is used univocally it has exactly the same meaning in each application, when it is used equivocally it has an entirely different meaning in each case, but when it is used analogically its meaning in one sense is to be explained by reference to its meaning in another sense. Thus to understand why we call accidents 'beings' we have to understand why we call substances beings; and we need to know what it means for a man to be healthy before we can understand a 'healthy' complexion, or a 'healthy' diet, for such a complexion is indicative and such a diet is productive of the health that belongs to a man.

It is the same with the case we are considering. For we have to refer to the use of 'God' to mean the true God in order to explain its use in application to things that share in divinity or which are supposed to be gods. When we say that something is a 'god' by sharing in divinity we mean that it shares in the nature of the true God. Similarly when we say that an idol is a god, we take this word to mean something that men suppose to be the true God. Thus it is clear that while 'God' is used with different meanings one of these

---

[1] *De Interpretatione* 1. 16a5

meanings is involved in all the others; the word is therefore used analogically.

Hence: 1. We say a word has different uses not because it can be used in different statements but because it has different meanings. Thus the word 'man' has one meaning and one use whatever it is predicated of, whether truly or falsely. It would be said to have several uses if we meant it to signify different things—if, for instance, one speaker used it to signify a man and another to signify a stone or something else. Thus it is clear that the Catholic, when he says the idol is not God, is contradicting the pagan who affirms that it is, for both are using 'God' to signify the true God. When the pagan says 'The idol is God' he is not using 'God' to mean that which is merely supposed to be God; if he were he would be speaking truly, as the Catholic does when he sometimes uses the word in that way, e.g., 'All the gods of the pagans are demons'.[2]

2, 3. The same reply can be made to the second and third objections, for these arguments have to do with the different statements that can be made with a word, not with a difference in meaning.

4. As to the fourth argument which takes the opposite point of view: the word 'animal' is not used wholly equivocally of the real animal and the animal in the picture. Aristotle uses the word 'equivocal' in a broad sense to include the analogical;[3] thus he sometimes says that 'being' which is used analogically, is used equivocally of the different categories.

5. Neither the Catholic nor the pagan understands the nature of God as he is in himself, but both know him as in some way causing creatures, surpassing them and set apart from them, as we have said.[4] In this way when the pagan says, 'The idol is God' he can mean by 'God' just what the Catholic means when he declares, 'The idol is not God'. A man who knew nothing whatever about God would not be

---

[2] *Psalms* 95:5   [3] *Categoriæ* 1, 1a1   [4] 1a. 12, 12

able to use 'God' at all, except as a word whose meaning he did not know.

Article 11. Is 'He who is' the most appropriate name for God?

THE ELEVENTH POINT: 1. It seems that 'he who is' is not the most appropriate name for God: the name 'God' is incommunicable, as we have said,[1] but the name 'He who is' is not. Therefore it is not the most appropriate name for God.

2. Dionysius says, *To call God good is to show forth all that flows from him.*[2] But what is supremely characteristic of God is to be the source of all things. Therefore the most appropriate name for God is 'The Good' rather than 'He who is'.

3. Every name of God should imply some relation to creatures since he is only known to us from creatures. But 'He who is' implies no such relation. It is not then the most appropriate name for God.

ON THE OTHER HAND we read in *Exodus* that when Moses asked, *If they ask me, What is his name? what shall I say to them?* the Lord replied, *Say this to them, He who is has sent me to you.*[3] Therefore 'He who is' is the most appropriate name for God.

REPLY: There are three reasons for regarding HE WHO IS as the most appropriate name for God.

Firstly because of its meaning; for it does not signify any particular form, but rather existence itself. Since the existence of God is his essence and since this is true of nothing else, as we have shown,[4] it is clear that this name is especially appropriate to God, for the meaning of a name is the form of the thing named.

---

[1] art. 9 above [2] *Divine names* III, 1. PG 3, 680
[3] *Exodus* 3:13 & 14 [4] 1a. 3, 4

Secondly because of its universality. All other names are either less general or, if not, they at least add some nuance of meaning which restricts and determines the original sense. In this life our minds cannot grasp what God is in himself; whatever way we have of thinking of him is a way of failing to understand him as he really is. So the less determinate our names are and the more general and simple they are, the more appropriately they may be applied to God. That is why Damascene says, *The first of all names to be used of God is* HE WHO IS *for he comprehends all in himself, he has his existence as an ocean of being, infinite and unlimited.*[5] Any other name selects some particular aspect of the being of the thing, but HE WHO IS fixes on no aspect of being but stands open to all and refers to him as to an infinite ocean of being.

Thirdly it is appropriate because of its tense: for it signifies being in the present and this is especially appropriate to God whose being knows neither past nor future, as Augustine says.[6]

Hence: 1. 'He who is' is more appropriate than 'God' because of what makes us use the name in the first place, i.e., his existence, because of the unrestricted way in which it signifies him, and because of its tense, as we have just said.[7] But when we consider what the word is used to mean, we must admit that 'God' is more appropriate, for this is used to signify the divine nature. Even more appropriate is the Tetragrammaton[a] which is used to signify the incommunicable and, if we could say such a thing, individual substance of God.

2. 'The Good' is a more fundamental name for God in so far as he is a cause, but it is not simply speaking more fundamental, for to be is presupposed to being a cause.

3. The names of God need not necessarily imply a relation to creatures; it is enough that they should come to be used because of the perfections that flow from God to creatures,

---

[5] *Orthodox faith* 1, 9. PG 94, 836

[6] *On the Trinity* v, 2. Peter Lombard, 1 *Sentences* 8.

[7] in the explanation   [a] cf art. 9 above, note *a*

and of thcsc thc primary one is existence itself, from which we get the name 'He who is'.

Article 12. Can affirmative propositions be correctly formed about God?

THE TWELFTH POINT: 1. It seems that affirmative propositions cannot correctly be made about God. For Dionysius says, *Negative propositions about God are true, but affirmative ones are loose.*[1]

2. Boethius says, *A simple form cannot be a subject.*[2] But God supremely is a simple form, as noted above,[3] hence he cannot be a subject. But whatever an affirmative proposition is about is its subject, therefore we cannot make such propositions about God.

3. Whenever the way something is understood is other than the way that it is we have error. Now God is altogether without composition in his being, as has been proved,[4] since therefore an affirmative statement is a conjoining of subject and predicate it would seem that they cannot be made about God without error.

ON THE OTHER HAND what is of faith cannot be false. Now some affirmative propositions are matters of faith, as for example that God is three and one and that he is almighty. Therefore some true affirmative propositions can be made about God.

REPLY: In every true affirmative statement, although the subject and predicate signify what is in fact in some way the same thing, they do so from different points of view. This is true not only of statements in which the predicate means something that only happens to belong to the subject, it is also true of those in which it expresses part of what the subject is. Thus it is clear that in 'a man is white' although 'man'

---

[1] *Heavenly hierarchy* 2. PG 3, 140
[2] *On the Trinity* II. PL 64, 1250   [3] 1a. 3, 7   [4] ibid

and '(a) white'[a] must refer to the same thing, they do so in different ways, for 'man' and 'white' do not have the same meaning. But it is also true for a statement such as 'man is an animal'. That which is a man is truly an animal: in one and the same thing is to be found the sensitive nature which makes us call it an animal and the rational nature which makes us call it a man.

There is even a difference in point of view between subject and predicate when they have the *same* meaning, for when we put a term in the subject place we think of it as referring to something, whereas in the predicate place we think of it as saying something about the thing, in accordance with the saying 'predicates are taken formally (as meaning a form), subjects are taken materially (as referring to what has the form)'.

The difference between subject and predicate represents two ways of looking at a thing, while the fact that they are put together affirmatively indicates that it is one thing that is being looked at. Now God considered in himself is altogether one and simple, yet we think of him through a number of different concepts because we cannot see him as he is in himself.

But although we think of him in these different ways we also know that to each corresponds a single simplicity that is one and the same for all. The different ways of thinking of him are represented in the difference of subject and predicate; his unity we represent by bringing them together in an affirmative statement.

Hence: 1. Dionysius says that what we assert of God is loose (or, according to another translation, 'incongruous') because no word used of God is appropriate to him in its way of signifying, as we have remarked.[5]

2. Our minds do not understand simple forms as they are in themselves, but as though they were concrete things in

---

[a] *Albus* here is used as we might use 'white' in speaking of the 'whites' in South Africa.

[5] 1a. 13, 6

which there is duality of the thing and the form that it has. In this way we treat simple forms as though they were subjects to which something can be attributed.

3. In the sentence, 'When the way something is understood is other than the way it is, we have error', 'other than' can refer either to the thing understood or the way of understanding. Taken in the former sense the proposition means that when a thing is understood to be in a way other than it is, we have error. This is true but irrelevant, for when we make propositions about God we do not say that he has any composition, we understand him to be simple. If, however, we take 'other than' to apply to the way of understanding then the proposition is false, for the way of understanding is always different from the way the thing understood is. It is clear, for example, that our minds non-materially understand the material things inferior to them; not that they understand them to be non-material, but that we have a non-material way of understanding. Similarly when our minds understand the simple things superior to them we understand them in our own way, that is on the model of composite things; not that we understand the simple things to be composite, but that composition is involved in our way of understanding them. Thus the fact that our statements about God are composite does not make them false.

APPENDIX 1

THE *SUMMA* AND THE BIBLE

1. IN THE first question of the *Summa* the terms holy teaching, *sacra doctrina*, and holy Scripture, *sacra scriptura*, are synonymous: this was common usage at a time when a master of theology or doctor of divinity was still called a *magister in sacra pagina*. Among his contemporaries Robert Kilwardby equated theology and Scripture, and St Albert spoke indiscriminately of holy Scripture, theology, and theological science, all three standing for the teaching we receive from God. Our attitude is not that of listening and then prepared to work things out for ourselves, but quite simply of taking what God tells us. So then, based on this obedience, Christian theology argues from authority. This is its characteristic to the highest degree, *maxime proprium*.[1]

Authority then still kept its original sense; it meant more the power of originating, giving, begetting, and cherishing, than of imposing an external pattern or of legally authorizing; *auctoritas* and *fontalitas* go together.[2] Later those writers or writings accepted as being authentically in the tradition and entitled to credit were called *auctoritates*; they could be appealed to even on matters that in theory could be allowed to speak for themselves, though such recourse was the weakest form of argument, *locus ab auctoritate infirmissimus*. On matters, however, beyond our ken where God speaks to us this was the proper method above all others for Christian theology.

Chief among these *auctoritates* are the canonical books of Scripture; indeed they alone are acknowledged as providing 'inside' and incontrovertible support, 'inside' because their thoughts are the thoughts of the Church, developed without

---

[1] 1a. 1, 8 ad 2
[2] 1a. 33, 4 ad 1. 3a. 16, 11; 55, 5. 2a2æ. 98, 3. 1 *Sent.* 29, 1, 1

addition or embroidery by the discourse of theology,[3] incontrovertible because they declare the word of the Lord. Holy doctors are witnesses who speak from within the living tradition of revelation; they are in the stream of the Church's own consciousness and, therefore, like the Scriptures, their writings can also provide 'inside' or 'proper' authorities. They do not, however, have the force of Scripture, or represent a final court of appeal; arguments based on them are 'probable', not conclusive, 'for our faith rests on the revelation made to the Prophets and Apostles, and not to others'. Last of all the writings of sages who neither belong to the specifically Christian tradition nor touch its mysteries may be treated as 'outside' authorities serving to recommend or confirm the conclusions come to by *sacra doctrina*.[4]

2. The place of Scripture is paramount in the *Summa*. A close and detailed familiarity with the letter and many of its senses is evident throughout. St Thomas's text was the Latin Vulgate according to the early thirteenth-century Paris exemplar; it seems likely that he consulted the corrected version, the Jacobin Bible, edited in his own community of Saint-Jacques. He included *Wisdom, Ecclesiasticus, Judith, Tobias,* and *Machabees,* on the principle that although their authenticity might be doubted their canonicity was warranted by their reception by the Church. He is not among the first rank of Biblical scholars of his time; his métier was not philology and he knew no Hebrew and the scantiest Greek, though he could have learned both languages from the Italian circles in which he moved. His own great commentaries, on St John's Gospel and the Epistles of St Paul, are directly theological in intention.

3. To appreciate the place of Scripture in theology—or more justly the place of theology in Scripture—according to St Thomas two extremes are to be avoided; on one side, of treating the Bible as the sole rule of faith, or as its systematic statement, or as a catalogue of the truths necessary for sal-

---

[3] *Summa*, Blackfriars, Vol. 1, Appendix 9, *Doctrinal Development*
[4] 1a. 1, 8 ad 2. Blackfriars, Vol. 1, Appendix 7, *Revelation*

vation, or as the title-deeds or charter of incorporation for the Christian Church giving chapter and verse for every item of its teaching, sacraments, and government; on the other side, of separating the sources of Christian teaching into two, namely Scripture and Tradition, even though their streams, like the Mississippi and Missouri, commingle. Both contain a truth, the first that objective revelation was completed with the Scriptures in the Apostolic Age, the second, that the Scriptures are silent about some necessary religious truths, for instance, about what in fact are the canonical books.

What are the precise relations between Scripture and Tradition is still an open question for discussion; here we content ourselves with some observations on how the position appears in the *Summa*. To treat the holy books as contemporary and alive in the Church is constant practice, and that theology, or holy teaching, draws the power of its arguments from them is never doubted. Furthermore, there is but one single body of doctrine, not an amalgamation of two, one a fabric of written law and the other more tenuously composed of unwritten custom, yet this single body displays a variety of phases, functions, and disciplines. It is not that part is scriptural and part traditional, for, as we shall see, all is Scripture and all is Tradition; to understand this coincidence of wholes in one situation we should refer back to St Thomas's theory of subordination.[5] Revelation was complete with the last of the Apostolic writings. The whole substance of its saving truth is to be found in the Bible. All the same this as a document is not a literary curiosity, born out of due time; it does not articulate every truth of revelation according to the needs and styles of later ages. Doctrines can be elicited from it without the warrant of a narrowly legalist or philological exegesis. This does not imply that the Church can improvise truths as it goes along, or tap undisclosed reserves. On the contrary the Church is grounded on the fact and content of Biblical revelation, and draws on the memory of this, so maintaining the identity of its thoughts. Dogmas are defined

---

[5] ibid, Appendix 6, *Theology as Science*

from the Church's dwelling on the Scriptures in mind and heart, not because another system of reference is invoked.[6]

4. Let us consider some representative passages from St Thomas, first about the unsystematic character of the holy Scriptures—not a shapelessness, but a power too deep to be formal, an appeal too wide to be bound by the etiquette of logic;[7] secondly about the factors determining the definition of doctrines from its richness when the Church, *the scribe instructed in the kingdom of heaven, is like a householder who bringeth forth out of his treasure new things and old.*[8]

When discussing the need of drawing up the articles of faith in a creed St Thomas raises the objection that holy Scripture is the rule of faith, which permits neither of addition nor of subtraction. He replies that 'holy Scripture contains the truths of faith spread out, *diffuse,* and in various manners, some of them obscure, so that to elicit them requires protracted application and schooling, *longum studium et exercitium,* beyond the opportunities of the majority of people occupied with other business. Nevertheless all must know the truth of the Christian faith. Hence there should be a plain statement concisely put together, *summarie colligeretur,* from what the Scriptures tell us, and this should be proposed for everybody's belief. Such a creed is not added to Scripture, but drawn from it.'[9]

If then there is nothing in the creeds that is not contained in holy Scripture, it will follow also that there is nothing in *sacra doctrina,* which as a science is based on the premises of faith, of which holy Scripture is not the source.

5. Next we inquire into why headings for belief are to be drawn from Scripture. Recall that the *Summa* treats objective *revelatio, sacra scriptura,* and *sacra doctrina* as co-extensive, for all three are about the same truth and truths. The distinction between them comes from our side, and lies

---

[6] ibid, Appendix 9, *Doctrinal Development*

[7] ibid, Appendix 5, *Sacra Doctrina.* Appendix 13, *Biblical Inspiration*

[8] *Matthew* 13:52   [9] 2a2æ. 1, 9 ad 1

in the different phases of closeness and clearness of the human mind with respect to God's truth. To this the mind comes by successive stages,[10] in which process the plan will appoint and promulgate this or that article to be expressly believed according to the situation;[11] more are given to us than to our ancestors, more to those in full visible communion with the Church than to others.

When inquiring whether the things we believe should be marked out in distinct articles, St Thomas puts the argument that we should have faith in all the things contained in Scripture, and these because of their multitude cannot be compressed into a limited series of statements.[12] He replies, 'that of the things to be believed some of themselves belong to faith, whereas others are purely subsidiary, for, as happens in any branch of knowledge, some matters are its essential interest, while it touches on others only to make the first matters clear. Now because faith is chiefly about the things we hope to see in heaven, *for faith is the first beginning of things hoped for,*[13] it follows that those things directly bearing us to eternal life essentially belong to faith; such are the three Persons of almighty God, the mysteries of Christ's incarnation, and other like truths. These are the heads for distinguishing the articles of faith. Some things, however, are proposed in holy Scripture, not as being the main matters of faith, but to bring them out; for instance, that Abraham had two sons, that a dead man came to life at the touch of Elisha's bones, and other like matters narrated in Scripture to disclose God's majesty or Christ's incarnation. These do not provide headings for the articles of faith.'[14]

Later on he picks up the same distinction and applies it to explicit belief. This we must have for the essential articles of faith, but not for the incidental and secondary matters contained in the Scriptures handed down to us. These we must accept by implication, *implicite,* or in readiness, *in præpara-*

---

[10] 2a2æ. 1, 2

[11] 2a2æ. 2, 5–8. For promulgation see 1a2æ. 90, 4.

[12] 2a2æ. 1, 6 obj. 1   [13] *Hebrews* 11:1   [14] 2a2æ. 1, 6 ad 1

tione animi, in that we are prepared to accept what divine Scripture tells us; only then are we held to explicit faith in them when we recognize as an established fact that they are entailed in the teaching of faith.[15]

6. Secondly, he touches on the principle of selection determining what truth from Scripture is to be put in the creed and so become an article or essential matter of faith. *Ubi occurrit aliquid speciale ratione non visum,* where a thing has a special quality of being unseen there a special *difficultas* occurs calling for a special effort of faith.[16] For instance, that our Lord was born of a virgin, that he was crucified, and that he rose again from the dead sound distinct notes, and therefore, unlike 'suffered, was crucified, dead, and buried' which all involve one another, are set forth in distinct articles. This formula, of a special *difficultas* or challenge setting up a new tension for a determinate act of faith, applies also when dissensions arise about the meaning of a point of faith and the Church must bring itself to an authoritative definition.[17] *I beseech you that there be no divisions among you, but that you be perfectly joined together in the same mind and in the same judgment.*[18] The degree of clarity and definition that is called for will depend on the psychological climate of the period and also on the temperaments of those caught up in the controversy: after all, under Providence the crisis has to be resolved then and there in current terms, and, although the definition is for posterity, a later generation of theologians may not themselves experience the urgency which gave that particular formula its edge.

7. Faith can cover everything in *sacra doctrina,* and this, as we have seen, is wider than the style of discourse adopted by scholastic theology and deeper than assents to propositions.[19] It implies so many concepts—Revelation, the deposit of faith, the living Gospel, the holy Scriptures, Tradition, theology both biblical and scholastic, all distinct, but not to be divided.

---

[15] 2a2æ. 2, 5   [16] 2a2æ. 1, 6   [17] 2a2æ. 1, 9 ad 2; 10
[18] 1 *Corinthians* 1:10
[19] *Summa,* Blackfriars, Vol. 1, Appendix 5, *Sacra Doctrina*

Revelation is the Word breathing Love, given to us and born in our physical world and in our minds and hearts, bringing us into God's presence and grace.[20] This revelation has been made to us not so much in the intimacy of the personal life (though this is the scene of the drama of acceptance or rejection) as in the life we share with God's people. We live it in and through the community which is now the body of Christ. It is declared by the deeds and words of God in a series of disclosures that closed with the Apostolic Age, leaving behind what is called (though not in the Middle Ages) the deposit of faith, or revelation in the objective sense. This is the παραθήκη,[21] committed to the stewardship of the Church, for its handing on, *traditio*, until the end of the world.

Faith, which is our response to the divine deed and the deposit that is left, does not stop at an initial assent of mind, but works through love, ἀγάπη,[22] and commits the whole person, who thereby does not shrink from affirmations on determinate points of truth or decisions on particular points of practice.[23] In doing so there is no consciousness of forsaking the premises of faith, but rather of extending them into an ever-widening field. They are not to be hoarded like a treasure. They are to be spent, on ourselves and others, though, like the widow's cruse, never diminished.[24] To hold the Christian faith is neither to adopt a vague and generalized outlook nor to hug a specialized secret. It is to be involved, body and soul, in the world blessed by God's incarnation. Reflections on the deposit of faith will be among the consequences, and these will be meditations on the words of God in Scripture. They will not remain either unformed or embryonic; they will take shape and be developed in our thoughts according to the processes of theology. These processes will not represent the lonely speculations of individuals however

---

[20] 1a. 8, 3; 43, 2, 3, 5, 6

[21] I *Timothy* 6:20; II *Timothy* 1:14

[22] *Galatians* 5:6. 2a2æ. 2, 2; 4, 3, 4, 7. Appendix 3, *The Dialectic of Love in the Summa*

[23] 2a2æ. 1, 2, 6; 2, 5   [24] III *Kings* 17:16

holy or eminent, but will have the social assurance of being conducted in the mind of the Church and being guarded by the unfailing witness promised by our Lord.

That at one stage the development presents conclusions arrived at by deduction will of course be more noticeable in scholastic and systematic theology, which starts from the articles of faith, than in biblical and liturgical theology, which is less abstractly engaged and takes the fact of revelation in the round. When the holy Scriptures, which form a wider, richer, more imaginative and more affectively-toned manifold than a compendium of doctrines in a creed, are the constant and immediate place of reference, then a type of theology develops which manifests a looser organization, employs methods more symbolic, rhetorical, and dramatic, and observes rules of evidence less severe than is the case with the intellectualism of scholastic theology.

The two theologies, biblical and scholastic, should not be separated, for they are complementary. Both are translations into different psychological media, or rather, expansions at different levels within man's single substance of the Gift of the Word and of the Spirit. Clearly the first is wider; which is the deeper need not be considered. Both at their best will be fused together, as in the *Summa*. Perhaps only in recent years have we recovered the sense of how profoundly Scriptural St Thomas's theology is, and redressed the balanced tilted by commentators and manualists of, let us say, a Cartesian temper of thought, who loaded the sacred ideology at the expense of the sacred historiography.

The heart of all Christian theology is the living Gospel, called by St Thomas the *lex evangelii* or *lex nova*.[25] How far it escapes from juridical conditions appears from his treatment,[26] when after long discussions on the details of the Old Law[27] he breaks out into this stirring overture to his questions on grace.[28] If we attend to its themes we shall be the better able to relate the words of the Bible and of the

---

[25] 1a2æ. 106 Prol.   [26] 1a2æ. 106–8   [27] 1a2æ. 98–105
[28] 1a2æ. 109–14

formularies of faith. Both compose the teaching of the Church, through which the Word continues to speak to us.

The Gospel Law is the *message of Christ ministered to us, written not with ink but with the spirit of the living God, not in tables of stone but in the fleshly tables of the heart.*[29] We are not merely told how to live, we are given the life; the Gospel is the only law which justifies, *of works? no, but of faith.*[30] In it the grace of the Spirit is overruling, *potissimum*, and foremost, *principale*; the Scriptures and documents of the faith are secondary, contributing method and order without themselves being the heart of the matter. *The letter killeth, the spirit giveth life;*[31] although the anarchism of the Joachimites was in the air, St Thomas followed St Augustine in taking the letter to mean any piece of writing existing outside us, even the moral precepts contained in the gospels.[32] If this be true of the written gospels even more is it true of the other canonical books; for the New Testament, though contained in the Old as a species in a genus—or as fruit in a thorn-tree—is higher and freer and less burdened with ceremonial and legalistic observances.[33]

8. The holy books or sacred Scriptures as such are not, then, the living Gospel; they are a sign, *sacramentum*, but not the thing, *res*, the written form, not the living revelation. *You search the scriptures for in them you think you have eternal life; they are they which testify of me.*[34] In this sense St Thomas stresses how Scripture is serviceable, *utilis*, ὠφέλιμος,[35] but is not an end in itself, for this is Christ; as Simon Peter confessed, *Lord, to whom shall we go? Thou hast the words of eternal life.*[36]

Consequently the complete source of *sacra doctrina* is not the collected sum of the scriptural texts themselves but divine revelation, delivered to the Church and embodied in holy Scripture. This revelation cannot be reduced to the senses that may be discovered by a detached scholarship

---

[29] II *Corinthians* 3:3   [30] *Romans* 3:27
[31] II *Corinthians* 3:6   [32] 1a2æ. 106, 1, 2
[33] 1a2æ. 107, 1, 2, 3, 4   [34] *John* 5:39
[35] *In* II *Tim.* 3, lect. 3   [36] *John* 6:69

working on its documentary remains, valuable though this approach certainly is; its meaning is found where it was given, conceived, and brought forth, that is in the mind of the Church. The meaning too of the holy books which contain it must be looked for in the same body, in and by which they were written. Promised by the prophets in the Scriptures, proclaimed by the mouth of Jesus Christ, the Gospel in its purity was committed to the Apostles as the source of all saving truth and moral instruction.[37] The revelation was then complete, and so it continues through the Church's memory to the Church's present consciousness and expectation of the future. No truth is added when it is unfolded in men's understanding, yet it is rather with the Biblical 'fact' than with the propositions of the Biblical record that dogmatic teaching is charged.[38] *For there are also many things which Jesus did, the which, if it should be written every one, I suppose even the world itself could not contain the books.*[39]

The Council of Trent speaks of the Church's written books and unwritten traditions,[40] but these last are Apostolic traditions; they are not of later origin, or described as sources of doctrine apart or diverse from Scripture. Theologians differ, and St Thomas is not precise, about the correlations between doctrinal definition and scriptural exegesis, yet the question comes into focus once you accept that the Church thinking traditionally is the Church thinking scripturally. The Scriptures as documents were written in the past, even so they are still alive and speaking; their full force, however, is not that of an immortal classic of literature, but as confronting us, as much now as ever in the past, as God's eternal covenant with his people. Similarly the Church's Tradition, which is not to be confused with ecclesiastical traditions however venerable, is apostolic preaching centred on the Gos-

---

[37] cf Council of Trent, Session IV. Denzinger 783

[38] *Summa*, Blackfriars, Vol. 1, Appendix 9, *Doctrinal Development*

[39] John 21:25   [40] Denzinger 783

pel and on nothing else, according to our Lord's charge, *Go and teach all nations, teaching them to keep all things whatsoever I have commanded you, and behold I am with you always, even to the end of the world.*[41]

---

[41] *Matthew* 28:19–20

APPENDIX 2

THE DIALECTIC OF LOVE
IN THE *SUMMA*

1. TAKE THE *Summa* as a text-book and you will find it professedly 'argumentative',[1] following the style of explanatory, not affective, theology. Yet the purpose is to help the whole man in living communion with God, not just to stock his mind with right ideas on the subject. In the first question St Thomas makes the first of his references to a way of perception closer to things, if more confused, than the notional knowledge acquired by rational study; there he speaks of judgment by bent, *per modum inclinationis*, in contrast to judgment by inquiry, *per modum cognitionis*.[2] Elsewhere he refers to this flair for the reality behind and the promise beyond abstract conceptualization as a sure discernment by kinship, *propter connaturalitatem*, rather than by the application of reasoning, *secundum perfectum usum rationis*; as a recognition rising from natural attraction rather than reached by rational choice, and setting up a relationship as it were of marriage, *affinitas*; as a familiarity from habit or second nature, *secundum habitualem dispositionem*, and physical disposition rather than from an effort of attention; as sympathy, *compassio*, and undergoing, *patiens*, rather than learning about, *discens*; as acting with instinctive sureness rather than with reflective certitude; as sharing in God's absolute and simple knowledge rather than reaching the truth through ratiocination; as a prompting, *instinctus*, touching, *contactus*, and real union; as a being made like, *assimilatio*, in an experience charged with love, *cognitio affectiva sive experimentalis*.[3]

---

[1] 1a. 1, 8 [2] ibid 6 ad 3
[3] III *Sent.* 35, 2, 1, 1; 33, 3, 3, 2 ad 2. 1a. 43, 5 ad 2. 1a2æ. 49,

Here is a judgment, not disinterested, but more committed, almost, one might say, partisan. Variously inflected according to the context in the *Summa* the burden is constant, that the mind can be loaded with knowledge deeper and wider than the forms represented in clear consciousness and that a reaching out to a thing, *appetitus, orexis*, distinct from the intaking movement of cognition, acts as the principal influence in effecting a union of knower and *thing*-known too intimate to be evaluated in rational terms. This perception, which will be discussed in touching on the Gifts of the Holy Ghost,[4] the effects of love,[5] and rapture,[6] is introduced here because the living discourse of Christian theology moves in the world of grace and depends on a loving intercourse with divine things, so much so that without devotion theology is like the faith from which it starts, which if *without works is dead*.[7]

For theology, as we have seen,[8] is not a rarified science, where inquiries are conducted with a proper air of detachment at a high level of abstraction. The medium in which it moves, the element in which it breathes, is God's saving revelation, and this is a continuous deed as well as a plan that will last until the end of the world; moreover its object is God's own substance, not merely the explanation of reality.[9] Allowing for the methodological need of treating surfaces and sections one at a time, also for the asceticism of logical discipline forbidding us to rush to conclusions but to keep the proper pauses in exposition, all things for theology are, or should be, entertained at depth and in the round, since they enter only as related to God.[10] Only? Indeed no divisive abstraction is implied, as though their being held in this relationship were but one aspect of them, not their complete being as it really is. For God's creative action produces the

---

3, 4; 57, 1; 68, 1 ad 4, 4 ad 3. 2a2æ. 9, 1 ad 1; 18, 4; 24, 11; 30, 1 ad 2; 45, 2; 97, 2 ad 2

[4] 1a2æ. 68–70. 2a2æ. 8–9; 15; 45–6   [5] 1a2æ. 28

[6] 2a2æ. 175   [7] *James* 2:17

[8] *Summa*, Blackfriars, Vol. 1, Appendix 6, *Theology as Science*

[9] 1a. 1, 1 ad 2; 3; 7   [10] 1a. 1, 7

whole of a thing, and the persons of the blessed Trinity take
up their abode as known and loved in the whole of a created
person.[11] Consequently mere thinking about God, however
exact and sustained, remains incomplete theology unless
charged with *dilectio*, or choosing to be in love with God as
he is in himself.[12] The putting of his creatures into an ordered scheme is scarcely more than theologico-legalism, an
administrative preliminary for getting to know them at a
deeper level, to hold theologically, and to mourn for their
creatureliness when separated from God, and to be comforted when that is taken into his society.[13]

2. The acceptance of the premises of theology by faith sets
a tone that continues throughout the discourse, and there the
proximate psychological determinant is appetitive, not cognitive. 'By the habit of faith we are moved by way of willing
not of understanding; it enables us to assent voluntarily without compulsion, though not to see what is believed.'[14] This
act of will, when arrested at an abstract moment in the genesis of Christian activity, is not yet the full love of God, since
faith is prior to charity and the other supernatural virtues.
Moreover, since sinners do not necessarily lose their faith, it
can remain as dead faith, *fides informis*, even when friendship with God has been broken because we have loved something else more, though not to the point of disbelieving or
denying his truth. Nevertheless living faith, *fides formata*,
quickened by charity and impelled by the understanding and
knowledge which are gifts of the Spirit, is faith in its typical
condition, an act in the body of Christ and setting the standard even for sick members.[15] 'All should reach to the measure
of faith proposed in the Creed by the activity of their living
faith. All the same a man with dead faith does not lie when
he professes the Creed, for this he does in the person of the
Church.'[16] A sinner is no hypocrite for subscribing to a truth

[11] 1a. 45, 3, 4; 43, 3
[12] 2a2æ. 27, 1, 3, 4, 5. 1a. 8, 3   [13] 2a2æ. 10, 4
[14] *In De Trin.* III, 2 ad 4   [15] 2a2æ. 4, 3, 4, 7
[16] III *Sent.* 25, 1, 2 ad 4

he does not carry into practice; if, while he is in that condition, he does not share in the loving life of the Church he is not altogether excluded from its promise. 'The profession of faith contained in the Creed, which is for all believers, is delivered in the person of the Church, and this is a loving and living faith, such as is found in all persons who worthily belong to the Church. With this sense is faith charged in the Creed, so that those of the faithful who lack this loving belief should try to attain it.'[17] Not faith alone but also the theological development of faith is an activity within the Church, and as for validity theology must think with the mind of the Church, since it is not a private exploration, so for completeness it must love with the heart of the Church.[18]

3. Faith, then, and the theology deriving from it cannot be appreciated apart from the total situation of his people being taken into the life of God. The Word and the Spirit of Love are sent to us, and all the words of the science of faith and all affections within divine friendship are so many echoes and refractions of their presence.[19] Mind and will are not divided, and the full meaning of theology is perceived only by those who are in love with divine things; *no man can say Jesus is Lord except in the Holy Ghost*.[20]

St Thomas goes to St Augustine, who lays his finger on the origins of this interplay of science and devotion. 'By grace the soul is made like to God, and therefore when a divine Person is sent there is implied a being made like to him by some gift of grace. Now because the Holy Spirit is Love, the soul becomes like to him through the gift of charity; consequently, love in the manner corresponds to the sending of the Spirit. Similarly because the Son is word, not any kind of mental utterance, but Word breathing Love, St Augustine says that the word he is proposing to consider is conceived

---

[17] 2a2æ. 1, 9 ad 3
[18] *Summa*, Blackfriars, Vol. 1, Appendix 5, *Sacra Doctrina*. Appendix 7, *Revelation*
[19] 1a. 6, 4; 14, 8; 34, 3; 37, 2 ad 5; 43, 5, 6; 1a2æ. 109, 1, 2; 2a2æ. 23, 2, 7, 8.
[20] I *Corinthians* 12:3

in company with love.[21] Consequently, what matches the sending of the Son to us is not any quality of mind, but that constitution or construction whereby the mind breaks forth into loving affection; as St John says, *Every man that hath heard, and learnt of the Father cometh to me*,[22] and the psalmist, *In my meditation a fire shall flame out*.[23] Therefore Augustine significantly remarks that, the Son is sent to somebody when he is known and perceived—perception here denoting real experience, *experimentalem quandam notitiam*.[24] And this is properly called wisdom, *sapientia*, as it were, relished science, *sapida scientia*.'[25]

Before turning to the loving experience of conclusions from faith through the working of the Spirit in the gift of knowledge, *donum scientiæ*,[26] let us first consider how love can modify knowledge.

Love-Knowledge

4. The question belongs largely to psychology. Here the guiding principle, often repeated by St Thomas, is that the active human subject is the whole person, the psycho-physical unity of an individual substance, and that we should guard against an exaggerated 'faculty-psychology' which makes powers or habits into 'manikins' by speaking of the mind doing this or the will doing that, of faith assenting to God and charity whole-heartedly loving him.[27] These powers and virtues are real, but they are not the thing engaged; they are qualities or modifications, *accidentia*, of the substance, for in creatures actual activity is distinct though not separable, from the power of acting, and the power of acting is not identical with their very being or substance.[28] When St Thomas's scientific psychology draws distinctions between

---

[21] *De Trinitate* IX, 10. PL 42, 969
[22] *John* 6:45   [23] *Psalms* 38 (39):4
[24] *De Trinitate* IV, 20. PL 42, 907   [25] 1a. 43, 5 ad 2
[26] Par 11 below
[27] 1a. 76, 1, 3, 4, 8. 1a2æ. 17, 4. 2a2æ. 58, 2
[28] 1a. 54, 1

these powers and virtues, the singleness of the acting substance is also maintained.

The acting subject is a substance, so also is the object for which it acts. Certainly this thing can wear different aspects or manifest the various 'formal objects' which differentiate the various powers that reach to it, for as something to be known it is not as such something to be loved,[29] and as something to be known it can exhibit different interests for different types of knowing, and as something to be loved it may be an end in itself to be valued, *bonum honestum*, or enjoyed, *bonum delectabile*, or a means to an end to be used, *bonum utile*,[30] nevertheless in activity the fundamental relationship is between thing and thing, and for human beings a polarization between person and person.

5. The only two general types of activity that we need consider here are knowledge and love, *cognitio* and *appetitio*. Now we are about to notice how at present the tug of real things on us is more strongly exercised through our love of them than through our knowledge, always observing our first guiding principle, that knowing and loving are not twin things or acting causes, but a doubled expression of one and the same thing or substance. Not only are they rooted in one single subject, but also as specific activities they can enter into one another: how intimately appears in the difference between merely registered and emotionally-toned sensation. The interpenetration can be even subtler and deeper between intelligence and will. So much so 'that Aristotle leaves it open to doubt whether choice is appetitively cognitive or cognitively appetitive'.[31] This interplay is studied at length in the analysis of a typical human act:[32] the conclusion in brief is that mind puts meaning into love, will puts movement into knowledge.[33]

6. Truth follows the intake of things by mind, and is, therefore, subject to the limitations of the knower. Because of the limitations attending the human mind in its present

[29] Notes *o* to 1a. 1, 1, *c* to 1a. 1, 3, *c* to 1a. 1, 7
[30] 1a. 5, 6. 1a2æ. 11, 3; 16, 3   [31] 1a. 83, 3   [32] 1a2æ. 8–17
[33] 1a. 82, 4. 1a2æ. 9, 1

condition truth is directly expressed as general, not particular; as common, not particular; as abstract, not concrete; as partial, not complete; in a mode representational, not original; as prosaically explained, not lyrically possessed; as an intermediate, not ultimate achievement of mind. On all these counts the profound impulse of its desire, *appetitus naturalis*, is disappointed. Lift 'meaning' to its status in the most elevated philosophy, and even beyond, to its existence in a world of bodiless forms or pure essences, and still the mind will not be content.[34] Such, however, is the satisfaction of 'meaning' that *cognitio* alone could almost stay with 'quiddity', or the answer to its question 'what?', but for the inner drive, the load of immortality, towards the thing behind the meaning. This drive is continued in the will towards the thing now presented as good as well as true. The will waits on the concepts proposed by the mind, yet they are needed more for the shaping, *specificatio*, than for the energizing, *exercitium* of desire.

'For loving draws us more to things than knowing does, since good is found by going to the thing, whereas the true is found when the thing comes to us.'[35] Love wants the substance, not the idea or form, the thing, not the thought of the thing.[36] It is on this desire for the ultimate thing that St Thomas founds his argument for the vision of God.[37] And it is the same desire that will not leave theology content to remain inside any formal system it may construct: *If any one thirst let him come to me, and let him who believes drink; as the Scripture says, out of him shall flow rivers of living water*.[38]

7. Love, then, supplies for a lack in knowledge in its human and rational condition in the lowest rank of intelligence, where its reception of intelligible forms can be compared to the reception of physical forms by *materia prima* in the lowest rank of reality.[39] Yet knowledge as such has not this lack,

---

[34] 1a2æ. 3, 6 & 7
[35] 1a. 5, 1, 2; 16, 1, 3, 4; 1a2æ. 22, 2. *De veritate* XXII, 4 ad 1
[36] *De veritate* XXII, 3 ad 4   [37] 1a. 12, 1; 1a2æ. 3, 8
[38] *John* 7:37–38   [39] 1a. 55, 2; 84, 6

for knower and known are one; Cajetan's formula, the knower is the known, seems preferable to that of John of St Thomas, the knower has the form of the known.[40] And given sheer knowledge unmixed with restricting factors the knower is the knowing and the knowing is the known, and the knower is the lover and the lover is the loving and the loving is the be-loved.[41] Only in creaturely knowledge is there an apartness, and it is this, which in human knowledge can be divisive and abstract, that calls for the uniting and adhering force of love, *vis unitiva et concretiva*.[42] The will can prompt the mind to know, yet not as remaining external to the mind, for love can flow into knowing, and bring there, as it were, its own reasons or motives; as the scholastics say, love can be not only *movens*, but also *specificans*.[43]

8. Then knowing and loving mutually include one an-other.[44] Before applying this to faith and theology let us glance at another instance of a fusion of knowledge and love. This is the response to the beautiful, *pulchrum*, καλόν, where the coincidence of the true and the good is intimately if inarticulately experienced.[45] Poetic experience offers a useful analogue to mystical experience (and the other way round, for saints have been more informative than poets in their retrospective accounts of preterrational processes, perhaps be-cause some of them have been trained in propositional sci-ence); neither, incidentally, should be regarded as abnormal or rare, for artists and saints are not special kinds of men or Christians, and all men, by nature and by grace, have it in them to respond to beauty or to God's presence. Significantly St Thomas's longest passage on æsthetics occurs in his com-mentary on the *De Divinis Nominibus* of the Pseudo-Dionysius, a neo-Platonist work that was a major influence on the writings of the mystical theologians in the Middle Ages. There he studies the chapter 'on the good, light, the beauti-

---

[40] *In 1am.* 14, 1   [41] 1a. 14, 4 & 8; 16, 5; 19, 1 & 4; 26, 2
[42] *CG* 1, 91. *In De Div. Nom.* IV, *lect.* 12
[43] See Par 10 below
[44] 1a. 16, 4 ad 1   [45] 1a. 5, 4 ad 1. 1a2æ. 27, 1 ad 3

ful, love, ecstasy, ardour, *zelus*, *zelos*.[46] Characteristically he does not slur over the note of mind, for the *pulchrum* is the *formosum*, manifested to intelligence in handsomeness, shapeliness, and radiance, *integritas*, *proportio*, *claritas*.[47] All the same this note is carried by a melodic line—as the chapter-title indicates—which moves from desire for the object single beneath its complexity to a delight that does not turn from one feature to another but rests in the whole thing as it is in itself.

9. What may then be called the existential impact of love on knowledge is also studied by St Thomas when, not confining himself to his plan of considering them as emotions or feelings, *passiones*, he treats of love and pleasure in wider terms.[48] He recognizes that love is more unitive than knowledge in seeking the thing, not the thing's reason; its bent is to a real union, though this can be constituted only by knowledge.[49] Other effects of love are enumerated: a reciprocal abiding, *mutua inhæsio*, of lover and beloved together; a transport, *extasis*, out of the self to the other; an ardent cherishing, *zelus*, of another; a melting, *liquefactio*, so that the heart is unfrozen and open to be entered; a longing in absence, *languor*, heat in pursuit, *fervor*, and enjoyment in presence, *fruitio*.[50] In delight, too, there is an all at once wholeness and timelessness that reflects the *tota simul* of eternity;[51] an edge of sadness similar to that of the Gift of Knowledge;[52] an expansion of spirit;[53] a complete fulfilment of activity without satiety, *for they that drink shall yet thirst*.[54]

These references to a somewhat neglected part of the *Summa* are worth consulting in order to catch some of the implications of a grace-given knowledge, affective as well as

---

[46] *In De Div. Nom.* iv, *lect.* 5–6, 8–10

[47] 1a. 39, 8. 2a2æ. 180, 2 ad 3   [48] 1a2æ. 26–34. 1a2æ. 29, 5

[49] 1a2æ. 26, 2 ad 2; 27, 2; 28, 1, 3, 4   [50] 1a2æ. 28, 2, 3, 4, 5

[51] 1a2æ. 31, 1, 2; 32, 2; 10, 1   [52] 1a2æ. 32, 4. 2a2æ. 9, 4

[53] 1a2æ. 33, 1   [54] 1a2æ. 33, 2. *Ecclesiasticus* 24:29

speculative, that fosters and is fostered by the love of God.[55]
*Now thanks be unto God who maketh manifest the savour of
his knowledge.*[56] 'Between ordinary science-knowledge and
faith-knowledge,' St Thomas comments, 'there is this difference. The first shines only on the mind, showing that God
is the cause of everything, that he is one and wise and so
forth, whereas the second enlightens the mind and warms the
heart, telling us that God is also saviour, redeemer, lover,
made flesh for us. Hence the savour of this knowledge, and
the fragrance spread far and wide. *Behold the scent of my
son is as of a field which the Lord hath blessed.'*[57]

10. The main difficulty in describing this experience is
that love lacks its own proper vocabulary; only by metaphor
are its motions translated into fixed meanings taken from
cognition not appetition.[58] For love, as already remarked,
does not stay with a meaning; taking up where knowledge
leaves off, indeed outstripping its requirements, we can love
better than we know,[59] and so, though we know God imperfectly and mediately in faith, we can love him perfectly
and immediately in charity.[60] In heaven the knowledge in
part will be done away with, yet the same love will remain.[61]

Nevertheless scholastic authors are sensitive—how sensitive
may come as a surprise to those who rate them arid—to the
straining of love at and into meaning and beyond. Love is
said to be discerning because it causes discernment in the
reason.[62] That however can be taken as a minimum description, of a man naturally seeking to know more about what
attracts him. The authors mean more than that love is a
stimulus working on knowledge, they are fascinated by its
working into knowledge; they mean that a thing can be perceived in and through the medium of the love-attraction or

---

[55] 1a. 64, 1   [56] II *Corinthians* 3:14
[57] *In* II *ad Cor.* 2, *lect.* 3. *Genesis* 27:27
[58] 1a. 27, 4; 28, 4; 36, 1
[59] 1a. 82, 3. 2a2æ. 27, 4 ad 1. *De veritate* XXII, 11 ad 5, 7
[60] 2a2æ. 26, 1 ad 1; 27, 3–6   [61] I *Corinthians* 13:8–13
[62] 2a2æ. 27, 2 ad 1

the love-possession, as well as in and through the concepts
formed by the mind; for instance when a crisis of chastity is
resolved in instincts of modesty and honour which are parts
of the habit rather than by the criteria of moral science.[63]
Again, when a man divines that he is in grace from the signs
that God is his love, the assurance is enough though the object is dark and the purely cognitive evidence is absent.[64]
*For I am not conscious to myself of anything, yet am I not
hereby justified, but he that judgeth me is the Lord.*[65]

The classical treatment of this question is found in John
of St Thomas.[66] He says in effect that the will applies itself
and our other faculties to activity by efficient causality. That
however is not enough for the love-knowledge arising from
sanctifying grace, where the will plays a second rôle as well,
namely of applying itself to the object, for that is its bent
and the want and burden of its nature. So appetite passes
into the very condition of the object, and in the experience
acts on the mind as a content-giving cause, *in genere causæ
objectivæ*. Purely rational exposition can go little farther.
John of St Thomas writes less drily than his master, yet the
full baroque of his style may perhaps be found better fitted
to describe the swirl of the experience, turbid rather than
limpid, to be expressed in terms of touch rather than of sight,
and of feeling rather than of sense.[67] Vallgornera, a younger
master of the period—it was that of Crashaw's hymn to St
Teresa—gives a list of names for it; 'Contemplation, rapture,
melting, being transformed, union, exultation, jubilation, to
be wrapped in darkness, to taste, embrace, kiss, to conceive
and bear, to be brought into the wine-cellar, to be drunk, to
follow a scent, to hear a call, to enter into the bedchamber,
to sleep in peace, and take your rest.'[68] Such also is the lan-

---

[63] 2a2æ. 45, 2; 144, 1; 145, 1–3

[64] 1a2æ. 112, 5   [65] 1 *Corinthians* 4:4

[66] *Cursus Theologicus in* 1am2æ. Disp. 18, art. 4

[67] 1a. 78, 3

[68] *Theologia mystica S. Thomæ* 1, 1. The subtitle—the Prince of
both theologies, scholastical and mystical—opens a division not found
in the *Summa*.

guage of the mystics, and of the Scriptures. *O taste, and see that the Lord is sweet.*[69]

The Gift of Science

11. St Thomas's doctrine of the Gifts of the Holy Ghost treats them as the complement of the theological and cardinal virtues. Virtues act in a human manner but they are touched by the gifts with superhuman genius.[70] As John of St Thomas puts it, by the virtues we walk, by the Gifts we fly. As held by faith the truths of God are now wrapped up in a human manner, but by the gifts they are the objects of more godlike contemplation.[71] It is not that more things are known, but that things are better known. The two Gifts directly corresponding to faith are Understanding and Knowledge;[72] their culmination in Wisdom is assigned to charity.[73] All three operate through love, and reach a perception unlike that of purely speculative knowledge in not being mediated by concepts.

Yet they take their names, *intellectus* and *scientia,* and their likenesses from two intellectual virtues. As theoretical understanding is the insight into first principles and definitions evident to the natural light of reason below the flow of experience so the Gift of Understanding by the light of grace, and by instinct not through clear ideas, recognizes the import of faith beneath the words and symbols of the creeds, and discerns, as it were, the 'what' of faith beneath them.[74] Thus the risen Lord in the inn at Emmaus *opened the understanding of the disciples, that they might understand the Scriptures. Thus it is written, and thus it behoveth Christ to suffer and to rise from the dead the third day.*[75] The Gift goes below the surface, *the Spirit searcheth the deep*

---

[69] *Psalms* 33:9

[70] 1a2æ. 58, 1, 2. CG III, 89, 92. 1a. 82, 4 ad 3. 1a2æ. 9, 4; 80, 1 ad 3; 109, 2 ad 1, 3a. 7, 2 ad 2

[71] III *Sent.* 35, 2, 1, 1 ad 1   [72] 2a2æ. 8 Prol.   [73] 2a2æ. 45
[74] 2a2æ. 8, 1, 2   [75] *Luke* 24:45–46

things of God,[76] to a depth only those in grace and love with God may reach. St Augustine attributes it especially to the clean of heart,[77] and St Thomas calls its opposite a blindness of mind and dullness of sense about spiritual and eternal good.[78]

Similarly the Gift of Knowledge matches the reasoned knowledge, ἐπιστήμη, that develops from natural intelligence, νοῦς. One might quite simply identify it with the science of theology, *scientia fidei*, but that it operates by instinct rather than by discourse; nevertheless it is certainly an indispensable part of theology. Nor is it precisely the 'science' enumerated by St Paul among the special graces, which enables the possessor to set out, recommend, and defend divine truths,[79] but rather a sure judgment in forming conclusions about the things which derive from God. One might almost call them the little things, dear but lesser than God. Moreover, short of the culmination of this Gift in the Gift of Wisdom, they are assessed and prized in themselves rather than in God.[80] It is a knowledge through compassion, συμπάθεια, a suffering with them without affectation of patronage. Such is the bitter-sweet blessing on the theologian, and particularly the scholastic theologian, who often seems called upon to work so far from his premises, taxing his patience and perhaps ours. For while he keeps his tenderness for all things real—*what God hath cleansed do not thou call common*[81]—and is sounding the heart of creatureliness and practising the asceticism demanded by any advanced technique, let him be warmed by the promise *to them that mourn, for they shall be comforted.*[82]

---

[76] 1 *Corinthians* 2:10   [77] cf 2a2æ. 8, 4, 5, 7

[78] 2a2æ. 15, 1, 2

[79] 1 *Corinthians* 12:8. 2a2æ. 9, 1 ad 1, 2; 177, 1

[80] 2a2æ. 9, 2 ad 3; 45, 1   [81] *Acts* 10:15

[82] *Matthew* 5:5. 2a2æ. 9, 4

APPENDIX 3

NATURAL AND SUPERNATURAL

THE FIRST question announces the theme, a harmony of nature and grace, reason and faith, to which the *Summa* will frequently recur; not, however, without paradox.

1. For St Thomas is simultaneously Aristotelean and Augustinian in his discourse about grace: not sometimes the one and sometimes the other, but both together; not oscillating between ill-matched propositions, but consistently and continuously. At the outset you may well wonder how the naturalism he shares with Aristotle, the respect for the movement from within things which would bear them to their ends, a movement which in the case of man points to the vision of God, can be reconciled with the thoroughgoing anti-Pelagianism that nothing we can do of ourselves will set us on the road there. Can worldliness accord with the heroism of holiness?

On the one hand he has been attacked for intruding nature into the economy of salvation; contemporaries secured his condemnation for fusing man's reason with earthiness, and later theological writers, emphasizing the challenge, indeed the affront, Christianity offers to nature, have found his rationalism lacking, to put it mildly, in religious awe and reverence. On the other hand, in the great controversies on grace during the sixteenth and seventeenth centuries his support would have been looked for more by those who preached justification by faith alone than by those who preached justification through works. He himself would not have allowed that the issue was accurately stated or that the alternatives were really exclusive, for as already noted, causes in subordination are not either-or cases:[1] in retrospect his school seems

---

[1] *Summa*, Blackfriars, Vol. 1, Appendix 6, *Theology as Science*. Appendix 9, *Doctrinal Development*

to stand on a position of somewhat lonely eminence, at once
denying Jansenism and maintaining that man's health is entirely God's free gift and mercy.

2. The clue is found in the double meaning of 'natural'
according to St Thomas's usage, namely the 'specific' and the
'intrinsic'.

The first draws a picture of an ordered universe divided, as
it were, by horizontal strata occupied by things according to
their kind; to take a simplified example, vegetable, animal,
human, angelic, and divine can be ranged at superimposed
levels. What is proper or natural to a higher is supernatural
relatively to a lower, and its form or quality is possessed because it is imparted, *per participationem*, not because it belongs there by nature, *per essentiam*. In this sense a nature
is constituted by its specific form and, in keeping with the
Latin genius and indeed with the Roman *gravitas*, the world
of natures is seen composed of things drawn up according to
their due position, settled rank, and status in planned discipline.

The second picture is full of movement. The lines, as it
were, are vertical, ascending through progressively realized
stages from lower to higher, or descending through diverse
degrees of participation: the evolution is epitomized in man
where the rational takes over the animal, and the animal takes
over the vegetable, and the vegetable takes over the merely
corporeal.[2] And the divine takes over the rational. The feeling, more Greek than Latin, Aristotelean than Platonic, biological than typological, is that parts within the universe are
open to one another. They communicate internally on the
ladder of Jacob's dream, *set up on earth and the top reaching to heaven*.[3] The hierarchies of Dionysius are in motion,
and all come to a head in the promise to Nathanael, *You shall
see heaven wide open, and God's angels ascending and descending upon the Son of Man*.[4] Hence the emphasis of
definition is on end, *telos*, the purpose of a thing in process,
rather than form, and if on form then rather as the inner

---

[2] 1a. 76, 3–6   [3] *Genesis* 28:12   [4] *John* 1:51

shaping principle, *morphē*, than as the thing's figuration, *eidos*, at a fixed moment of observation. The notion of a thing's nature becomes less enclosed; it is the principle of a thing's own appetite, the inner spring of its activity for what is not itself.[5]

3. St Thomas notes and accepts both senses of the word nature,[6] and uses a duel system of references in consequence. When 'nature' indicates a thing's specific constitution, then the world-order is ranked according to different kinds and modes of being, each with their appropriate kinds or modes of activity. In this respect things are typologically fixed, and the lower cannot of itself pass into the higher; sense of itself cannot evolve into reason, or reason into angelic intelligence, or angelic intelligence cannot reach to the mind of God.[7] In this connection we may note that even the God of philosophy does not, as it were, represent the highest layer of reality, since he is beyond all classification,[8] and his activity is not that of a first or initial cause within a series of causes.[9]

When set in this diagram of natures in gradation, our sharing in God's life by grace is termed supernatural, and beyond the unaided power of any creature.[10] When, however, 'natural' points to the principle of motion from within, then in the case of living things spontaneous activity is released, which in the case of intelligent things issues into voluntary activity in its full sense.[11] Then the *naturale* means the *voluntarium*, and as an intrinsic motion is contrasted, not with the supernatural, but with the *violentum*, or compulsion by an extrinsic force,[12] and with the *artificiale*, or imposed pattern of action.[13] In the light of internal finality a theology of salvation avoids the rhetoric which makes grace look menacing to nature, or merely though impressively legal, or a powerful

---

[5] *In Physic.* III, *lect.* 1 (III, 1. 200b10)   [6] 3a. 2, 1

[7] 1a. 12, 4   [8] 1a. 3, 5

[9] 1a. 44, 1; 45, 2; 104, 1; 105, 5

[10] 1a2æ. 109, 2, 3, 5; 110, 1. *Summa*, Blackfriars, Vol. 1, Appendix 5, *Sacra Doctrina*

[11] 1a2æ. 6, 1, 2   [12] 1a2æ. 6, 5

[13] 1a2æ. 21, 2 ad 2. CG II, 23, 75, 89

convention of the super-ego, or preternatural, or queer. That *wisdom reacheth from end to end mightily and ordereth all things sweetly*[14] was a favourite text with St Thomas to show the connatural working of grace within us.[15] The foundations of heaven are not laid on the ruins of earth.

4. This background to the relations of faith and reason goes to explain how he can be so firm on the distinction between them yet refuse an abrupt separation. They do not exclude one another, on the contrary, for if reason can operate without faith, faith cannot operate without reason; hence his confidence that science remains science when suffused by revelation, just as sensation and emotion are none the worse but better off when caught up by intelligence and friendship. The supernatural does not derogate from the natural, but witnesses to our human dignity, for if impotent of ourselves to scale the heights, our impulse is towards them. It is this nobility that grace takes, and makes capable of glory.[16]

---

[14] *Wisdom* 8:1
[15] e.g. 1a2æ. 110, 2. 2a2æ. 23, 2
[16] *De veritate* XII, 3 ad 12

APPENDIX 4

THE MEANING OF THE WORD 'GOD'

TIMOTHY MCDERMOTT, O.P.

1. 'WHEN WE argue from effect to cause,' St Thomas says, 'the effect will take the place of the definition of the cause in the proof that the cause exists; and this especially if the cause is God. For when proving anything to exist the central link of the argument is not what that thing is (we cannot even ask what it is until we know that it exists). The central link is rather what we are using the name of the thing to mean. Now when demonstrating from effects that God exists, we are able to start from what the word "God" means, for, as we shall see, the names of God are derived from these effects.'[1] What is meant is that in proving men to be mortal, say, it is possible to start from a grasp of what existent men are, from a grasp of the nature of man arrived at through experience. But to prove that men exist, one could not use such a starting-point, for it already begs the question; one would start rather with a notion of how to use the word 'man', and search experience for traces of creatures to which the name could apply.

St Thomas also says, 'Because they observe that the course of nature follows fixed laws, and that law depends upon a lawgiver, men as a rule perceive that the things they observe have a lawgiver; but from such general considerations it is not immediately obvious who or what the lawgiver of nature is, or whether he is only one. So too when we observe a man moving and performing actions, we perceive that there must exist in him a cause of this behaviour different from that existing in other things; and we call this cause a "soul", though as

---

[1] 1a. 2, 2 ad 2.

yet we do not know what the soul is (whether it be a body), or how it causes the observed behaviour.'[2]

2. We shall expect then that the ways of proving God to exist will start from experience and examine it for traces of such a being as could be called 'God', where 'God' ought to have the meaning it has in ordinary everyday language. Now we do in fact find that the structure of the 'ways' is one of argument from experience: 'Some things in the world are certainly in process of change: this we plainly see', 'In the observable world causes are found to be ordered in series', 'Some of the things we come across can be but need not be', 'The fourth way is based on the gradation observed in things', 'An orderedness of actions to an end is observed in all bodies obeying natural laws'. Again, when these observable beginnings have been identified as traces of some newly-disclosed being, we appeal to everyday ordinary language for the name of this being: 'this is what everybody understands by God', 'to which everyone gives the name "God"', 'and this we call "God"'.

3. It has sometimes been felt that the being disclosed would not have been recognized by the ordinary man as his 'God', and that St Thomas is guilty of jumping the gun. Some commentators suggest in fact that only at the end of Question 11, when there has been proved to be only one God, shall we be at liberty to give what we have proved to exist the name 'God'. St Thomas, a little more realistically, connects the giving of the name with such general considerations as are referred to in the quotation above from the *Contra Gentes*, considerations which do not yet make it obvious, as he says, 'who or what the lawgiver of nature is, or whether he is only one'. For the ordinary man is not in fact usually clear as to whether there is one God or many, and it is only the ordinary man overawed by Christianity that now takes it for granted that there is one.

4. Another cause of difficulty is that the name 'God' is given in the first 'way' to 'some first cause of change', in the

---

[2] CG III, 38

second to 'some first cause', in the third to 'the cause that other things must be', in the fourth to 'something which causes in all other things their being . . .', and in the fifth way to 'someone with understanding (directing) everything in nature to its goal'. It has been suggested that here we have five different ways of assigning the name 'God'; none of them, moreover, 'ordinary', but all rather philosophical. And yet one finds it difficult to distinguish the 'different' modes of assignation in the first four ways; and as regards the fifth way one would have said it showed forth a very 'ordinary' way of conceiving God. The first four ways are obviously concerned to trace the existence of *ultimate* causality, a cause behind *everything*, and the fifth way adds the note of intelligence which transforms that 'first cause' into a 'providence'.

5. It is fairly clear that this is what St Thomas thought most people meant by the word 'God': a providence at the causal beginning of the world we see. 'For everybody who talks of God uses the word to name that which exercises a universal providence over things. . . . It is used to signify something transcending all things, at the beginning of all things, separate from all things: it is this to which people using the word 'God' wish to refer.'[3] And however undeveloped this is as a notion, it is not difficult to see that all five ways arrive at it, and that it provides the basis for the further developments of the questions that follow. We shall see that the notion of God as a first origin, *primum principium*, the fount of being, becomes very quickly the ruling notion of the whole treatise, a fact to which St Thomas himself draws our attention later, when discussing the Trinity: 'Creatures can lead us to God only as effects to a cause. So natural reason can know about God only that which must belong to him as the first beginning of everything that exists; and this was the basis we used when considering God earlier.'[4]

---

[3] 1a. 13, 8 c. & ad 2   [4] 1a. 32, 1

APPENDIX 5

THE FIVE WAYS

1. THESE FIVE arguments, the *quinque viæ*, are reasoned ways which open out the prospect of the world caused by God. Their starting-points are distinct, yet how soon they converge is a matter of some debate. Some see them, as it were, as marking traffic-lines on the same road, from the composite to the simple, from the many to the one, from the parts to the whole, and, looking back from an insight they feel no need to analyse, may doubt the value of mapping them separately: indeed an early manuscript is content to speak of a passage by five modes or manners, *quinque modis*. Others, more deliberative in discovery and more attentive to the letter of the text, delay over the distinct conclusions that are reached.

That all five amount to the same thing is shown later, notably in the following Question which meditates on the simplicity of God.[1] Then, as it is meant to be, preceding ratiocination is stilled in understanding, like motion in rest and choosing in enjoying;[2] a single recognition that the world as a whole depends on God succeeds reflection about its parts. Remember, too, that the philosophical theism which is developed in the *Summa,* though as thoroughgoing as that of Plotinus and using no substitute where reason can serve, is subsumed, according to its opening promise,[3] in the *sacra doctrina* of faith responding to God's revelation of himself in Christ.

2. We are tempted either to overstate or understate the force of the arguments. It is a temptation to the temper of philosophical mechanics that prevailed before Hume woke Kant from his dogmatic slumbers, and that still persists where flatly-conceived logic provides a board on which solidified

---

[1] 1a. 3. cf Blackfriars, Vol. 2, Appendix 12
[2] 1a. 79, 8; 83, 4. *In De Trin.* VI, 1   [3] 1a. 1, 1, 3, 7, 8

metaphysical entities can be moved like chessmen, to treat them as though they offer brisk and quasi-geometrical demonstrations for anybody, except a complete empiricist, who is prepared to think hard. On the other hand, the contemporary feeling that rationalism lies outside a truly religious approach is prone to write them off—all very well as providing an admissible hypothesis for the theist mentality that asks their sort of question, but for the rest profane exercises that have little or nothing to do with our cleaving to the living God.

Kant says that it is very necessary that we should be convinced of God's existence, but not so necessary that we should prove it. St Thomas would agree. All the same he thinks that divine truth can be proved, and for some of us should be proved by the theoretic reason; it is not merely a postulate of the practical reason. Admittedly rational theory is no more than penultimate, all the same, as appears in the introductory question to the *Summa*, it is an intrinsic part of *sacra doctrina* and neither irrelevant nor irreverent to the Christian mysteries. The arguments about to be considered display his characteristic combination of modesty and confidence; the power of reasoning is not overloaded to bear more than it will carry nor relegated to a rhetoric of religion.

They display a philosophical effort of construction, or of road-making towards what lies behind appearances. Inevitably the job is not complete, but it has to be done, and while a fideist may be excused if personally he finds the work unnecessary, so also an agnostic if he finds it too perplexing and the results unsatisfactory, a dogmatic atheist may well be challenged to show equal stamina of reason in sustaining his negation.

3. Before looking at the common build-up of the five proofs let us take from earlier works two parallel passages on what may be called inchoate theism. The first refers to the general observation that natural things follow a set order and the inference that therefore they are ordered by something. 'But who or what this is, or whether it be one or not, cannot be gathered from this initial general appreciation. Thus when we observe a man moving and functioning we judge there is a cause in him of this activity, and this we call *soul*, without

yet knowing what it is, whether it be a body or not, or how it effects the activity.'[4]

The next passage, which acknowledges its debt to Avicenna, carries the same caution. God's existence is self-evident in itself but not to us, for though somehow implicit in all our knowledge, since every truth reflects and shares in the exemplar truth of God, *secundum suam similitudinem et participationem*, what we first recognize is truth manifested in things of sense, not in God's own substantial being. 'We observe sense-objects and do not reach God except by advancing from them as things which are caused and therefore require an efficient cause, and this ultimately cannot be a body. So we do not arrive at God except by process of argument, which is never demanded for the self-evident.'[5]

4. In these two portmanteau arguments are compressed the four stages that are more clearly marked in the *quinque viæ*. They are: (1) a reading from what we experience through our senses, namely that things are changing, dependent, temporal or contingent, limited, and directed; (2) that something else is implied; (3) which turns out to be itself unchanging, independent, eternal or necessary, unlimited, and not directed by another; (4) and this we call 'God'.

5. Before commenting on each in turn, remark that the ways can be taken in two manners, directly as they are discovered, *in via inventionis*, and reflexively as interpreted, *in via judicii*.[6] To start with they point to something far beyond our experience, yet what this is, or rather what this is not, still remains much in the dark, and, though we give it the name 'God', is not manifested as the God we worship. Then later, when they are drawn together and the mind contemplates the qualities of uncreated and created being,[7] their evidence grows wider and yet more formed, deeper and yet clearer.

---

[4] CG III, 28. That the vague ideas men have about God are not enough for happiness. Note also the next chapter, that demonstrative knowledge takes us only a little further

[5] I *Sent.* 3, 1, 2   [6] 1a. 79, 8, 9   [7] 1a. 2–13; 44–9

This goes to explain a difference among the commentators. Some, keeping close to the history of the arguments and their position in the *Summa*, do not move far from the context of medieval science and are content with a limited objective. Others, fearing distraction from the true bearing of the dialectic, take it into an ampler metaphysical setting, and, for instance, would free the first argument from ballistics, the second from our consciousness of being acted on, the third from existence in time, the fourth from degrees of physical extensity and intensity, and the fifth from a designed pattern in things: they may even feel that the article does not show St Thomas writing at the top of his form.

The opposition, which goes back earlier than to the age of High Thomism of Cajetan and Bañez in the sixteenth century and will reappear in other appendices, is about where and when to lay the emphasis in commenting on the *Summa*; it will be seen in proportion if we allow that all the qualifications of an argument need not appear at the outset so long as they are made during the course of development. For the arguments can be set in three periods, of *scientia* which discovers a conclusion, of philosophical *sapientia* which takes a more total view and judges the conclusion in its highest rational causes, and finally of the wisdom of *sacra doctrina* when the highest cause is *veritas prima* accepted by divine faith.[8] These periods are abstractions which can be distinguished, not separable situations for someone who, like St Thomas in the *Summa*, is a Christian thinking single-mindedly about God.

Note that the second reading does not represent the argumentations, for all their display of logical analysis, as directed to pure concepts, forms, or essences, but as searching, throughout, into an existing world, and beyond to the being who supports it. The natural theology that results does not compose a system merely of meanings; it is about things as they are, and in the *Summa* it is an overture to the study of God's revelation in history. In St Thomas's mind the thought

---

[8] cf 1a. 1, 6, 7; 79, 9. 1a2æ. 57, 2

rises from living experience, and its translation into our minds
has to accept some embarrassments from its original exemplification. From these it can escape, yet without finding refuge
among the ideas of Descartes or Leibniz or Wolff.

THE FIRST WAY

1. PLATO, THE father of philosophical theology, writes in the *Laws* as an old man who regards atheism as a piece of youthful extravagance and has hardened in his condemnation of the crime of false theological tenets issuing from the theories of Ionians and Sophists. Arguing for the divine government of the world, he discovers motions of soul, *psuchē*, behind the unintelligent motions of the corporeal universe. His proof, which elaborates the *Phædrus* on immortality, turns on the examination of motion, *kinēsis*. This is divided into communicated motion and its source in spontaneous motion, which last is alive, *empsūchon*. Soul or mind is the cause of all cosmic movement, but although this may culminate in the perfectly good soul, *aristē psuchē*, the reasoning disregards the question, rarely felt by the Greeks to be capital, whether there be only one God or many.[1]

Aristotle gets behind self-initiated movement to a still more ultimate cause, the unmoved first mover of others, *akinēton kinētikon d'eteron*. The steps of the argument are worked out in the *Physics*,[2] and are more theologically presented in the twelfth book of the *Metaphysics*, which has the appearance of having been composed as a separate work:[3] both places are systematically studied in St Thomas's commentaries.[4] Aristotle's theology is Plato's, but written in the terms of a physicist, not a moralist. As to whether his God moves as a final or an efficient cause, it is enough here to remark that these are not alternatives,[5] and that the ultimate object of desire is treated as a present force, not merely an anticipated ideal.

2. The theology seems to be committed to a particular

---

[1] *Laws* x, 896A   [2] VII–VIII. 241b24–267b26
[3] XII, 6–7. 1071b3–1073a14
[4] *In Physic* VII, lect. 1–9; VIII, lect. 1–23. *In Meta*, XII, lect. 5–8
[5] cf 1a. 103, 1, 5; 105, 3, 4, 5

astronomical theory, that of Eudoxus, and can be regarded, not unfairly, as an appendix to physics. The same could be said, in a preliminary and partial sense, of the argument presented by St Thomas. He took it in the first place from the Arabic Aristoteleans; when genetically isolated it can be criticized, as it was by the Scotists, for its adoption of a middle term from physics. Two classical commentaries are much exercised on this point; Ferrariensis twists and turns,[6] and Cajetan resigns himself to the immediate conclusion that the first mover is no more immobile than the human soul.[7] Set the argument, however, in its complete background, against the overhanging questions on God's immutability and eternity,[8] and charged with the metaphysics of actuality and potentiality at the heart of created beings, then one agrees with Bañez that the middle term covers all motion, even the application of spiritual power to activity and the attraction of final causes.[9] As such it moves on a plane where it is neither confirmed nor impugned by theories about projectiles or by the laws of thermodynamics.

3. The *prima via,* described by St Thomas as the most open, *manifestior,* of the five, though for us it has become congested with traffic-blocks, starts from Aristotle's faithfulness to fact: movement cannot be regarded as illusory, and if we seek to explain it we arrive at something itself exempt from movement. 1. It examines what is meant by movement; 2. reflects that what is in movement much be set in movement by another, and furthermore that 3. no explanation is reached by infinitely prolonging the series of movers and moved; 4. and infers that a first mover exists which is not subject to movement, and this is what everybody understands by 'God'. These four steps call for separate examination.

4. The *Summa* sometimes uses *motus,* movement or motion, in the widest sense to include life and spontaneous activity, and the term is applied to God and the immanent

---

[6] *Summa Contra Gentiles, cum commentariis* 1, 13. Paris, 1552

[7] In 1am. 2, 3. Venice, 1508.   [8] 1a. 9–10

[9] *Scholastica Commentaria.* In 1am. 2, 3. Salamanca, 1588

acts of knowing and loving.[10] As such, the *actus perfecti existentis*, it is contrasted with what is dead, inert, potential and non-actual.[11] Here, however, it is restricted to change, *mutatio*, the transition or process from one condition to another.[12] Change is taken according to Aristotle's resolution of the opposition between Heraclitus and Parmenides, *he tou dunatou he dunaton entetecheia*, or in St Thomas's words, *actus imperfecti scilicet existentis in potentia inquantum hujusmodi*, which can be rendered, incomplete actualization, namely of something still as such really potential.[13] The clumsiness of the description is recognized and unavoidable, for perhaps movement can be movingly expressed only by metaphor, but it brings out the composition within change of dual principles, the potential and the actual. There is a being not yet completed but able to be completed (*ens in potentia*) with respect to a being completed (*ens in actu*). These two are already joined in a process of becoming, which, as it were, is a flow of being half-potential, half-actual. The thing in movement is a subject, *motum et patiens*, of what is really going on because of the presence of a force, *movens et agens*. The process is indicated rather than defined, since rational terms arrest meanings, and we tend to speak of a state of motion which, etymologically at least, is a contradiction in terms, since state implies stability and motion the reverse.

Motion so understood is not confined to local motion, but applies also to transformation of substance, as when one kind of thing becomes another, to instantaneous changes of accidents, as when a man is converted from non-loving to loving, as well as to successive changes, such as the alteration of qualities, the addition or subtraction of quantities, and the movement from one place to another.[14] Consequently the argu-

---

[10] 1a. 9, 1 ad 1; 14, 2 ad 2; 18, 3 ad 1; 58, 1 ad 1. 1a2æ. 31, 2 ad 1. *In De anima* III, *lect.* 12 (Aristotle 431a6)

[11] 1a. 9, 1 ad 2; 18, 1–3   [12] cf 1a. 45, 2 ad 2; 3

[13] *Physics* III, 1–2. 201a10, 201b4, 202a7. *In Physic.* III, *lect.* 2–3. *Metaphysics* XI, 9. 1065b5–1066a35. *In Meta.* XI, *lect.* 9

[14] We neglect here the questions of creation (1a. 45, 2) and transubstantiation (3a. 75, 3–7)

ment does not hinge on debated questions of celestial mechanics, though they may be involved for the historian of science and philosophy, but abstracts the universal implications of change as such, that is of *fieri* or becoming in terms of *esse* or being.[15]

5. Next, by reduction to the principle of contradiction it is impossible for the potential as such to be the actual as such, or for the becoming fulfilled to be the being fulfilled at the same time at the same spot. Hence you look outside the being in motion for the principle imparting the motion, or rather, since the analysis transcends the ordinary commonsense image of space, you conclude that the moving principle is 'other' than the principle in motion, according to the formula, everything in motion is set in motion by another, *omne quod movetur ab alio movetur, hapan to kinoumenon hupo tinos kineisthai*.[16] Note that this should be taken with formal precision; it means that the passive is not as such the active, not that one and the same thing or substance may not initiate its own movement within a particular system of reference, as is the case with living things. Nor at this preliminary stage does it suppose or state, as has sometimes been thought, the numerical diversity of things: were the world one substance and it was agreed that change was real you would still have to posit somewhere a principle for change which is exempt from change.

6. The argument now enlarges its depth of focus. What is being looked at is movement as a single situation where *actio-passio* are conjoined in one thing or one real universe, not as a transmission of particles along a line of units or a tide of waves of energy. Moreover, this situation is not confined to the initial passage, but extends to the whole condition of being in motion. The full argument performs a kind of 'lumping-together', so that the entire universe is considered as in motion: this will appear later in the *Summa*, and especially in the passages on returning to God.

---

[15] cf 1a. 2, 3 ad 2; 79, 4; 105, 5. 1a2æ. 9, 4
[16] *Physics* VII, 1. 241b24. *In Physic.* VII, *lect.* 1. *In Meta.* V, *lect.* 14

What we are looking for is the principle into which the change can be resolved, and if many factors are involved then they must be arranged in essential subordination, thus chisel, muscles, nerves, senses, artist, Michelangelo. What we should not look for is the first mover within a series of things each giving and receiving the same sort of movement, thus chisel number one, number two and so forth. Such a series is said to be in accidental subordination, for though the units follow one another they do not depend on one another for their movement. We shall return to this point in considering the argument from causality in the next appendix.

In the meantime let us refer to the question of a series of items stretching endlessly backwards. There are problems about infinite magnitudes and numbers,[17] but whichever way they are solved bears no relation to the need of having to stop, *ananchē stēnai*, at the first mover of the world in process of change. St Thomas himself held that it was impossible for the reason to demonstrate that the world had started once upon a time. In other words the concept of an infinite series is admissible: a closely reasoned process of elimination shows that created reality and everlasting reality are not mutually exclusive concepts.[18] So in the *prima via* he is not attempting to follow a chain of movers-in-motion to the end. The first mover he arrives at is not number one of the series, but outside it. As you watch a long train of goods wagons clattering past your surmise is that they are being pulled by some other force, not a leading wagon, and you will still require something like a locomotive even if it is suggested that the train of trucks needs neither to have had a beginning nor to be going to have an end. The mover-moved relationship, then, is understood not by a repetition of antecedents before consequents keeping always at the same level, but by rising above it; hence any being in motion will serve to take us directly to the being which is not in motion. This will appear more clearly when movement is explicated in causality, and the first

---

[17] 1a. 7, 3–4
[18] Opusc. *De æternitate mundi contra murmurantes.* cf 1a. 46, 1–3. CG II, 31–8

cause is seen to be immediately operative in every effect.[19]

7. The argument leads to a first mover which is not itself in motion, *primum movens immobile*. Notice the moderation of the conclusion, which claims no insight into God's own existence, but merely says that there is source of motion, *archē kinēseōs*, and this we understand to be God.

Lest a contradiction be suspected here, namely that what commences to move another cannot itself be immobile, observe that the mover-moved relationship is taken according to what is essentially implied, and is not defined by a transference of energy from one thing to another or by our experience of particular kinds of movement. That the mover itself should have been moved by another is incidental, *per accidens*; as such and *per se*, as Aristotle notices, the mover is immobile.[20] For to move another is to actualize, and therefore as such to be actual and not to be potential.

Also lest such an immobile principle be thought of as too inhuman for devotion, and too static to bear any resemblance to the living God, reflect that its stillness is that of pure activity. If Aristotle's God may seem remote, especially if *noēsis noēseōs* is translated a thinking on thinking,[21] in St Thomas, heir to the Christian humanism of Chartres and therefore to the gracious spirit of Plato, this *actus purus* is invested with the nobility of every perfection,[22] and holds the unbounded life of eternity,[23] sought in every desire and exemplified at the heart of every delight.[24] But this is to anticipate. Let us return to the mover and the moved, and end with the echo of the psalm. *The heavens declare the glory of God*,[25] when St James looks beyond the revolutions of the heavenly bodies and tells us that *every good gift and*

---

[19] Appendices, 3, 7, 11

[20] *Physics* VIII, 5. 256a3–257a33. *In Physic.* VIII, *lect.* 9. Action as such is motionless; cf 1a. 41, 1 ad 2; 53, 1 ad 2. The strength of God is his immutability; 1a2æ. 61, 5

[21] *Metaphysics* XII, 9. 1074b34. *In Meta.* XII, *lect.* 11

[22] cf *Summa*, Blackfriars, Vol. 2, Appendix 13

[23] cf *Summa*, Blackfriars, Vol. 2, Appendix 16

[24] 1a2æ. 30, 4; 31, 2   [25] *Psalms* 18:1

every perfect gift is from above, and cometh down from the Father of lights, with whom there is no variableness, neither shadow of turning.[26] The text in effect is a packed comment on the *prima via*, and how warm it is and how accurate.

---

[26] James 1:17

THE SECOND WAY

1. HERE ST THOMAS, one may hold, comes more into his own, for the middle term is now enlarged from motion, as in the *prima via*, to the sustained dependence of the activity evident in our surroundings. The argument turns on things being operative, productive, or effective, rather than on things undergoing a process of change, and on producing, *actus motoris*, rather than on becoming produced, *actus mobilis*: these notes, while not representing diverse elements, are at least distinct enough to provide grounds for two discussions.[1]

In both cases, however, the course of the argument goes through the same stages. Accordingly we shall look at 1. experience and causality; 2. indicate that the 'cause' which is correlative to the 'effect' (from *ex-facere*, to work out) is other than it; 3. that an infinite causal series is impossible; and 4. the conclusion that a first uncaused cause exists, to which everybody gives the name 'God'.

2. The second way begins, 'In the world of sense we find there an order of efficient causes': note the implication that a causal order is discovered in experience, not there disclosed. As we shall soon see, causality in the full sense is a metaphysical conclusion, not an extremely abridged account of empirically registered facts. The later Alexandrian sceptics denounced the search for 'causes', and their criticism finds famous expression in Hume—register your facts, induct your laws, and then remember that as a philosopher you have reached your goal. That events follow a pretty regular course is accepted and that they will continue to do so is expected; hence the sciences, concerned with the co-ordination of items in their own respective systems, rightly rely on some sort of necessary succession of antecedents and consequents, and will

---

[1] Note in anticipation that creatures are not wholly active or productive, since their substance or being is not identical with their activity. cf 1a. 44, 1, 2

want a system of prediction for the operation of apparently random factors.

This, however, does not amount to the causality considered by St Thomas. The critique of science, more aware of the difference between 'plain facts' and 'scientific facts', and of the construction that has gone into the latter, is nowadays less inclined than formerly to accept the old empirical account of scientific method, and even to admit that 'theory' must come in before any 'observation' can be made, and that some sort of deduction is prior to argumentative induction. Nevertheless we can risk over-simplification and say that if philosophy is ruled out then causality does little more than promulgate a general law, written in a kind of shorthand and often in mathematical notation, summing up the results of induction from cases of 'this' constantly following after 'that'. Afterwards an *ad hoc* explanation for this happening may be attempted by a scientific hypothesis, which, however, will be regarded less as true or false than as good or bad, that is as likely or far-fetched, neat or inelegant, timely or out-moded, useful for advance or unpromising.

All the same the scientist is a man, and man is an animal who hunts for real reasons, and so is driven ever deeper to find explanations; he begins to think of 'things', not merely of 'happenings'. And then, as soon as he begins to ask 'why?', and answer 'because', he is entering philosophy and warming to the idea of 'cause'. True, he may shy off when told that he is thinking metaphysically, partly perhaps because he has learned a lesson from the unfortunate history of metaphysicians intruding their own concepts into a field where, though not unexemplified, they offer no substitute for the proper concepts of the particular science concerned, and possess no heuristic value. Professional metaphysicians do not stand alone in venturing such spurious terms, for all scientists except the closest and narrowest specialists seek wisdom by breaking out into the widest views,[2] and qualify as metaphysicians, if with an amateur status. Indeed controlled im-

---

[2] cf 1a2æ. 57, 2

agery is the due tribute we pay to the analogy of being, and it can be doubted whether terms are spurious so long as they do not displace the proper terms for the discipline in question and are not too stiffly applied—and we are aware of transferring their specific meaning from one subject to another.

Let us admit, after all, that thinking about the general comes easier to us than thinking about the particular, if thinking means theory: Aristotle and St Thomas say as much. The more abstract the interest the simpler it is; inasmuch as it is less complicated the difficulties offered call more for subtlety than for hard work, for understanding at depth more than for calculating, for discerning the essential conditions of being more than for systematizing its diverse and heterogeneous manifestations in phenomena.

3. Some such sort of preface serves to lead into the meaning causality has for the *Summa*. It is not concerned with two events, nor even with two diverse things, pictured as one here and the other there in space, the first, as it were, firing into the second and scoring hits that can be registered and recorded. Causality is discerned as a transaction within one being as motion or change is discerned within its subject; and this being caused, like the being changed, though found not to be self-explanatory, is not escaped from, but remains the object of interior examination. Moreover this is inspected, not in its pure idea, but in a judgment that refers to an existing thing: in the case of the *secunda via* to an active thing.

All the same if real and active in itself the thing is not so of itself. Judged to be neither simply self-existing nor wholly self-acting, in both respects it is inferred to depend on an existing and acting 'other', which is its cause.

A cause is a real and positive principle from and on which another proceeds and depends for what it actually is and does. There are four types of causes, final, efficient, material, and formal; here in the *secunda via* the argument immediately engages only the efficient cause. This is the *agens*, the active and executive principle producing the effect, to which it is prior in nature though not necessarily in time, and into which it does not enter as a component part. Efficient cause is a stronger term to a philosopher than to a scientist, who may require no more than an antecedent map-reference or a condition favouring the appearance of an *event*, without thinking of it as exerting and maintaining influence on the inner nature of an *effect*. It is also a stronger term than 'occasion', or juncture of opportune circumstances for something to be done or made. Furthermore its meaning is more 'universal' in philosophy than in a particular science, since it is translated into the abstract medium of 'being'; there it belongs to a full efficient cause to produce and conserve a thing completely, both as to its *esse* and to its *agere*.

4. For an effect to be intelligible (or, to use a terminology later than St Thomas, to have 'sufficient reason') we have to look into its being and activity, and then through and beyond to its spring of being and activity, that is to its cause. Now in a series of causal dependents you cannot go back indefinitely. The text of the argument is clear, perhaps too clear, for when you read that without a first cause you cannot have an intermediate cause (or intermediate causes) and a last cause (namely the one posited as present), you might presume that the clause refers to causes linked together in the same chain or to a series of agents of the same kind, starting with 1, going on to 2, 3, 4, &c., and ending, let us say, with 55, taken to stand for the last effect (namely the one confronting us).

Such a causal series is said to be in accidental subordination, that is to say, such causality as 1 exerts on 2 is incidental, *per accidens*, to such causality as 2 exerts on 3, and 3 on 4, and so forth. Such is the case with human generation, when, as St Thomas says, a man begets a child because he is a man, not because he is the son of his father.[3] In this type of series you cannot infer from the present existence of the last the present existence of the first; what is more, and no less a disqualification for philosophical theism, you cannot infer a first cause at all. For human genealogy, St Thomas adds, can possibly stretch back indefinitely.[4] If a halt in the past has to be called it will not be in the name of causality; it may be be-

---

[3] 1a. 46, 2 ad 7   [4] ibid

cause of problems involved in natural science by infinite magnitudes or multitudes,[5] and for Christians it will be because of faith. That things started once upon a time is admissible and to be believed, but not capable of proof, *credibile, non autem demonstrabile vel scibile.*[6]

The first cause the argument is seeking is therefore of another kind. If human generation be the starting-point, this causal origin will not be our first parents but a reality outside the series, like the mover with respect to things in motion. Outside, but not remote, for the prime will be as close to any subsequent generation as to the inaugural generation, and closer to the generating now than this is to the generating then. The series in question is of causes in essential subordination or related *per se*, namely when one exists actively in virtue of the active existence of another and therefore 'higher' being.

The continuity is along the line—if that is not too thin a word—of causation, not of objects that happen in succession, which so far as causality may be concerned may march without beginning in the past or end in the future. When, however, we are resolving a properly causal series, and are faced with a dependent or derived action, we may in the first place uncover another dependent or derived action to account for it, and then go on to uncover more of the same sort, yet eventually we must come to a stop and conclude that there exists an action which is neither dependent nor derived, though what the agent is we do not as yet know. We shall gather during later developments of the argument that the sequence is not prolonged through a great number of factors; accordingly to speak about extending the series is here better avoided. If causation be taken metaphysically, that is purely in terms of *esse* and *agere*, then the highest or the deepest cause (the *causa altissima* judged by wisdom) is swiftly reached from any one exemplification of causation. St Thomas does not treat causation as a number of successive changes strung together, but as the co-presence of effect and

---

[5] cf 1a. 7, 3, 4   [6] 1a. 46, 2

cause in one proceeding; he is forming a whole, not searching for the first of a class, and so he looks, not from one action to the previous action, but deeper and deeper into one action within which a higher principle contains a lower. The origins are soon found to lie as deep as divinity.

The world is caused because now it depends on God, not because it was started in the past. He is not another world but of the same sort as ours; then there would be no truly causal dependence, for, though according to popular speech like causes like, if the likeness is univocal, as between members of the same species, one individual may indeed cause another individual to come about (*causa secundum fieri*) but does not cause its nature nor conserve its being (*causa secundum esse*):[7] a full cause is an *agens æquivocum*, and the likeness between it and the effect is analogical.[8]

God might then be supposed to be another world, but of a higher kind than ours, indeed of the highest and best kind. Although at first sight the *quinque viæ* might appear to carry us no further than to such a pantheon, reflection shows that they are not concerned with another world at all—if that means an order of things that bears sufficient resemblance to our world to enable us to deal with it in something of the same way and ask its cause. They all point to something of which the question, 'what caused it?' cannot be asked. The commentators may differ about the speed at which they should be taken, but not about the implications of their conclusions, or, when they have met together, of their common conclusion. Then a broader way leads us to the conclusion that God is not a kind of thing at all; he is not in a genus since he is pure being and the fount of all being, *principium totius esse*; he is outside and beyond every genus and can consequently cause every kind of thing, *extra omne genus et principium omnium generum*.[9]

5. The opening argument, St Albert remarks, proves only that God exists in the manner of a cause.[10] The religious

---

[7] 1a. 104, 1   [8] 1a. 4, 2, 3; 6, 2. CG 1, 29, 31
[9] 1a. 3, 5; 4, 3 ad 2   [10] *Summa Theologiæ*, 1, 3, 18

appeal of the conclusion is limited, but not inconsiderable. God is named from our universe, and we are not told what God is in himself, though soon we are told a lot about creatures and how in some ways they are like him.[11] Later St Thomas will try to show that in speaking about God we can surpass this creaturely reference, so that when we declare that he is good we mean more than that he is the cause of goodness:[12] an effort that will become easier when, writing specifically as a Christian theologian, his understanding is founded on faith in God's revelation of himself.

---

[11] 1a. 4, 3   [12] 1a. 13, 2, 6

THE THIRD WAY

1. CAUSALITY RUNS through all five arguments. The first has taken the actualizing of the effect, the second the acting of the cause; now attention shifts and deepens to the finite being of the effect, considered in its duration by the third, and in its sharing, *participatio*, in existence by the fourth: the fifth can be expanded to consider all finite being as tending to an end.

2. Plato reasons that were nothing deathless nothing now would be alive;[1] Plotinus and St Augustine pick up the same theme.[2] The distinction between necessary and contingent predication is essential to Aristotle's logic, and the existence of ungenerated and indestructible heavenly bodies is cardinal to his natural philosophy, yet for the conclusion that there exists a metaphysical ground of reality that cannot be otherwise St Thomas owes more to the Arabic philosophers than to him, or to Boethius and the *Liber de Causis*. His wording echoes Maimonides, who took the proof from Avicenna.[3] Everything that is exists either as a 'bound to be' or as a 'possible', this last seeming to signify, for Avicenna and also for Averroes, an essence to which existence is added as an incidental predicate.

3. The difficulty is that existence, *esse*, is not strictly speaking a predicate. Though some may be of the opinion that the *Summa* text lays itself open to the charge of treating existence as a predicate, St Thomas elsewhere makes it evident that his distinction between essence and existence is not between the conceivable and the real, but between the potential and the actual within real created substance: the tenor of the third argument should be read accordingly.

---

[1] *Phædo* 72. *Phædrus* 245–247

[2] *Enneads* IV, 7. *Confessions* XI, 4

[3] *The Guide of the Perplexed*. Ed. M. Friedländer. London, 1925, Part II, p. 152. Aristotle argues to the same effect for an indestructible 'heaven' in *De cælo* I, 11 sqq

The meaning of three terms he commonly uses may be touched on, namely *ens, esse,* and *essentia. Ens,* or being, can be treated, like *studens,* either as a noun or as a participle. As a noun it is applied to anything, and signifies that which is, *id quod est*; as such it can be treated as an essential predicate only of a necessary or *per se* being. As a participle it signifies primarily existence, *esse,* that whereby a thing is, *quo est,* and secondarily the subject or essence, the what which a thing, *res,* is, *quod quid est,* hence *quidditas,* an abstract construction like *entitas,* and also *realitas,* not one of St Thomas's terms.

4. *The tertia via,* given in the *Contra Gentes* as an argument for divine eternity,[4] follows the order of the first and second ways, and starts from the plain fact that things are born and die away. Yet were everything perishable, without anything to keep it from perishing, once there would have existed nothing at all, and consequently nothing would exist now. Instead we must posit a necessary being, which exists of itself, *per se,* and possesses what the Latin translator of Avicenna called the *vehementia essendi.*

5. A thing's necessity is either caused by another or not. If not, then we have the conclusion; if caused, then to explain that causes recede *ad infinitum* is like taking refuge in the old myth that the earth is supported by a giant who stands upon a great tortoise who squats on the back of a great elephant whose legs reach all the way down. Therefore a being exists necessary of itself, which has no cause for its necessity but is the cause of the necessity of other things.

6. Three comments on the argument. First, there are various kinds of necessity. The main distinction lies between absolute and conditional necessity.[5] This last ranges from fact to theory; if something has happened, however contingently, it achieves the necessity that now it cannot be otherwise;[6] again the rules of logic admit no alternative, for instance a

[4] CG I, 15

[5] 1a. 19, 3, 8; 82, 1; 116, 3. CG I, 67

[6] 1a. 25, 4. cf 1a. 16, 8 ad 4

valid conclusion drawn from a negative premise is bound to
be negative; again, a hypothetical necessity invests means if
an end is to be obtained; then again, our thoughts may reflect the unchangeable reasons for things in the divine mind,
as when we judge that the whole is greater than the part,
reality obeys the law of contradiction, friendship is fair in
itself, and lying is always wrong.

Many modern philosophers hold that 'necessary' applies
only to statements, but it is perfectly sensible to talk, as St
Thomas does, about necessary beings, that is things not liable
to go out of existence. His argument is about things, and
points to the absolutely necessary existent, which requires no
condition at all for its necessity, and is implied in every other
necessity in things and in statements about them. In brief, if
God does not exist nothing is possible.

7. Next, despite some similarity with the Anselmic argument,[7] fallacious reasoning from the conceptual to the real is
absent. Existence is not regarded as a predicate that can be
inferred from another predicate. (Note that non-existence
can be inferred about an object to which incompatible predicates are assigned.) From the beginning and throughout the
Summa, arguments are about things, and proceed from one
manner of existence to another. Here the middle term of the
argument is not the notion of beings that conceivably can be
or not be, but the existence of such beings. In working from
the world to God it works from one existent to another.

8. Finally, like the others, you can take this proof both
directly from the beginning or reflexively from the end, or
like a prelude about creatures of time and like a coda about
creatureliness in a duration beyond time. At first it is
enough, Cajetan cautiously observes, that it introduces prime
necessary being, without bothering whether this be one or
many, though it is evident from the argument itself that it
cannot be a collection of contingent things, and from the
prima via that it is not a steady flow underlying phenomena.
Nor would a mental 'law of necessity' meet the case, for what
is sought is basic being, not a notional reflection of it.

---

[7] 1a. 2, 1 obj. 2

If, however, you read on and then return to the proof, enjoying a deeper insight into the perfection implied where essence is existence,[8] you will then concentrate on the inherent
inadequacy of contingency to explain itself, be less involved
with time and less hampered by the difficult third and fourth
sentences of the text, and conclude to one single necessary
being. Whereas at first the 'possible not to exist' will be read
as the 'possible to go out of existence in time', as in the letter
of the text and in the knotty argument, closely analysed by
St Thomas, in Aristotle's cosmology where he tries to show
that something which always existed and will exist is something which must exist,[9] later the *possibile* will be related to
esse and *non esse* as such, not to *esse tale* and *non esse tale*,
this or that kind of existence possessed by things subject to
generation and corruption. While the human mind in its
present condition starts the argument from looking at ordinary things perishable in time, the blessed in heaven could
turn to their timeless yet profoundly contingent surroundings
and frame the same metaphysical argument—if they cared to.

---

[8] 1a. 4, 4; 4, 2. CG I, 28
[9] *De Cælo* I, 11–12. 281a–283b26. St Thomas *in loc. lect.* 25–6

THE FOURTH WAY

1. THIS ARGUMENT, which appears more imaginative than the last as gazing not at the duration but at the perfection of things in existence, notably at the 'good' that is in them, a good that promises the 'best', is anticipated by Plato,[1] St Augustine,[2] and St Anselm.[3] Elements of it appear in Aristotle.[4] St Thomas stresses the factor of causal dependence in the texture of existing things, not merely of ideas: this is its strength.

The stages are similar to those taken by the preceding proofs: 1. the observation of degrees of being; 2. the reflection that 'more or less' implies a 'most'; 3. that the most and noblest being is cause of all other being and good; 4. and this we call God.

2. 'More or less' is taken by analogy for quantity to signify the comparative gradation of forms and perfections;[5] form may be taken to represent any sparkle of being for knowledge, and perfection any attraction for love.

Either quality or substantial being may express perfection. In the first case it can vary by extent or by intensity; extensive growth is measured by the objects covered, intensive growth by the depth of rooting in the subject, thus we can understand or love more and more things and we can grow more and more understanding or loving. Substantial being may be signified by the specific or generic nature of a thing, and in this narrow typological sense perfections do not vary; cats and catmint exhibit the same essentials of vegetable life, and all men are equal not as persons, but as specimens of human nature. Addition here or subtraction changes the species, for species, Aristotle often tells us, are like numbers. Such a

---

[1] cf *Phædo* 75, 77, 93, 100. *Republic* v, 476; vi, 506–7

[2] *De Trinitate* viii, 3. cf *De civitate Dei* xi, 16

[3] *Monologium* 1–4

[4] *Metaphysics* iv, 5. 1008b31–1009a5. St Thomas *in loc. lect.* 9

[5] 1a2æ. 52, 1.

formal perfection is predicated univocally, or in the same
sense, of all who possess it, and for such a form, bound up
with matter, there is not a 'most', still less a causal 'most';[6]
as already noticed, a full cause is above or beyond the species
of the effect.

If, however, the perfection is not such as to be definable
specifically by genus and difference it can be shared in or 'participated' with a constancy of meaning that admits differences
of degree.[7] Thus the transcendental attributes of being—
truth, unity, goodness, and perhaps beauty. These perfections
are called analogical, that is they can be predicated variously
of diverse subjects, and it is with these, despite the possibly
misleading reference to 'the greatest hot thing' that the argument is concerned.[8] Recall the distinction we have drawn
between two periods for the *quinque viæ*, namely when they
lead out of a particular cosmological background and when
they are retraced in the light of what has been learned. At
this second or metaphysical period St Thomas is spared the
embarrassment of Platonists who do not distinguish between
univocal and analogical perfections; he is not looking for a
'most' horse, but for a 'most' being, not for the best of a kind,
but for the best being above all kinds.[9]

3. That 'more or less' implies a 'most' does not remain
with the grammar of comparatives and superlatives but is
drawn into philosophical insight. Where a perfection is found
in diverse things and at various strengths then it is involved
a) with multiplicity, because it is repeated, and *b*) in composition, because it is not pure. When the same perfection is
possessed by things of themselves diverse then all cannot
possess it of themselves.[10] Where a perfection is possessed
but with a limitation or qualification there it is received in
the potentiality of a subject. On these counts we ascend *a*.

---

[6] 1a. 44, 3 ad 2   [7] 1a. 13, 3 ad 1

[8] cf 1a. 6, 2 ad 3. CG II, 15, for 'fire' as the hottest of things and
the cause of heat

[9] *In Meta.* II, *lect.* 2 (993b25–30). 1a. 13, 5, 6, for analogy of
terms used of creatures and God

[10] *De potentia* III, 5

from the many to the One possessing the perfection of itself, and *b*. from the composite to the Simple, where the perfection is sheerly actual without admixture of potentiality.[11]

4. The argument, which is not an unattached piece of conceptual analysis, hinges on perfections really existing, and opens to the existing of their cause. Though the temper of the dialectic is Platonic, it is content to indicate how the world about it is charged with a strength not its own, or rather not from itself, without proposing an escape to another world of pure forms.

5. All perfections referred to are ultimately resolved into the perfection of existence, *esse*. This is not taken according to its meaning in the logic of statements, as when we say that this is that; nor vaguely and generally to indicate being at one or two removes from non-existence, as when we say that something merely is, but to refer to the actuality of every form or nature, the culmination of every perfection.[12] The way is prepared for the next question, on the existential essence or essential existence of God, who alone is pure act and *ipsum esse subsistens*.[13]

6. Other arguments exemplify this ascent from participated being to pure being and sometimes in a warmer atmosphere; they can be regarded as applications of the *quarta via*. Thus the inference from intelligence to first intelligence,[14] and from truth to eternal truth,[15] dear to St Augustine, suggested here and there in the *Summa*, and kindled by the oratory of Bossuet and Fénelon. Thus also the inference from the good and desirable to the best and supreme object of desire, *to ariston, to prōton orekton*,[16] and from law to the Eternal Law.[17]

---

[11] 1a. 3, 7; 65, 1. CG II, 15. *De potentia* III, 8

[12] 1a. 3, 4; 4, 1 ad 3; 2 ad 1. CG I, 28   [13] 1a. 3, 4

[14] 1a. 14, 4; 16, 2; 79, 4   [15] CG II, 84, 1a. 16, 6, 7

[16] 1a. 60, 5. 1a2æ. 1, 4, 6; 2, 8; 3, 1, 8; 5, 8

[17] 1a2æ. 19, 4; 91, 1, 2

THE FIFTH WAY

1. SINCE TELEOLOGY is so conspicuous a feature of Aristotle's theory of the structure and history of nature, you might expect from him the conclusion that things move towards the fulfilment of some divine plan. Despite a few traces here and there of this line of thought, for instance when the order of the universe is compared to a household or army and is assigned to the head or general, or when a providential activity for the maintenance of species is allowed, or when Anaxagoras is praised for introducing reason as the cause of the ordered disposition of things, unlike Plato he never speaks of foresight or providence, *proroia*, in God. His concept of purpose relates to ethics and deliberate choice, whereas *to heneka*, 'that for the sake of which', or the final cause, corresponds rather to the biological concept of function in the light of the whole organism. As a biologist he is mainly interested in the 'internal directedness' of organic development. Sometimes he contrasts the works of thought and of nature. And though without a mind somewhere directedness is at most unconscious purpose, and unconscious purpose is no purpose at all, his language suggests that, like many modern thinkers, he does not feel the difficulty.[1]

2. In approaching the question St Thomas's mind was of course informed by the Christian doctrine of divine Providence. This is a matter of biography, not of philosophy: the student might expect him to strain the rational evidences, but may well conclude that in fact he does not.

His starting-point, as with the other arguments, is an observed composition, this time of means and ends, not of the changeable and the changing, of the able to act and the acting, of the possible to be and the being, of being partial and not wholly perfect. Like the other arguments, too, it can be

---

[1] *Physics* II, 8. 198b10–199b34. St Thomas *in loc. lect.* 12–14

taken in two manners, initially as it appears in the text, and reflexively in the context of the metaphysics of final causality. In the first manner it might almost seem to be the argument from design, perhaps not too well compressed, which proves at most that there is some sort of directing mind in the universe: this, for Cajetan, is sufficient at this early stage. In the second manner it need not be based on an observed scheme of associated things nor be restricted unconscious action which seems directed to a purpose, but can proceed, like the other arguments without pursuing a series of subordinates, from any one example of a thing or things where activity as a function of being can be explained only in relation to an end not yet achieved, or a more complete whole not yet disclosed. As such it is read in the light of the four preceding proofs, all of which are variations on the principle that the potential is causally actualized only by the actual, and notably in the light of the fourth proof, in which all 'desire' is interpreted as a response to the ultimate object of desire. This may be the reason why St Thomas puts this argument last, though of all its appeal is the most popular.

3. It turns on the truth that means cannot be directed to ends except by an intelligent cause. How is the means-end composition brought about? The terms are not yet united, otherwise we should not see things acting as they do, 'questing' as it were, or at least not yet at rest. Yet the terms are related. Where then if not in some sort of prevision? This implies intelligence. Consequently, since we find things without intelligence related to ends, we infer a directing intelligence outside them. The text of the *quinta via* confines itself to these limits, but the argument can be amplified to refer to all functions that need to be resolved into a deeper whole than they constitute taken alone and apart: the scientist here goes some of the way, but not so deeply as the philosopher. Hence the argument applies to all things that do not of themselves possess their ends, that is to all creatures.[2] To appeal

---

[2] 1a. 103, 1. 1a2æ, 1, 8. CG III, 16

to chance instead of purpose is to take a blinkered view, to
appeal to blind necessity is to take no view at all.[3]

4. Note first that St Thomas does not say that things are
for an end, and so, though he abounded with the medieval
humour of accounting for things by reasons *ex convenientiis*,
or recommendations from the analogies running through a
Christian world-view, his argument is spared the necessity of
answering the question why mosquitoes exist. His formula is
that activity is for an end, *agere est propter finem*.

Note secondly the implied distinction between external
and internal finality.[4] External finality lies, outside the relationship of an activity to its own proper end, in a combined
operation by different and diverse things achieving an ordered
plan, pattern, or design. This is not finality as such, the inner
motion of the partial towards the more complete which concerns the fulfilment of being or substance through activity,
or to *esse* as expressing itself in *agere*, but the collective tendency, often presumed, of a group of beings or substances
which may override their own particular inclinations; it may
be credited with greater social importance, yet is not granted
the same metaphysical status, for the *bonum commune* of a
group is not the true *bonum universale*.[5]

A group of substances is an accidental unity (not that it
has come about by accident, or even merely by convention,
but that it consists in an arrangement of diverse substantial
unities), and to base the argument for finality on this incurs
the same weakness that attends argument from a series of
accidentally subordinate movers or causes. We may well be
at a loss to assign the purposes of many things within the

---

[3] 1a. 49, 3. *Physics* II, 8. 199b19–26. 9. 200a30–68. CG I, 13. *De
veritate* v, 2. *In Physic.* II, lect. 12–15. *In Meta.* VI, lect. 3

[4] 1a. 65, 2

[5] The *bonum commune* can be a collective notion of the good
within the group; in its strongest sense it is the *bonum separatum*,
the 'outside' universal good which is the cause of good in each and
all together. cf *In Meta.* XII, lect. 12. 1a. 103, 2. 1a2æ 109, 3. CG
III, 17

world-order; in fact the bleak strength of argument from
finality has been damaged by its association with anthropo-
morphic evocations, both humanist and religious, of a universe organized for man's comfort, dignity, or salvation.

Internal finality is the relation of an acting thing to its own
completion; it is easier to see how mosquitoes are organized
for their own conservation and reproduction than to appreciate their place in the scheme of things. The fifth argument
is about internal finality, and therefore can begin wherever
potentia is found ordered to *actus*. We need not consider
whether the pattern exists for the benefit of any one type
of its components; until we can quote with conviction the
text that *all things work together for good to those that love
God*,[6] the argument does not prove that the teleological universe is particularly good for man.

5. Whenever there is activity there is reason for activity,
and therefore intelligence. The argument shows that tendency
is 'intended', and that the *opus naturæ* is the *opus intelli-
gentiæ*.[7] St Thomas would have us see love running through
the universe; though properly speaking only present with intelligence, love enters also into things which lack even sense-
awareness, for these can be said 'not to know naturally, but
to love and desire naturally'.[8]

This is not a flower of speech, an example of the pathetic
fallacy of reading our emotions into non-human things, but
a conclusion from the metaphysics of potentiality and actuality applied to all active being. Love supposes an adaptation
and fitting together, *adaptatio, co-aptatio*, of distinct things,
an adjustment that springs from direction, not chance.[9] There
is a natural setting towards completion even behind our conscious volitions and choices which quickens all we do; we are
not responsible for this inborn purpose, but only for the
modifications and applications we give it.[10] That ultimately
this desire is communicated by one supreme good and in-

---

[6] *Romans* 8:28   [7] I *Sent.* 25, 1, 1   [8] III *Sent.* 27, 1, 4 ad 13

[9] 1a2æ. 27, 4. *De potentia* I, 5

[10] 1a2æ. 10, 1. *De veritate* XXII, 5, 6

telligent will awaits later proof,[11] as also does the conclusion that all purposes conspire in one ordered universe ruled by a single providence.[12] The fifth argument is not complete until, placed in its total theological context, it is seen to promise the disclosure of a lover.

---

[11] 1a. 6, 2, 4; 11, 3; 19, 4; 20, 2; 44, 4. 1a2æ. 1, 8
[12] 1a. 22, 2; 47, 3; 103, 3

APPENDIX 6

ANALOGY

HERBERT MCCABE, O.P.

ST THOMAS is concerned to maintain that we can use words to mean more than they mean to us—that we can use words to 'try to mean' what God is like, that we can reach out to God with our words even though they do not circumscribe what he is. The obvious objection to this is that in e.g. *God is good*, 'good' must either mean the same as it means when applied to creatures or something different. If it means the same, then God is reduced to the level of creatures; if it does not mean the same then we cannot know what it means by knowing about creatures, we should have to understand God himself; but we do not, hence we do not understand it at all —we only have an illusion of understanding because the word happens to be graphically the same as the 'good' we do understand. St Thomas wishes to break down this either-or. It is not true, he says, that a word must mean either exactly the same in two different uses or else mean something altogether different. There is the possibility of a word being used with related meanings.

We might ask why he is not content to say simply that our language about God is metaphorical. He does not say this because he wants to distinguish between two different kinds of thing that we say about God; between statements like 'The Lord is my rock and my refuge' and statements like 'God is good'. The first of these is quite compatible with its denial—'Of course the Lord is not a rock', whereas the second is not. We would not say 'God is not good', though we are quite likely to say 'God is good, but not in the way that we are'. It is an important point about metaphor that while we can easily say 'God is not really a rock' we cannot so safely say 'The Lord is not a rock in the way that Gibraltar is'. For one thing there is only one way of being a rock, but more importantly, being a rock in the way that Gibraltar is is what the poet has in mind. Unless we think of God as being just like Gibraltar—although of course not really being a rock—we betray the poet's meaning. Qualification emasculates his meaning in a way that flat contradiction does not. In the case of 'good', however, since there are in any case many ways of being good amongst creatures, there is nothing incongruous in saying 'He is good, though not in our way'. What makes it possible to be confident that the word 'good' is in some meaning applicable to him is that he is the cause of the goodness of creatures. It does not, as St Thomas insists, follow from this that to call God good is to *say* that he is the cause of goodness, it is to say, he thinks, that there is something we can only call goodness in God—goodness is the best word available for signifying this although it does so imperfectly.

He attaches great importance to the idea that such words apply 'primarily' to God. The point of this seems to be that when you 'try to mean' God's goodness by using the word 'good' of him, you are not straying outside its normal meaning but trying to enter more deeply into it. His objection to the metaphor theory of theological language is that in metaphor the primary use of the word is a literal one, so that words would always apply primarily to creatures and to use them of God would be to move outside their ordinary meaning.

No metaphor is the best possible metaphor—you can always say 'I don't really mean that'. But some things we say of God even though they are imperfect cannot be improved on by denying them; their imperfection lies in our understanding of what we are trying to mean.

GLOSSARY

abstraction: the formation from relative and mixed experience of an object in human knowledge which can be considered simply in itself apart from its real accompaniments or concrete exemplification. And so 1. the consideration of the general in the particular; 2. of a form apart from its material subject.

accident: 1. as a mode of being real, that which cannot exist as a thing but only as of a thing which is its real subject or substance, thus a smile; one of nine categories enumerated by Aristotle, and accordingly called a 'predicamental accident'. See *categories*. 2. as a manner of predicating, or attributing a predicate to the subject of a proposition, not necessarily or essentially, but contingently, incidentally, and in point of fact, thus 'white' applied to 'man', and accordingly called a 'predicable accident'.

action: the doing of something, strictly, of producing an effect; contrast with *passion*.

activity: translates *operatio*, and is a wider term. It may be unaccompanied by change, thus knowing or loving as such.

actuality: indicates any sort of really being or acting, often as the fulfilment of some prior potentiality.

æon: the measure of duration of non-material creatures, as time is that of material creatures.

analogical term, idea, value: common to diverse objects but with a distinct pitch or intensity of meaning, thus beauty as applied to God, to Helen of Troy, a ship-of-the-line under full canvas, etc., all of which, simply speaking, are diverse. The likeness is not purely verbal or *equivocal*, nor yet *univocal*, that is amounting to exact generic or specific sameness. Hence *analogical cause*, which possesses a fuller being than that of its effects.

analogy: the method of drawing on such meanings for literary effect (metaphor and simile) and striking parallels for scientific discovery: thus the philosophical analogies which run throughout the *Summa*. The reader is referred to specialist studies—and controversies—for an appreciation of their range and variety.

appetition: the response to being good as cognition is that to being true. The bent or tendency of anything potential to what will make it complete and actual is called 'natural appetite'; as such it is unconscious. When this end is somehow apprehended the appetite is called 'animal', that is, psychic; it works at the two levels of emotion, sensitive appetite, and will, rational appetite. Appetite remains even when desire is fulfilled.

beatitude, happiness, bliss: the final cause, end, and perfection of an intelligent being. Objective beatitude, the object giving completion, thus God; subjective beatitude, the act of attaining it, thus the vision of God.

being: that which is. Anything can be said to be, and each *is* in a sense peculiar to itself. Nevertheless the senses of 'being' compose graded sequences of analogical meanings, in which that of being-a-substance is a kind of paradigm for the others. The best summary is to be found in Aristotle's *Metaphysics* v, 7. 1017a7–b9.

categories: the irreducible modes of existence, and consequently of predication, for natural philosophy: the usage is Aristotelean and differs from the Kantian. Aristotle listed the following ten modes or categories of being: being a substance (e.g. a baboon), being quantified (large), being qualified (black), being related to (the leader of a troop), being in action (scratching), being acted upon or passion (being scratched), being in place (on the mountain), being in time (yesterday afternoon), being in a posture (doubled up), and having something on (mud). Of these categories substance, quality (which includes disposition and activity), relation, and quantity are the most important for philosophical theology.

cause: a real principle on which the being of something depends. This something is another being in the case of two of the four main types of cause enumerated by Aristotle, namely 1. the final cause or end, that on account of which something is or acts; 2. the efficient cause or agent, the producer of the effect. The other two are 3. the material cause, that out of and in which something is made; and 4. the formal cause, its inner shaping principle or form. The form of a thing as an idea in the mind of the maker is called the exemplar cause. These notions are analogical, and delicately subdivided in scholastic philosophy.

change, movement: the passage or process from a condition of potentiality to that of actuality but not yet complete. Substantial change, from one thing to another; accidental change within the same things from one mode of being to another. Alteration, change of quality; growth and shrinking, change of quantity; local motion, change of place. Change may be instantaneous or successive. Change regarded as being from an agent is action; the same change as undergone in a thing is passion.

comprehension: 1. the knowing of an object as much as it can be known; thus God alone comprehends himself. 2. the real embracing of an end; thus the blessed in heaven are said to comprehend God.

definition: nominal definition states what a term indicates, and in so doing may touch on its etymology. Real definition expresses what a thing is by giving its proximate genus and specific difference, or if this is not possible by getting as near as may be to a proper and peculiar description.

demonstration: a discourse of reason which makes clear the necessary connection between a predicate and a subject by exposing the link or middle term. Contrasted with induction, which is seeing a general truth in particular facts or working to it from them. Deduction is of two types, from cause to effect, and from effect to cause, which roughly correspond to *a priori* and *a posteriori* proofs respectively.

difference: the distinction between the specific and the generic, or between two species of the same genus.

distinction: any type of non-identity, sometimes between aspects of one single thing. Real distinction, between elements or real principles there; virtual or conceptual distinction, between real meanings we may see there. Other distinctions may be logical or even purely nominal.

diversity: the otherness of this thing compared to that thing.

efficient or agent cause: the First or Uncaused Cause causes secondary causes. These may be true principal causes, which produce in virtue of what they really are, thus a man is the principal agent of his responsible actions, or instrumental causes, which act from the motion they receive from a higher principal, thus a man may be the instrumental cause of a miracle.

equivocal: having the same name, usually taken for the merely equivocal, the occasion for the fallacy of equivocation, when an identical word covers quite different meanings (terms, but not ideas, can be equivocal in this sense), but sometimes for the designedly equivocal, or analogical, when a common meaning is inflected by diversity. Thus equivocal cause, which exists outside the class to which its effect belongs, though the effect is really related to and in some way like the cause.

essence: the 'what' or *quid* of an object, signified by the definition; its intelligible principle.

eternity: the all at once whole and complete possession of unending life.

existence, esse: the act of being real, not merely intelligible. Note, however, that the classical essence-existence distinction is not that between the ideal and the real, but between the real as potential and as actual.

faith: assent to an object not determined by its inner evidence perceived either immediately, as with insight or understanding, or mediately, as with the scientific knowledge of a conclusion. To be committed without wavering to God's own truth in revealing himself is the theological virtue of faith.

final causes: by analogy with efficient causes may be divided into the ultimate end or good and intermediate and subordinate goods. These last may be true ends in themselves, thus a human friend, or just means to an end, thus having a tooth extracted.

form: literally 'shape' by contrast with 'stuff' or matter; the inner determining principle by which something is what it is, its *morphē*; that which renders it intelligible, its *eidos*; hence extended to the cognitional form through which it is reached by mind or sense.

individual: strictly speaking a singular, not a particular material object, thus Abelard, not just a doctor of divinity.

infinite: the non-determinate or unlimited. Material infinity of imperfection, because of absence of form. Formal infinity of perfection, because of non-contraction by matter.

matter: that which bodily things are made of. Usually signifies prime or bare matter, the subject of and potentiality for substantial change, which can never exist save under some substantial form. Corpuscular matter is called matter stamped with quantity.

nature: 1. as essence, constitution, kind, thus human nature; in this sense it can be contrasted with 'supernatural'. 2. as the principle of motion from within, spontaneous motion in living things, 'voluntary' motion in conscious things; in this sense nature is not contrasted with grace, but with the artificial or violent.

object: rarely said with reference to a grammatical subject, but generally to the activity of a verb. Material object, that which it is about; formal object, the specific interest there engaged.

opposition: contradictory terms imply a flat denial, thus black, not black; contrary terms imply a common basis, which can take on an intermediate condition between them, thus black, white.

participation: the sharing in a property or mode of being which belongs primarily, essentially, and underivatively to another, and therefore the not possessing it to its fullest extent of existence.

particular: a restricted general term, one, some, most. Often used, however, for the individual.

passion: one of the categories of being, a being acted upon; any change regarded as belonging to the thing in which it occurs.

place: one of the categories of being, the determinateness of a thing in relation to other bodies in space, its immediate environment.

potentiality: being as correlative to actuality. The Latin word *potentia* is used both for the active power of doing or making, the capability of acting upon another thing, and for passive potentiality, the capacity for being acted upon by another thing.

practical knowledge: knowledge ordered to the doing or making of something, contrasted with theoretic knowledge, also called speculative or, better, contemplative, which is for the sake of its truth.

predicament: a category of being.

principle: any starting point, whether in the order of reality or in that of thought; a wider and more generic term than cause.

privation: the absence of a form which could—and, in moral matters, should—be present.

property: that which belongs to something, and, strictly speaking, that which is a necessary or essential characteristic though no part of its substance, essence, or nature, thus a sense of humour is proper to a rational animal.

quality: one of the categories of being: any modification of a substance inherent in that substance.

quantity: one of the categories of being: the property of being divisible into parts without qualitative change while yet being actually undivided.

relation: the 'being to another' of a thing. The following division is a somewhat rough and ready simplification. A 'predicamental relation' consists in being a relation and so is distinct from the thing which is its subject, thus to be a father. A 'transcendental relation' consists in being a relative subject, thus to be a creature.

science: in its most pointed and Aristotelean sense, the knowledge of a demonstrated conclusion. But often it means any knowledge, and particularly when this surpasses opinion.

single: one substance, whether simple or composite.

species: 1. a kind or class of being, and notably of physical being, determined by the addition of a specific difference to a proximate genus. 2. in the theory of knowledge; the 'look' or form or likeness of an object present in mind or sense when it is known. Note that such a 'species' is not itself the direct object of knowledge; it is rather the opening out or relation of the knower to the known.

subsistence: existing as a complete substance, not as a partial substance, e.g. an animal soul, nor as an accident, e.g. a thought or a wish.

substance: the capital category of being, contrasted with accident: that which exists in itself and not in another as in a subject. First substance, a thing as a thing. The word 'substance' is sometimes used as equivalent to essence, especially in its adjectival and adverbial forms.

theology: in this volume means Christian theology, of which the premises are revealed truth, and which subsumes philosophical or natural theology.

time: one of the categories of being; the determinateness of an occurrence in relation to other occurrences before and after, a measure of successive change.

universal: that which is common to many and can be predicated of each.

universal cause: an agent which transcends the class or classes of effects it produces.

univocal: a term or idea which can be applied to more than one object with exactly the same mathematical, juridical, generic, or specific meaning. Thus triangle, murder, mammal, rational animal, but not being, true, good.

INDEX

The discourse is so shot through with analogies and pre-sents such a crisscross of subject matters as almost to defy an index of manageable size, except for proper names and main headings. In consulting the following summary, the student is advised to go hunting for himself the harmonics of the ideas that occur to him.

abstract, 197, 276
   and concrete, 78, 195, 197
abstraction, 121, 176, 193, 220, 243, 295
'accident,' 82, 83, 131, 223, 246, 295
accidental, 30, 69
   as incidental, 227, 228
   mode of existing, 140
action, 295. *See* activity; agent; cause
actio-passio, 269, 270
activity, 76, 145, 247, 257, 295
actual being, 73, 90, 269, 270. *See* existence
actuality, 68, 73, 75, 90, 98, 270, 295
adverbial qualification, 179
'aeon,' 151–56, 295
aesthetics, 249
affective knowledge, 244, 246. *See* love, dialectic of
affirmative propositions, 199, 200, 227, 228, 229
agent, 92, 93, 103, 104, 276. *See* cause
   analogical, 95, 112, 207. *See* analogical
   univocal, 94, 95, 206, 207. *See* univocal
agnosticism, 34. *See* negative theology
Alan of Lille, 200, 211

Albert the Great, St, 15, 231, 279
Alexander of Hales, 152
Alexandrian sceptics, 274
Algazel, 124
allegorical sense of Scripture, 58, 59, 60. *See* metaphorical usage
allegory, 59, 60
Amaury of Bène, 87
ambiguity, 58, 60. *See* equivocal
Ambrose, St, 53, 105, 108, 135, 202, 212, 217
anagogy, 59, 60
analogical
   cause, 208, 209, 279
   term, 95, 109, 205, 206, 208, 210, 223, 224, 286, 287
analogy, 18, 28, 59, 60, 130, 205, 208, 209, 210, 223, 275, 279, 285, 290, 293, 294, 295
   double, 208
Anaxagoras, 286
angels, 27, 131, 142, 154, 173, 175, 176, 183, 187, 188
Angevins, 14
Anselm, St, 33, 63, 283, 285. *See* ontological argument
anthropocentrism, 291
anthropomorphism, 34, 202, 203, 291
apologetics, 54, 55, 56

Apostles, 56
appetite, 243, 296
  natural, 168, 248
appetition, 97, 110
  contrasted with cognition,
      247, 248, 249, 252
Arab aristoteleans, 15, 29, 120,
      268, 281
Aratus, 55
argument, 54
argumentative theology, 53, 54,
      55
aristoteleanism, 29, 46, 255
aristotelean logic, 281
Aristotle, 12, 15, 24, 29, 102,
      116, 117, 150, 267, 272,
      276, 281, 284, 285
  cited
      Categories, 213
      De Anima, 75, 172, 183,
          191
      De Coelo et Mundo, 135,
          147, 149
      De Interpretatione, 196,
          203, 209, 229
      De Partibus animalium, 49
      Metaphysics, 42, 46, 48,
          49, 63, 70, 81, 88, 90,
          99, 101, 102, 106, 113,
          116, 139, 149, 150, 156,
          157, 161, 165, 206, 210,
          215, 216, 218
      Meteorologia, 103
      Nicomachean Ethics, 49,
          51, 97, 107, 110, 111
      Physics, 83, 103, 117, 118,
          119, 121, 128, 144, 152,
          156, 164
      Posterior Analytics, 45, 52,
          63, 134
      Topics, 187
article in Summa, 18, 19, 20
articles of faith, 43, 47, 53, 66,
      234, 235, 236. See faith;
      theology
artificial, 257
astronomy, 43

Athanasian Creed, 146
attribution, 84. See predication
  causal, 211, 212
  formal, 200, 201
  literal, 198, 202, 203
  negative, 200, 201
  primary, 209, 210, 211
  secondary, 209, 210, 211
Augustine, St, 24, 29, 105, 106,
      138, 154, 182, 245, 254,
      281, 285
  cited
      Christian teaching, 97, 103,
          201
      City of God, 87, 171
      Confessions, 60, 185, 188
      83 Questions, 127, 145,
          178
      Enchiridion, 70
      Epistles, 56, 60, 135, 148,
          172
      Nature of good, 105, 107,
          139
      On Genesis, 105, 106, 137,
          140, 151, 185, 187, 189,
          190
      Retractations, 192
      Sermons, 181
      Soliloquies, 190
      Trinity, 44, 50, 84, 112,
          115, 135, 145, 148, 169,
          187, 189, 191, 206, 213
      True religion, 188
      Usefulness of believing, 58
augustinianism, 15, 138
authorities, theological, 23, 231,
      232, 233
authority, 231
  argument from, 23, 55, 231
Averroes, 24, 80, 92, 203, 207,
      281
Avicenna, 15, 24, 124, 159, 264,
      281, 282
awareness of God, 63, 64
axioms, 24, 64

Bañez, D., 265, 268

bare matter, 90. *See* matter
Baroque, 14, 252
Barth, K., 33
base things of world, 58
bathos, 58
Bazaine, A., 11
beatific vision, 33, 177, 185, 186, 188. *See* light of glory; vision of God
beatitude, 296
beauty, 103, 104, 249, 250
before and after, 152
being, 76, 80, 96, 97, 277, 296
  as noun and participle, 282
  degrees of, 69, 70
  good, 96, 97, 98, 226
  not a genus, 81
  one, 158, 159, 160
  true, 99, 286
Bernard, St, 165
best, 286, 287
'be, to,' verb, 80. *See* existence
Bible, *Summa* and, 231–41
biblical,
  criticism, 240. *See* Scripture
  theology, 231. *See* theology
blessed knowledge, 33. *See* beatific vision
bodies, 72, 73, 130, 131
  heavenly, 141
  mathematical and physical, 124, 125, 126. *See* extension
bodily and spiritual, 57, 58
body, 73, 74
  extended, 72, 136
Boethius, 24, 54, 64, 83, 96, 98, 113, 115, 129, 143, 150, 152, 191, 227, 281
Bonaventure, St, 152
Bossuet, J. B., 287

Cajetan, T. de V., 194, 249, 265, 268, 283, 289
canonical writings, 56, 232, 233
Cassino, 14
categories, 296

Catholic truth, 39
causal, 87
  relation, 100
  series, 68, 69, 125, 271, 273, 277, 278
  terms, 199, 200, 201, 210, 211
causality, 26, 66, 68, 69, 70, 92, 93, 103, 104, 110, 111, 206, 207, 209, 261, 274, 275, 276, 277, 281
  and demonstration, 26, 65, 66, 260
  and knowledge, 184, 191, 192, 259
  divine, 50, 68, 69, 70, 260, 261
causation, 68, 103, 104
  of good, 102, 103, 104. *See* good
cause, 129, 133, 134, 275, 276, 296
  analogical, 208
  efficient, 68, 69, 103, 289. *See* agent
  final, 103. *See* end
  formal, 103. *See* form
  material, 102. *See* matter
  metaphysical and physical concept of, 265, 278, 284. *See* metaphysics
  univocal, 208
causes
  intermediate, 68, 69, 128. *See* causal series
  knowledge of, 50. *See* wisdom
  the four, 102, 103
Causes, Book on, 97, 99, 146, 147, 281
certainty, 42
certitude, 42, 48
change, 68, 69, 137–42, 144, 269, 270, 296. *See* motion
  measure of, 149, 150, 152, 153. *See* time

change (cont'd)
  of accidents, 140, 141
  of substance, 140, 141, 153
charity, theological virtue, 55,
    179, 182, 244, 251
Chartres, humanism of, 30, 271
choice, 142, 242, 247
Christ, 36, 62, 239
  Body of, 53
  Revelation complete in, 233–
    40
Christology, 17, 36, 53
Chrysostom, St John, 166, 168
Church
  and Israel, 25
  and philosophy, 11
  and Revelation, 11, 234
  and Scripture, 232, 233, 239,
    240
  and Tradition, 240
  defining rôle of, 234. See ar-
    ticles of faith
  living continuity of, 23, 24,
    239, 240
  mind of, 23
  theology in, 244, 245
Cicero, 107
Cologne, 15
commentaries, Thomist, 39
common good, 290
comparative and superlative, 69,
    70
comparison, 93
complex judgment of simple ob-
    ject, 204, 205, 227, 228
component, 87
compositeness, 84, 85, 86, 87,
    114, 144, 145, 159
composition to simplicity, 70
composition, types of, 84, 85
comprehension, 67, 168, 180,
    181, 182, 296
conceptual knowledge, 242, 243
  about God, 50, 53, 193, 202
concrete, 176, 197, 198, 220,
    221

  and abstract, 78, 195, 196,
    198
condition, form, and order, 105,
    106
conservation of things by God,
    128, 140
contemplation, 47, 244
contingency, 69, 284
continuity in change, 12
continuum, 121
contradiction, principle of, 270
'convenience,' argument from,
    26, 27
corpus articuli, 20
creation, 132, 133, 134
'creator,' 209, 210, 211, 212–15,
    216
creaturely perfection, 211, 244
creatures, 12, 45, 56, 58, 169,
    170, 171, 176, 177, 183,
    185, 186, 191, 192, 216,
    261, 274, 280
  composition in, 114
  in theology, 48, 53, 191, 196,
    197, 201, 244
  likeness of to God, 78, 93, 94,
    95, 205
  mutability of, 140
  proportion of to God, 164
  relation of to God, 95, 214,
    215, 216
credibility, rational, 66. See faith
creed, 234, 238. See articles of
    faith

Damascene, St John, 52, 53, 63,
    66, 118, 141, 217, 218,
    226
David of Dinant, 87
debate, 20, 21
deduction, 67, 238
definition, 53, 80, 81, 117, 196,
    218, 297
  and infinite, 117
  of dogma, 236
degree and kind, 286

degrees of being, 69, 70, 285, 286, 287. *See* analogy

delight, 250

delightful good, 107, 108, 247

demonstration, 26, 33, 64, 181, 259, 297
  by causality, 26, 64–70, 192
  definition in, 53, 65, 82
  effect in, 66
  two types of, 66

deposit of faith, 22, 236, 237

Descartes, R., 238, 266

design, argument from, 289, 290. *See* finality

desirable good, 97, 98, 100

desire, 103, 289. *See* love

development of Christian doctrine, 235, 237, 238

devils, 129

devotion and definition, 237, 242, 244

dialectic,
  and syllogistic, 26
  of love, 242–58

difference, 297
  specific, 80, 81, 82

differentiation, 88

dimensions, 72, 74, 121

Dionysius, the pseudo-, 51, 57, 59, 74, 87, 88, 91, 92, 93, 95, 99, 100, 101, 111, 139, 141, 156, 158, 160, 167, 170, 173, 183, 190, 192, 195, 202, 203, 205, 207, 210, 218, 249, 256

disputation, scholastic, 21

distance, 127, 129

distinction, 205, 297

diversity, 80, 297

division, 159, 161, 162

dogma, 234. *See* articles of faith

Dominicans, 14, 35

double-meaning, 28

'double-truth' theory, 14

doubt, religious, 48

duration, 143, 145, 146, 147, 148, 149, 150

ecstasy, 185

effect, 64, 274. *See* cause
  argument from, 65, 66, 67, 191, 192, 277
  in cause, 92
  like cause, 92, 94, 95
  naming cause from, 218, 219, 274, 276, 277, 278, 280

efficient cause, 68, 69, 276. *See* agent
  instrumental, 13
  principal, 13
  secondary, 13

either-ors, 25, 255

embracing perfection as cause and pure existence, 92

end, 100, 102, 256. *See* final cause
  activity for, 290
  foreknown, 42, 70
  penultimate, 13

Enlightenment, the, 14

equivocal, 28, 206, 223, 224, 299
  cause, 208, 209
  term, 205, 206, 207, 223

equivocation, fallacy of, 208

essence, 76, 77, 79, 282, 299
  and existence, 78, 79, 80

essences, 29, 30, 248

essential property, 79

eternal law, 287

eternity, 143–58
  in delight, 250

ethics, 46

etiology, 59, 60

etymology, 217, 218

Eudoxus, 268

everywhere, 130, 131, 132, 133, 134, 135

evidence, in itself and to us, 64

evil, 18, 67, 70, 100

eyesight, 171, 172, 173

examples, moral, 44

exegesis, Scriptural, 58, 59, 60
existence, 33, 63, 66, 71, 76, 79, 80, 81, 90, 93, 95, 96, 97, 98, 99, 100, 101, 102, 114, 118, 120, 130, 144, 152, 153, 158, 159, 161, 176, 225, 226, 281, 282, 283, 284
    as intelligible, 171, 174–75
    as perfection, 79, 90, 91, 92, 93, 101, 128, 130, 226, 287
    derived and underived, 79, 114
    not a genus, 81, 82
    not a predicate, 281, 283
    not univocal, 82, 83
    unspecified, 78, 80, 93, 226
existential essence and essential existence, 287
experiential knowledge, 51, 246, 253, 254
extension, 72, 73, 74, 117, 118, 119, 121, 122, 123, 131

'faculty-psychology,' 246
faith, 23, 33, 42, 66, 182, 193, 194, 227, 235, 237, 245, 298. See Revelation; theology
    and philosophy, 11
    and propositions, 237
    and reason, 12, 22, 53, 54, 55, 56, 258
    and Scripture, 54, 235, 236
    and theology, 33
    articles of, 26, 48, 66, 235, 236
    as embodied, 25
    darkness of, 25, 65, 193, 194
    doubts and, 48
    from hearing, 25
    in relation to Prophets and Apostles, 56
    loving and living, 244
    presupposes rational knowledge, 66

provides principles of theology, 54, 55
    rule of, 233, 234
    transcends confessional formulation, 12
    within Church, 11, 234, 237, 245
fallibility of reason, 42
Fathers of Church, 23, 30, 232
Fénelon, F., 287
Ferrariensis, S., 268
'fifth way,' 70, 288–91
figures of speech, 34, 57
final cause, 103, 298. See end
finality, 70
    external, 27, 290
    internal, 291
finite and infinite, 65, 167, 181
first and final causes, 50, 68, 69, 70, 260, 261
first principles of thought, 63, 64
'first way,' 68, 267–73
'five ways,' 68–70, 260, 261, 262–92
flesh and spirit, 12
Florence, Council of, 30
form, 74, 75, 76, 77, 87, 94, 105, 106, 107, 118, 119, 120, 250, 257, 298
    and matter, 75, 87, 141
    definition by, 119, 120
    in mind, 169, 170, 174, 175, 248
    resemblance by, 94
    subsisting, 141, 220
formal
    cause, 103
    expression, 29, 30
    interest, 30, 45
    object, 247
Fossanuova, 15
'fourth way,' 69, 70, 285–87
Friedländer, M., 281

genus and species, 80, 81, 82
geometry, 121, 123, 126

Geyer, B., 35
Gift of Knowledge, 253, 254
Gifts of the Holy Ghost, 27, 51, 243, 253
Gilbert de la Porrée, 139, 214
Gilby, T., 12, 15, 36
Gilson, E., 15, 87
glory, light of, 169, 170, 171, 176, 177, 179
glosses, Scriptural, 132, 189, 193, 221
Gnostics, 151
God, 52, 53
    and causality, 68, 69, 70, 110, 111
    and creatures, 45, 57, 94, 95
    and language, 90
    and natural theology, 92
    and theology, 52, 53
    as cause of creatures, 50
    as fount of being, 50
    as happiness, 64, 167
    as represented, 27
    as supremely knowable, 167, 168
    attributes of, 84, 199, 200, 201
    author of Scripture, 37
    beyond all categories, 80, 81, 82
    bodiless, 73, 74
    essence and existence in, 64, 79
    'essence' of, 77, 78
    eternity of, 143–49
    existence in, 78, 79, 93, 175, 225, 226
    existence of, 33, 62–70, 83, 262–92
    first cause, 85
    fount of being, 261
    free mercy of, 23
    goodness of, 110–16
    how he is not, 32
    immanence of, 127–36
    immobility of, 138, 272
    immutability of, 71

    infinity of, 71, 117, 118, 119, 120
    knowledge about, 50, 53
    knowledge in, 46, 47, 50
    meaning of word 'God,' 63, 65, 259–61
    names of, 78, 93, 217–26
    negatively known about, 62, 65, 71
    no accidents in, 83, 84
    not in genus, 81, 82, 279
    not self-evident to us, 64, 65
    one for philosophy and Scripture, 16
    perfection of, 71, 89–94
    plurality of perfections in, 84
    presence of, 132, 133
    primary attribution of perfections to, 210, 211, 293, 294
    pure actuality, 83, 138
    pure form, 85
    relation to creatures, 215
    simplicity of, 72–88, 229
    subsistent existence of, 92, 175
    that he is, 32–66
    transcendence of, 12, 30, 81, 82, 95, 113, 168, 278, 279
    unity of, 71, 158–65
godhead, archetypal cause, 88
good, 96–108. See end
    by nature, 113, 114
    by participation, 114, 115, 116
    causality of, 102, 104
    division of, 107, 108, 109
good man, 104
Gospel
    law of, 239
    living, 238
grace, 132, 134, 255
    and nature, 12, 13, 22, 25, 55, 255, 256
    knowledge of God through,

grace (cont'd)
193, 194, 250, 251. See
vision of God; faith
presence of God by, 134, 136
reassurance of, 251
Greek temper, 29, 30, 267
Gregory the Great, St, 54, 90,
131, 132, 183, 184, 189
Grosseteste, Robert, 53
ground of necessity, 69
guidedness in nature, 70

happiness, 64, 167, 168, 181
heavenly bodies, 141, 153
hell, 149
Hellenism, 15
Heraclitus, 29, 269
Hilary, St, 79, 85
history, 60
Hohenstauffen, 14
hope, 182
Hugh of St Victor, 24, 53, 60
Hume, D., 262, 274

Ideas Platonic, 115, 116
idolatry, 222, 223, 224
imagery in divine vision, 190.
See metaphor
images and thoughts, 191, 192
imagination, 171, 173
immobile, 138, 272
immutability, 137–42
Incarnation, the, 23, 33, 237.
See Word of God
indefinite, the, 118, 119, 168.
See matter
individual, 44, 75, 76, 77, 174,
220, 221, 299
and science, 43
and specific nature, 77, 78
indivisibility, 130, 131, 159,
160, 161, 162, 165. See
unity
induction, 67, 275
indwelling of God, 132, 133,
134
infinite, 118

and finite, 65
series, 68, 69, 271, 272, 278,
279, 282, 299
infinity, 117–27
actual, 125, 126
by form, 118, 120, 168
by matter, 118, 119, 120, 168
potential, 125, 126
innate knowledge, 64, 188
instantaneous whole, 144, 150
instantiation, 174, 220
intellect, unlimited range of, 120
intelligence and purpose, 289,
290, 291
intensive and extensive growth,
285
intermediate cause and mover,
68, 69, 277
Ionians, the, 267

Jacob, 188, 190, 256
Jacobin Bible, 232
Jerome, St, 47, 56, 148
Joachimites, 239
John of St Thomas, 249, 252,
253

Kant, I., 12, 262, 263
Kilwardby, Robert, 331
knowable in so far as actual, 167
knowing, 167, 168, 214, 216,
247
and loving, 243
as relation, 214
through sympathy, 242
knowledge, 174, 248
inequality of, 178, 179, 180
influence of love on, 250, 251,
252
of God from effects, 191, 192
proportionate to being, 167,
168
through form, 168, 171
through likeness, 169, 170,
185, 186, 248
through real presence, 185,
186

Knowledge, Gift of, 253, 254

language, 196. *See* words
  metaphorical and symbolical, 27, 202, 203
  theological, 34, 195–229
Latin spirit, 30
law, 46
legalism, 11, 233, 244
Leibniz, G. W., 266
Leo XIII, 35
Leonine *Summa*, 35
letter and spirit, 239
light of God, 169, 170
likeness, 94, 95, 169, 170, 171
  in knowledge, 248
limitation, 118, 119, 120
limits. *See* definition
  by form, 118
  by matter, 118
literal attribution of terms, 202, 203
literal sense of Scripture, 59, 60, 61
living body, 73
'Lord' applied to God, 213, 216
love, 237, 247, 250, 291. *See* good
  dialectic of, 243–54
  effects of, 250
  for thing, not meaning, 248, 277
  in love with God, 244
  of God in all desire, 111, 289
  without vocabulary, 251
love-knowledge, 246
loving and knowing, 179, 243, 245, 248
Lucretius, 151
Lyons, Council of, 15

McCabe, H., 36
McDermott, T., 36
magnitude, 121
Maimonides, Moses, 24, 200, 207, 281
man, 26. *See* Revelation

single substance, 25
  to God's image, 74, 206
Manichees, 133
manner of knowing and being, 179, 229
many, 160, 161, 162
  to one, 70
Marx, K., 12
material cause, 102
materialism, 13, 14
mathematical and physical science, 122, 123
mathematics, 33, 43, 44, 101, 102, 122, 123, 164
matter, 74, 75, 90, 102, 118, 119, 120, 299
  and form, 75, 77, 87, 118, 141
  indefinite, 118, 120, 123
  primordial, 90
meaning, 29, 30, 45. *See* definition; form
  and etymology, 201, 211, 217
  mode of, 196, 197, 203, 229
  reference and, 196, 202, 217, 218
means to end, 289
measure, 105, 106, 107
measurement, 82, 157
medium
  of knowledge, 176, 177
  of science, 43
metaphor, 202, 203, 209, 210
metaphorical usage in theology, 34, 56, 57, 59, 60, 75, 139, 145, 203, 210, 211, 219, 293, 294
metaphysics, 42, 54, 265, 274, 275, 277, 278, 284
middle term, 66, 268, 274
miracle, 190
mirror, 184
  seeing God in, 169
  seeing God through, 183
monism, 12
moral
  science, 51

moral (*cont'd*)
   sense of Scripture, 58
   theology, 17, 47
Moses, 188, 190, 192
motion, 68, 124, 138, 267, 269.
      See change
movement as change and as ac-
      tivity, 138, 268, 269
multiplicity and unity, 205
music, 43
mystery of God, 24

name, common and proper, 219,
      221
names, divine, 220, 221, 222
Naples, 14
Nathanael, 256
natural, 299
   and supernatural, 255–58
   contrasted with intelligent,
      291
   contrasted with voluntary, 70,
      257
   desire, 168, 184, 248
   different senses of the word,
      257
   knowledge of God, 191, 192,
      193
   theology, 42
   truths of religion, 42, 66
nature
   and grace, 22, 25, 55, 255,
      256
   as essence, 76, 77
   as intrinsic, 256, 257, 299
   as specific, 220, 256, 299
   as substance, 82, 200
necessary, 69, 281, 284
   and contingent, 69
   being, 282, 283
necessity, absolute and condi-
      tional, 282
negation and definition, 144
negative
   knowledge of God, 17, 58, 71
   terms, 199, 200
   theology, 34, 58, 199

New Law, 27, 46, 59
newness, 152, 153
non-existence, 100, 161
'nothing,' 214
notional knowledge, 51, 242,
      248, 264
nouns, 195, 196, 198, 219, 220
   about God, 198, 221
'now,' 149, 150, 151, 152, 153
number, 136, 156, 164, 165
   infinite, 124, 125, 126
numbering, 155, 156

object, 299
   formal, 30, 45, 52, 53
objections in *Summa*, 20
occasion, 277
Ockham's Razor, 67
Old Law, 27, 46, 59
omnipotence, 129
omnipresence, 127, 128, 129,
      130, 131, 132, 133
ontological argument, 63, 283
opinion, 181, 182
opposition of perfections, 91
optics, 44
order, 106, 107
   of nature, 164, 259, 260
Origen, 156

pantheism, 87, 88, 128, 129,
      134
parabolical sense of Scripture,
      59, 61
Parmenides, 29, 269
participation, 69, 70, 79, 113,
      115, 116, 256, 299
participles, 196
   about God, 198
particular cause, 299
parts, 145
party line in theology, 11
passion, 299
patristic theology, 55
Paul, St, 182, 186, 190
Pegis, A. C., 15
Pègues, T., 35

perfection, 89, 105, 106, 202, 203
  pure and mixed, 203, 210, 211, 221, 286, 287
  variation within, 286, 287
perfection-words, 207
Peter, St, 239
Peter Lombard, 53
phenomena, 26
philosophers as theological authorities, 54, 55
philosophy
  and theology, 11, 55
  excision of from theology, 13, 21
  of religion, 33
physical science, 43
Piana Summa, 35
Pius V, St, 35
place, 129, 130, 136, 299
Plato, 12, 29, 116, 159, 267, 272, 281, 285
platonism, 15, 138, 147, 255, 286, 287
Platonists, 100, 102, 120, 138, 151
pleasurable, the good as, 107, 108
Plotinus, 263, 281
pluralism, metaphysical, 12, 115
poetic experience, 249
poetry, 16, 28, 56, 57
possible being, 69, 284
potential being, 68, 73, 90, 102, 269, 270, 289
  not lack of being, 100
potentiality, 68, 73, 74, 75, 90, 299
  active and passive, 140
power, 119, 133, 140
practical,
  and theoretical, 46
  knowledge, 300
  science, 46, 47
predicate and subject, 64, 100
predication, 64, 80, 85, 198,

207, 227, 228. See attribution
proper and metaphorical, 219
premises of theology as science, 44, 54
presence of cause, 127, 129
  causal, 132, 133
  objective, 132, 133
  of God, 127–35, 173
principal cause, 13
principles, 300
privation, 300
probability, argument from, 16
probable opinion, 182
Proclus, 97. See Causes, Book on
pronouns, 196
  about God, 198
property, 79, 300
prophecy, 190
proportion, 168, 169
prospectus of Summa, 31, 32
Providence, divine, 57, 133, 218, 261, 288
purpose, argument from, 70, 289, 290
  in world, 70
Pythagoras, 159
pythagoreans, 90

quality, 300
quantity, 121, 300. See extension
Question in Summa, 17, 18

rational credibility, 55. See faith
rationalism, 13, 263
reason and faith, 25, 66
reason for existence and for knowing existence, 66
reasoning for understanding, 262, 263, 265
recommending arguments, 26, 27
reference and meaning, 202, 203, 204
regularity of events, 274

relation, 212, 213, 214, 215, 216, 300
relative terms, 199, 200, 212, 215, 216
resemblance, 94, 95
resurrection, 54, 173
Revelation, 50, 193, 194, 237, 243. *See* faith; Scripture
  and Scripture, 235, 236
  as presence of the Lord, 237
  completion of, 233, 240
  embodied in rational animals, 25, 26, 57, 58
  for all, 40
  given to Prophets and Apostles, 23, 240
  includes many objects, 45, 57, 58
  need for, 42
  public, 17, 237
  social fact, 17, 25
  to whole man, 25, 33
  unifying principle in Christian theology, 45
  within Church, 239, 240
Roccasecca, 14
Roman Law, 29

'Saviour' applied to God, 215
Scholasticism, 19, 21, 30
Scholastics, the, 251
Scholastic theology, 238
science, 43, 44, 53, 258, 300
sciences
  diversification of, 43, 45, 46
  practical, 46, 47, 48
  theoretic, 47, 48
scientific method, 275
Scotists, 268
Scripture, 23, 42, 231, 238. *See* Revelation
  and Tradition, 232, 233
  as Revelation, 234
  as sacrament, 239
  authority for theology, 54, 55
  canonical, 55, 56
  for all, 24, 57

language of, 173
metaphorical usage in, 61, 72, 74, 139, 173
record of Revelation, 232, 234
senses of, 58, 59, 60
signifies God's will for us, 23
variety in, 233, 234
within Church, 233, 234
Scripture
  quoted
    Acts, 55, 254
    I *Corinthians*, 39, 50, 51, 54, 163, 169, 179, 180, 188, 236, 245, 252, 254
    II *Corinthians*, 51, 55, 128, 185, 239
    Daniel, 147
    Deuteronomy, 50, 148, 163, 217
    Ecclesiastes, 148
    Ecclesiasticus, 41, 43, 56, 152, 250
    Ephesians, 172, 210
    Exodus, 67, 146, 189, 196, 225
    Ezra, 155
    Galatians, 221, 237
    Genesis, 72, 94, 188, 207, 251
    Hebrews, 25, 59, 65, 72, 75, 235
    Hosea, 57
    Isaiah, 42, 50, 72, 94, 101, 128, 172
    James, 46, 137, 243, 272
    Jeremiah, 73, 130, 181, 204, 212
    Job, 72, 132, 133, 149, 171
    John, 53, 63, 73, 77, 148, 166, 174, 179, 239, 240, 246, 248, 256
    I *John*, 94, 167, 169, 177, 178
    I *Kings*, 237
    Lamentations, 110
    Luke, 111, 253
    Malachy, 137

Scripture (cont'd)
    Matthew, 58, 60, 89, 99,
        111, 128, 193, 241, 254
    Micah, 144
    Numbers, 188
    II Peter, 219
    Philippians, 180
    Proverbs, 48, 50, 195
    Psalms, 64, 72, 73, 75, 93,
        127, 128, 149, 171, 177,
        216, 219, 221, 224, 246
    Revelation, 177
    Romans, 50, 57, 66, 144,
        174, 191, 208, 238, 291
    Song of Solomon, 132, 182
    II Thessalonians, 43
    I Timothy, 101, 237
    II Timothy, 42, 237
    Titus, 54
    Wisdom, 45, 78, 104, 123,
        135, 137, 219, 258
secondary cause, 13
'second way,' 68, 69, 274–80
sectarian thinking, 12, 13
sed contra, 20
self-evidence, 63, 64
sensation, understanding from,
    57, 191, 192
sense and passion in thought, 25
senses, 46, 170, 172, 174, 175,
    176
sensus communis, 46
series, causal, 271, 278, 279,
    282
shape, 118
signification, and mode of, 203
simple things known by com-
    posite things, 78, 144
simple things not differentiated
    by addition, 88
simplicity, 72–88, 145
size, 122, 123
Sophists, the, 267
soul, 73, 267
    human, 174
space, 124

species
    as class, 81, 300
    as form, 106
    as knowledge-form, 300
specification, 80
    changed by addition, 285
Speusippus, 90
Spinoza, B., 12
Spirit, Holy, 12, 245, 246
spiritual and material, 25
spiritual sense of Scripture, 59,
    60
subject and predicate, 64, 100,
    227
subordination, 12, 233, 271, 272
    accidental and essential, 277
    of causes, 278, 279
    of sciences, 44, 48, 54
subsistence, 30, 197, 201. See
    existence
substance, 82, 83, 84, 102, 164,
    200, 301
    as existent thing, 98, 223, 248
    as possessed of a nature, 82,
        198, 200, 201
    creaturely, 246, 247
    non-material, 156
succession, 144
sufficient reason, 277
Summa Theologiae, 12, 15
supernatural, 42, 177
    and natural, 255, 256, 257,
        258
supreme, 112, 113
    absence of dichotomies in, 25
    and Bible, 231–41
    dialectic of love in, 242–54
    dialogue within, 20, 21
    foreword to, 39
    medievalism of, 16, 17
    method of, 21–27
    movement of, 16, 256
    outline of, 31, 32, 36
    spirit of, 12, 33
    structure of, 15–21, 36, 62
    style of, 16, 28, 29, 39
symbolism, 56, 57

sympathy, knowing through, 51, 254

synonyms, 204, 205

systematic theology, 33, 54, 55, 238

teleology, 70, 288, 289

terms implying time, 212, 213, 214, 215, 216

Tetragrammaton, 221, 226

theism, inchoate, 64, 263, 264

theodicy, 43

theology, 26, 33, 41, 231
   affective, 21, 51, 242, 244, 245
   aim of, 39, 62
   and a cosmology, 267, 268
   and articles of faith, 53, 54
   and contemplation, 243
   and faith, 11, 23, 33, 44, 51, 53
   and figures of speech, 27
   and other sciences, 24, 43, 47, 49, 51
   and philosophy, 11, 13, 16, 21, 23, 24, 55
   and proof, 53, 54
   and reason, 22, 54, 55, 56
   and Scripture, 23, 231-41
   and symbolism, 57, 58
   appeal to authority in, 22, 23
   as scientific, 26, 44
   as wisdom, 48, 49, 50, 51
   Christian and natural, 23, 42, 43, 301
   derivation from blessed knowledge, 33
   derivation from faith, 23, 33
   functions of, 24, 54
   in Church, 11
   method of, 53, 54, 55
   natural, 191, 192
   negative and symbolical, 58
   not axe-grinding, 13
   not hybrid, 21, 22
   not mere thinking, 242, 243, 244
   practical, 47
   principles of, 22, 44
   stammering about God, 90
   talk about God, 52, 53
   theoretic, 47, 48
   types of, 238
   unity of, 12, 22, 27, 45, 46
   versatility of, 47, 55, 236, 243

theophanies, 34

theory and practice, 46, 47

thing, subsisting, 30, 248

'third way,' 69, 281-84

Thomas Aquinas, St, 14, 232, 288. See Summa Theologiae
   position of, 11
   spirit of, 13, 29, 35
   style of, 13, 20, 28
   Commentary on the Metaphysics, 20
   Disputations on the Power of God, 213
   Summa contra Gentes, 42, 282

Thomism, secular, 21

thoughts about single thing, 205

time, 122, 124, 144, 145, 149, 150, 151, 152, 153, 154, 155, 156, 213, 214, 215
   and eternity, 149, 150
   infinite, 125

Tradition, 237, 240
   and Scripture, 232, 233, 234

traditions, ecclesiastical, 240

transcendental properties of being, 97, 98, 286. See being

Trent, Council of, 240

Trinity, the blessed, 18, 23, 27, 62, 244

tropology, 60

true and real, 99

truth, 286
   necessity of, 63, 143, 283
   thing to mind movement, 247, 248

understanding and sense, 175
Understanding, Gift of, 253
unending, 143
unity, 114, 158, 159, 160, 162, 165
  in variety, 12
  of a science, 16
  of universe, 164
  philosophical and mathematical, 164, 165
universal, 175, 301
  cause, 209, 301
  good, 290
  term, 29
univocal, 301
  cause, 206, 208, 209
  term, 206, 207, 208, 209, 222, 223, 286
unlimited, 119–26
  knowable, 169, 181
useful good, 107, 108, 247
utrum, 19

Vallgornera, T., 252
value, 107, 108, 247
Varro, 87
verbs, 196, 198
  about God, 147, 198

violent, the, 257
virtues, 253
vision of God, 148, 169, 170, 171, 173, 177, 182
  inequality in, 179, 180
  not in this life, 189, 190
volume, 121
Vulgate, 35, 232

ways of knowing and being, 174, 179, 229
wherever, 136
whole, 131, 143, 145
  homogeneous and heterogeneous, 162
will, 104, 247, 248
Winchester notions, 29
wisdom, 49, 50, 51, 138, 275
Wisdom, Gift of, 254
Wolff, C., 266
Word of God, 25, 86, 88, 148, 237, 239, 245
  made flesh, 25
words, 196, 205, 206, 207, 293, 294
  and faith, 244
words, human and God, 59, 196
worthy good, 108

OTHER IMAGE BOOKS

THE IMITATION OF CHRIST – Thomas à Kempis. Edited with an Introduction by Harold C. Gardiner, S.J. (D17) – $1.25

ST. FRANCIS OF ASSISI – G. K. Chesterton (D50) – $1.25

VIPER'S TANGLE – François Mauriac. A novel of evil and redemption (D51) – 95¢

THE CITY OF GOD – St. Augustine. Edited by Vernon J. Bourke. Introduction by Étienne Gilson. Specially abridged (D59) – $2.45

RELIGION AND THE RISE OF WESTERN CULTURE – Christopher Dawson (D64) – $1.25

THE LITTLE FLOWERS OF ST. FRANCIS – Translated by Raphael Brown (D69) – $1.75

THE IDEA OF A UNIVERSITY – John Henry Cardinal Newman. Introduction by G. N. Shuster (D75) – $1.65

DARK NIGHT OF THE SOUL – St. John of the Cross. Edited and translated by E. Allison Peers (D78) – $1.25

THE PILLAR OF FIRE – Karl Stern. A psychiatrist's spiritual journey from Judaism to Catholicism (D83) – 95¢

A POPULAR HISTORY OF THE REFORMATION – Philip Hughes (D92) – $1.25

THE CONFESSIONS OF ST. AUGUSTINE – Translated with an Introduction by John K. Ryan (D101) – $1.75

A HISTORY OF PHILOSOPHY: VOLUME 1 – GREECE AND ROME (2 Parts) – Frederick Copleston, S.J. (D134a, D134b) – $1.75 ea.

A HISTORY OF PHILOSOPHY: VOLUME 2 – MEDIAEVAL PHILOSOPHY (2 Parts) – Frederick Copleston, S.J. Part I – Augustine to Bonaventure. Part II – Albert the Great to Duns Scotus (D135a, D135b) – $1.45 ea.

A HISTORY OF PHILOSOPHY: VOLUME 3 – LATE MEDIAEVAL AND RENAISSANCE PHILOSOPHY (2 Parts) – Frederick Copleston, S.J. Part I – Ockham to the Speculative Mystics. Part II – The Revival of Platonism to Suárez (D136a, D136b) – $1.45 ea.

A HISTORY OF PHILOSOPHY: VOLUME 4 – MODERN PHILOSOPHY: Descartes to Leibniz – Frederick Copleston, S.J. (D137) – $1.75

A HISTORY OF PHILOSOPHY: VOLUME 5 – MODERN PHILOSOPHY: The British Philosophers, Hobbes to Hume (2 Parts) – Frederick Copleston, S.J. Part I – Hobbes to Paley. Part II – Berkeley to Hume (D138a) – $1.45; (D138b) – $1.75

A HISTORY OF PHILOSOPHY: VOLUME 6 – MODERN PHILOSOPHY (2 Parts) – Frederick Copleston, S.J. Part I – The French Enlightenment to Kant (D139a) – $1.75; (D139b) – $1.45

OTHER IMAGE BOOKS

A HISTORY OF PHILOSOPHY: VOLUME 7 – MODERN PHILOSOPHY (2 Parts) – Frederick Copleston, S.J. Part I – Fichte to Hegel. Part II – Schopenhauer to Nietzsche (D140a, D140b) – $1.75 ea.

A HISTORY OF PHILOSOPHY: VOLUME 8 – MODERN PHILOSOPHY: Bentham to Russell (2 Parts) – Frederick Copleston, S.J. Part I – British Empiricism and the Idealist Movement in Great Britain. Part II – Idealism in America, the Pragmatist Movement, the Revolt against Idealism (D141a, D141b) – $1.45 ea.

THE SPIRITUAL EXERCISES OF ST. IGNATIUS – Translated by Anthony Mottola, Ph.D. Introduction by Robert W. Gleason, S.J. (D170) – 95¢

WE HOLD THESE TRUTHS: Catholic Reflections on the American Proposition – John Courtney Murray, S.J. (D181) – $1.25

LIFE AND HOLINESS – Thomas Merton. Exposition of the principles of the spiritual life (D183) – 85¢

AMERICAN CATHOLICISM – John Tracy Ellis. A comprehensive survey of the American Church (D190) – 95¢

THE COUNCIL, REFORM AND REUNION – with a new Introduction by Fr. Hans Kung (D198) – 95¢

WITH GOD IN RUSSIA – Walter J. Ciszek, S.J., with Daniel L. Flaherty, S.J. (D200) – $1.45

THE TWO-EDGED SWORD – John L. McKenzie, S.J. Outstanding interpretation of the Old Testament (D215) – $1.45

NO MAN IS AN ISLAND – Thomas Merton (D231) – $1.45

CONJECTURES OF A GUILTY BYSTANDER – Thomas Merton. A collection of notes, opinions, reflections (D234) – $1.45

THE NOONDAY DEVIL: Spiritual Support in Middle Age – Bernard Basset, S.J. A funny-serious book of spiritual direction (D237) – $1.25

UNDERSTAND THE BIBLE – J. Holland Smith (D238) – $1.25

HEALTH OF MIND AND SOUL – Ignace Lepp (D239) – 95¢

RELIGION AND PERSONALITY – Adrian van Kaam, C.S.Sp. (D240) – $1.45

RELIGIONS OF THE WORLD (2 Volumes) – John A. Hardon, S.J. An account of the history, beliefs, and practices of the major religions of the world (D241a) – $1.75; (D241b) – $1.45

THE RELIGION OF TEILHARD DE CHARDIN – Henri de Lubac, S.J. (D242) – $1.65

CHRISTIAN RENEWAL IN A CHANGING WORLD – Bernard Häring, C.SS.R. (D244) – $1.45

OTHER IMAGE BOOKS

THE NEW TESTAMENT OF THE JERUSALEM BIBLE: Reader's Edition – Alexander Jones, General Editor (D253) – $1.65

CHRISTIAN SACRAMENTS AND CHRISTIAN PERSONALITY – Bernard J. Cooke, S.J. (D246) – $1.25

THOUGHTS IN SOLITUDE – Thomas Merton (D247) – $1.25

NEW TESTAMENT ESSAYS – Raymond E. Brown, S.S. (D251) – $1.45

TEILHARD DE CHARDIN AND THE MYSTERY OF CHRIST – Christopher Mooney, S.J. (D252) – $1.45

THE FOUR GOSPELS: AN INTRODUCTION (2 Volumes) – Bruce Vawter, C.M. (D255a, D255b) – $1.25 ea.

THE PROTESTANT CHURCHES OF AMERICA – Revised Edition – John A. Hardon (D259) – $1.95

EXISTENTIAL FOUNDATIONS OF PSYCHOLOGY – Adrian van Kaam (D260) – $1.75

THE CATHOLIC EXPERIENCE – An Interpretation of the History of American Catholicism – Andrew M. Greeley (D261) – $1.45

MORALITY FOR OUR TIME – Marc Oraison (D266) – $1.25

SUMMA THEOLOGIAE – Thomas Aquinas – Thomas Gilby, O.P., General Editor
Volume 1: The Existence of God; Part One: Questions 1–13 (D270) – $1.45
Volume 2: The Mind and Power of God; Part One: Questions 14–26 (D271) – $1.45

THE MIDDLE AGES: A POPULAR HISTORY – Joseph Dahmus (D274) – $1.95

HISTORY OF ETHICS – Vernon J. Bourke (D275b) – $1.45

THE GOSPELS AND THE JESUS OF HISTORY – Xavier Léon-Dufour, S.J. (D276) – $1.75

INTRODUCTION TO THE OLD TESTAMENT (2 Volumes) – André Robert and André Feuillet (D278a, D278b) – $1.95 ea.

THE SEVEN STOREY MOUNTAIN – Thomas Merton (D281) – $1.95

THE PSALMS OF THE JERUSALEM BIBLE – Alexander Jones, General Editor (D283) – $1.45

CONTEMPLATIVE PRAYER – Thomas Merton (D285) – 95¢

THE CHALLENGES OF LIFE – Ignace Lepp (D286) – $1.25

THE ROMAN CATHOLIC CHURCH – John L. McKenzie (D287) – $1.75

BEING TOGETHER: OUR RELATIONSHIPS WITH OTHER PEOPLE – Marc Oraison (D289) – $1.25